ANTHROPOLOGICAL PAPERS OF
THE UNIVERSITY OF ARIZONA
NUMBER 48

Pre-Hispanic Occupance in the Valley of Sonora, Mexico

Archaeological Confirmation of Early Spanish Reports

William E. Doolittle

I0894276

THE UNIVERSITY OF ARIZONA PRESS
TUCSON
1988

About the Author

WILLIAM E. DOOLITTLE, a geographer, has conducted field work in northern Mexico, especially in Sonora, and in Arizona, New Mexico, and Texas. His principal interest is cultural ecology, particularly the analysis of prehistoric and traditional present-day agricultural ecosystems, land use patterns, and settlements. He obtained Bachelor's degrees in government and geography from Texas Christian University (1974), a Master's degree from the University of Missouri-Columbia (1976), and his Doctor of Philosophy degree from the University of Oklahoma (1979). Although his graduate degrees are in geography, he received extensive training in anthropology. He was Assistant Professor of Geology and Geography at Mississippi State University for two years prior to moving to the University of Texas at Austin in 1981, where he is an Associate Professor of Geography. He has published papers on prehistoric and traditional agriculture and agricultural development theory.

Cover: Aerial view of the Valley of Sonora near the town of Banamichi. The hilltop feature at center, Cerro Batonapa, is a cerro de trinchera site, Son K:4:22 OU. (Photo by Edwin J. Surman B.)

THE UNIVERSITY OF ARIZONA PRESS

This book was set in 10/12 Linotype CRTronic Times Roman
Manufactured in the U.S.A.

Library of Congress Cataloging-in-Publication Data

Doolittle, William Emery.
Pre-Hispanic occupance in the valley of Sonora, Mexico: archaeological confirmation of early Spanish reports

(Anthropological papers of the University of Arizona: no. 48)
Bibliography p.
Includes index.
1. Indians of Mexico—Sonora River Valley—Antiquities. 2. Indians of Mexico—Sonora River Valley—Agriculture. 3. Land settlement patterns, Prehistoric—Mexico—Sonora River Valley. 4. Sonora River Valley (Mexico)—Antiquities. 5. Mexico—Antiquities. I. Title. II. Series.
F1219.1.S65D66 1988 972'.17—dc19 87-30040

ISBN 0-8165-1010-5 (alk. paper)

British Library Cataloguing in Publication data are available.

In Memory
of

John F. Bobb
William M. Comer
Ronald L. Doolittle
Douglas G. Morton
David A. Pearson
and the other mates whom I saw fall,
and all the others . . .
up against "The Wall."

Contents

FIGURES

TABLES

Preface

> We remain a part of the organic world, and as we intervene more and more decisively to change the balance and nature of life, we have also more need to know, by retrospective study, the responsibilities and hazards of our present and our prospects as lords of creation (Sauer 1969: 104).

The Valley of Sonora is a region in which Carl Ortwin Sauer (1889–1975) and his students from Berkeley conducted a great deal of work over fifty years ago. With this study, my intent was not to replicate the endeavors of my predecessors but rather, with the benefit of five decades worth of additional materials, ideas, and methods, and the perspective that time offered, to reinvestigate items they studied previously. James J. Parsons, a prominent member of the Berkeley School, partially justified such action when he said: "It pays to keep going back to an area, a people . . . significant phenomena or relationships continue to present themselves" (Parsons 1977: 14). I went to the Valley of Sonora, in part at least, to take another look for Mr. Sauer.

The research on which this work originated was part of a National Science Foundation funded project entitled *Economic Networks: Mesoamerica and the American Southwest* (BNS 76–16818). The co-directors were Richard A. Pailes, Department of Anthropology, University of Oklahoma, and Beatriz Braniff C., then of the Instituto Nacional de Antropologia e Historia, Hermosillo, Sonora. The Rio Sonora Project, as it is familiarly called, conducted archaeological surveys and excavations throughout eastern Sonora and especially in the middle portion of the Rio Sonora Valley, the Valley of Sonora. As the principal surveyor for this project during the summers of 1977 and 1978, I had the opportunity to examine in detail every mesa or terrace overlooking the floodplain and most of the similar locales overlooking the large arroyos in the Valley of Sonora. Numerous prehistoric settlements were found. The field crew took notes, made a systematic surface collection of cultural materials, including ceramics and lithics, and drew a sketch map noting the location, size, and composition of the structures of each site. Archaeological data collected during this survey constitute the basis for this research. Numerous excavations by other members of the project provided essential information concerning the identification and dating of relic features.

Although this work is based principally on archaeological data and ethnohistorical evidence, ethnographic analogs are also incorporated. Some of the ethnohistorical data were gathered as part of the Rio Sonora Project. Many, however, have been obtained since the termination of that project. Grants from the University Research Institute, The University of Texas at Austin, facilitated collection and analyses of these data, as well as manuscript typing. Archaeological and ethnohistorical data on agriculture are in some respects incomplete. Accordingly, ethnographic parallels based on present-day traditional agricultural practices in eastern Sonora are used as analogs where necessary. This information was collected in 1980, 1981, and 1982 as parts of projects funded by the Vice-President for Graduate Studies and Research and the Biological and Physical Sciences Institute, both of Mississippi State University; by the Andrew W. Mellon Foundation in conjunction with the Institute of Latin American Studies of Tulane University; and by the National Science Foundation (SES–8200546).

Certain materials included here have been published elsewhere. For the right to republish I thank the Association of American Geographers; the American Geographical Society; Academic Press, Inc.; the *Journal of Field Archaeology*; and the Trustees of Boston University.

Acknowledgments

My work could not have been completed without the help of numerous people. I am indebted, above all others, to B. L. Turner II for his supervision and to Richard A. Pailes for providing the initial opportunity to carry out field work.

In Mexico my research was facilitated through the help of personnel at the Centro Regional del Noroeste, Instituto Nacional de Antropologia e Historia, Hermosillo, Sonora, especially Beatriz Braniff C., her husband and then director of the institute, Arturo Oliveras M., and current director Cynthia Radding de Murrieta. Guillermo Salas, former Profesor de Geologia, Universidad de Sonora, and Edwin J. Surman B., IFEX Internacional, S.A., Hermosillo, Sonora, provided geological maps and aerial photographs, respectively. Ricardo and Jesus Loera and Francisco Herrera Romo of Baviacora provided local aid and support. Alfonso A. Daco, Jefe de Exploracion, Cia. Minerales Sotula, S.A. de C.V. (Campbell-Resources, Inc., Toronto, Ontario, Canada) of Huepac, Sonora, helped with the geological assessment and was instrumental in locating many archaeological sites. I thank all these people for both their courteous assistance and their friendship.

Many people in this country also gave essential suggestions, assistance, and services during the completion of this project. Campbell W. Pennington and Carroll L. Riley provided cultural information about northwestern Mexico that only they possess. J. Charles Kelley and the late Donald D. Brand offered suggestions about conducting archaeological surveys that proved to be most beneficial. Charles W. Polzer S.J. provided information about and assistance in the collection of ethnohistorical data from the early Spanish era. Woodrow Borah and Gary Paul Nabhan shared insight on evaluating the accuracy of Spanish records for reconstructing demographics and traditional arid land agricultural ecosystems, respectively. Frederick M. Wiseman offered suggestions concerning ecological analysis. Thomas L. Bell and Carole L. Crumley commented about the applicability of spatial models to prehistoric settlement data. Karl W. Butzer offered cogent comments concerning the ecological basis for cultural development. T. H. Lee Williams provided assistance with remote sensing techniques. Thomas J. Wilbanks, James R. Bohland, Stephen I. Thompson, and Beverly Beaty-Benadom provided valuable administrative aid that I greatly appreciate. Johnnie Gentry supplied a plant press for field use. Guy R. Muto and Lois E. Sanders provided soil testing equipment. Clement W. Meighan and P. I. Vanderhoeven of the Obsidian Hydration Laboratory, Department of Anthropology, University of California at Los Angeles provided obsidian hydration analyses. B. L. Turner of the Plant Resources Center, The University of Texas at Austin, identified some plant samples, and R. C. Koeppen, Center for Wood Anatomy Research, Forest Products Laboratory, Madison, Wisconsin, identified wood samples.

I thank all the members of the Rio Sonora Project: botanists James Vaughn and Suzy Gerlach; palynologist Adrianne G. Rankin; and archaeologists Daniel T. Reff, Richard Crump, Kent Buehler, Robert Nespor, Jeanne Simonelli, Jeanne Vaughn, Pat Hardin, Stephen Gugler, Richard Wilson, Marsha Smith, Kathleen Roy, Victoria Dirst, Craig Gerlach, Charles Pyle, Monte Tidwell, Merle Hunsaker, and Ruth Hunsaker. Linda Turner helped my wife and children while I was in Mexico during the second field season. Appreciation is expressed to my colleague and friend, Robert C. Balling, Jr., whose competitive spirit is always an inspiration, and to Paul W. English for his support and encouragement.

A number of individuals also contributed to the successful completion of this monograph by reading parts of various drafts. Edward J. Malecki, James M. Goodman, William C. Johnson, Terry G. Jordan, James A. Neely, Richard E. W. Adams, Jack D. Elliott, Jr., and John O'Hear offered comments on earlier drafts, and Carol A. Gifford edited the final manuscript. I especially thank the Univeristy of Arizona Press, directed by Stephen F. Cox, for the fine production of this volume and for making this material available in monograph form.

Finally, I extend special gratitude to my parents and sister, Karen, for providing moral and financial support in times of need, and to my wife Diane, and sons William, David, and John Galen for their love, patience, and sacrifices.

William E. Doolittle

CHAPTER ONE

Early Settlements in Northern Mexico

The prehistory of nearly all of northern Mexico remains poorly understood; it is the "*terra incognita*" between the American Southwest and central Mexico (Sauer 1954: 554; Doyel 1979: 554). To a large extent the quantity and the quality of data collected to date are to blame for the problem. Basically, two kinds of data exist—archaeological and ethnohistorical. Although both kinds are extremely sparse and often contain numerous inconsistencies and discrepancies, the single greatest problem is that they are often contradictory.

THE ARCHAEOLOGICAL EVIDENCE

Northern Mexico has long been perceived by archaeologists as a region inhabited during pre-Hispanic times by small groups of "barbarians" (Di Peso 1979: 152–161). Known collectively as the Chichimecs (Riley and Hedrick 1978), these people are commonly thought to have been dominated by the more advanced Casas Grandes culture in the present-day state of Chihuahua (Di Peso 1974). This generalization is probably the result of disparities in the distribution and intensity of archaeological investigations to date. Without doubt, the intensive excavations and surveys by Di Peso at Casas Grandes constitute the most comprehensive research carried out in the expansive Gran Chichimeca.

With the exception of one study recently completed in Rio San Miguel Valley immediately west of the Valley of Sonora (Braniff C. 1984, 1985), archaeological research in eastern Sonora has consisted mainly of extensive regional surveys. Reconnaissance trips by Bandelier (1890, 1892), Lumholtz (1902), Amsden (1928), Sauer and Brand (1931), Ekholm (1939), Sauer and Haury (1946; West 1979: 124), Lehmer (1949), Noguera (1958), and Wasley (1967) were directed to the discovery of large or special types of sites (for example, early man and *cerros de trincheras*). Employing state of the science methods during those days of limited funds and harsh travel conditions, these people surveyed several kilometers each day with relatively few arbitrarily chosen locales selected for investigation. Indeed, Donald D. Brand once recalled that the locations of many sites recorded during his and Sauer's three day journey in the Valley of Sonora correlate with places where the model-T Ford they were using broke down.

The settlement data collected during such endeavors have led most archaeologists to believe that the population of the region was small and its culture rather simple (Johnson 1966: 35). Recorded architecture was of limited variety and the settlements themselves were few, small, and showed no evidence of planning or design. Occupation was interpreted as dating late in pre-Hispanic times, because adobe surface structures similar to pueblos dating to late periods in other parts of the Southwest were the principal structures discovered.

Perhaps the most graphic account of archaeological conditions came from Amsden (1928: 38, 39), who noted: "On a broad level mesa . . . , where I expected from the appearance of it to find a large site, there were a few scattered sherds, but I could locate no traces of houses." He went on to say: "In the valley again, we soon passed an 'island' standing on the edge of the stream, upon which I rode to look for a ruin, but was disappointed. Farther upstream I climbed to the top of a *mesita* and was again disappointed." Ekholm (1939: 8) echoed similar sentiments in saying: "sites are rather rare and difficult to find."

When encountered, settlements were often identified as little more than a scattering of houses "not placed in any very definite order," according to Amsden (1928: 47). Bandelier (1892: 487) noted that "villages" were comprised of houses "irregularly scattered" and "not connected together." Sauer and Brand (1931) stated in one place that the people of Sonora "did not have impressive individual towns . . . , their agricultural villages, here closely clustered, there sparsely strewn" (p. 72); in another citation, that "there were scattered ruins of single houses or small clusters" (p. 102); and in yet another, that "in general they are irregular assemblages of small house clusters" (p. 114).

Most frequently, houses were identified "by the rectangular outlines of 'foundation' stones, called *cimientos* by the Mexicans. Invariably the rooms were rectangular or square" (Sauer and Brand 1931: 114; see also Ekholm 1939: 8). According to Amsden (1928: 47): "rooms are always rectangular, eight by ten or ten by twelve feet in size," and "mounds of adobe . . . indicate that the use of that material for house-building was practiced." Bandelier (1892: 487) argued that the rock alignments visible on the surface were the foundations of wattle and daub, jacal, or reed mat houses. However, he provided no physical evidence to support that interpretation. Sauer and Brand (1931: 114–115) felt that in some cases semisubterranean structures, known generically today as pit houses, were also used prehistorically. "We saw walls exposed here and there by native treasure hunters, in which the stone foundations appeared as the surface expression or denudational remnants of walls of pit houses. The rooms were made by excavating to a depth of several feet and by lining the excavation with cobbles set in adobe mortar, to prevent caving. Slight depressions are still common within the enclosures." For the most part, however, stone foundations of small, rectangular, single room houses, and the presence of adobe "melt" have been used as evidence that surface structures were the principal form of architecture.

Discovered sites tended to be small. The only researcher to actually include house counts was Bandelier (1892: 487–488), who noted that sites ranged from "ten to fifty small houses," and that "none of the villages . . . could have sheltered more than a few hundred people."

Part of the reason for their small sizes, according to Bandelier (1892: 487), was environmental. "The river bottom is not fit for permanent habitation." Accordingly, "villages stand upon terraces so cut up by gulches that only room for small pueblos is found on their surface." Sauer and Brand (1931: 114) also confirmed that "the most numerous settlements are located on natural terrace spurs (mesas)."

The archaeologocial evidence uncovered to date suggests that prehistoric occupation was relatively late. On the basis of architectural remains, but apparently overlooking the significance of pit houses that have been dated quite early in the Southwest, Sauer and Brand (1931: 73) noted: "The ruins in Sonora . . . do not appear to belong to the earlier phases." Lehmer (1949: 5), using other evidence, concurred, saying: "One of the most interesting facts we gathered is that pottery is apparently quite late in most of Sonora." In addition to being late, it has been argued on the basis of "the absence of rubbish mounds at any of the sites" that "their period of existence was brief" (Amsden 1928: 49). These conditions, when viewed in light of events that occurred in other parts of the Southwest, led to the interpretation that eastern Sonora was populated by migrants from other areas. Most archaeologists have concluded that people moved into the region from either the north or the east.

Amsden (1928: 49) argued that migration was the result of the collapse of the northern cultures in Pueblo IV times, A.D. 1300 to 1450. Looking at a different source area, Brand (1935: 305) used ceramic data as evidence that people moved into the region around A.D. 1400 as nomadic tribes from the east drove formerly Chihuahuan people westward. Modified versions of Brand's theory have gained momentum and have a number of proponents. Di Peso (1974, Vol. 3: 799), for one, considered the aboriginal people of eastern Sonora to be descendants of migrants from Chihuahua following the demise of Casas Grandes about A.D. 1350. His contention is based in part on the need to explain where the residents of the "fallen" city went. Only one scholar, who used materials excavated from caves in the far eastern part of the region rather than surface evidence from throughout the area, argued for an early migration and, therefore, a long period of occupation. Lister (1958: 112–115) presented evidence that some, probably small, migrations may have occurred as cultures in the upper part of the Southwest were expanding southward in pre-Mogollon III times, prior to A.D. 900. Unlike the others, however, he made no claims concerning the size of the population and the degree of development in other parts of the region at the time of Spanish Contact.

THE ETHNOHISTORICAL EVIDENCE

Archaeological interpretations of a small, scattered population occupying the region briefly in late pre-Hispanic times stand in marked contrast to the evidence provided by the early Spanish explorers. Indeed, long after his own field work was completed, Sauer himself (1954: 555) argued that archaeologists "neglected" documentary evidence of advanced cultures scattered throughout northern Mexico. Many scholars who have traced the explorers' routes, such as historian Bolton (1949), accept the view that eastern Sonora was the densely populated, legendary "maize country" visited and described by Alvar Nuñez Cabeza de Vaca, who in 1536 was the first Spaniard to enter the Southwest. After gleaning the explorer's reports for ethnographic information and synthesizing the evidence contained therein, Riley (1980, 1982) concluded that the inhabitants of eastern Sonora were divided into discrete but related groups defined largely by the sections of the river valleys they occupied. At Contact, each of these groups had attained a modified chiefdom form of social organization that Riley (1979) termed "statelets." The exact nature of their organization is unknown, but statelets are argued to have had a social and political structure more complex than that of the Pueblo Indians (Riley 1980: 42).

Indeed, the narratives of the early Spanish explorers contain allusions to ceremonies and a celestial religion that involved a priesthood. A complex trading network that included the sale of slaves and organized warfare are also mentioned, suggesting a high degree of social stratification (Riley 1976a). Although he carefully avoided using value-laden and problem-ridden terms such as "level of development," Riley did not define statelets clearly. Accordingly, his classification has been criticized for adding to rather than resolving existing confusion (Naylor 1983: 121). The most tangible, and archaeologically verifiable, evidence Riley used for establishing statelets was ethnohistorical documentation of settlements and settlement patterns.

The Spanish explorers who entered the region in the mid-1500s described a complex settlement system with a variety of architectural forms, including some public structures, and numerous settlements of different size and function. Cabeza de Vaca wrote in the 1542 *Relacion* of his 1536 observations that "Some houses are of earth, the rest all of cane mats"

(Smith 1871: 167; also see Bandelier 1905: 156; Nuñez Cabeza de Vaca 1942: 81; Covey 1983: 119). Juan Jaramillo, one of the chroniclers of the 1540 expedition led by Francisco Vazquez de Coronado, said: "Their dwellings are huts made of frame poles, almost like an oven, only very much better, which they cover with mats" (Winship 1904: 224). Being "like an oven" suggests that mat houses were circular. The *Relacion postrera de Cibola* bears out this observation in saying that "houses built of reed mats . . . are round and small, a man hardly able to stand up inside" (Hammond and Rey 1940: 308). The *Relacion del suceso* provided even more insight, stating that mat houses were "almost underground" (Hammond and Rey 1940: 287). Clearly these ethnohistorical accounts suggest that "pit houses" were common in eastern Sonora at the time of Spanish Contact.

In addition to the references to pit houses are statements mentioning above-ground adobe "pueblos." The version of the Cabeza de Vaca party's *Joint Report* transcribed by Gonzalo Fernandez Oviedo y Valdez in 1537 stated that the people "lived in small adobe houses with flat roofs" (Hedrick and Riley 1974: 61; also see Davenport 1924–1925: 58 and Theisen 1972: 253). Little information about houses came from the Coronado expedition mainly because his chroniclers were strictly forbidden from entering native towns (Riley 1982: 40). However, Cabeza de Vaca's observations were repeated by others, particularly in the 1565 entourage of Francisco de Ibarra. Antonio Ruiz, one member of Ibarra's expedition, mentioned terraced or flat-roofed houses (Sauer 1932: 53). Baltasar de Obregon, the chief chronicler for Ibarra, frequently reported "terraced houses." In two places he specifically said they had "walls one and a half *estado* high" (Hammond and Rey 1928: 160, 173; Cuevas 1924: 156). Sauer (1932: 42) interprets estados as floors or flats. Obregon himself confirmed this interpretation, saying that in one town there were "houses of two and three stories." (Hammond and Rey 1928: 197).

In addition to what were undoubtedly dwellings, there exists evidence that some structures within the towns were ceremonial in nature, or at least were used by the public. Pedro Castañeda de Najera, Coronado's principal chronicler who apparently was at least on one occasion exempt from the ban on entering towns, noted that "dignitaries of the pueblos stand on some terraces which they have for that purpose . . . instructing the people. . . . They have their temples in small houses [kivas?], into which they drive numerous arrows, making them look like porcupines on the outside" (Hammond and Rey 1940: 250). The famed Spanish colonial historian Bartoleme de las Casas, who probably drew his information directly from personal interviews with Cabeza de Vaca and Fray Marcos de Niza (Riley 1976a; 25), also reported "very tall stone and mud temples for idols and for the entombment of principal personages" (de Las Casas 1967, I: 281).

Although the architecture reportedly varied, the layout of the towns seems to have been most consistent. Descriptions are less than ideal, but the towns appear to have been of clustered though not necessarily contiguous houses. According to the Cabeza de Vaca party's *Joint Report*, houses "were together and not spread out, one here and the other over there" (Theisen 1972: 356). Ibarra's chronicler stated that houses were not only "excellently grouped" (Hammond and Rey 1928: 160), but they were also situated along "well planned streets" (Hammond and Rey 1928: 173). In one case he even alluded to the presence of a central plaza, saying that houses were "built in the form of a square. They are large and strong, with stout walls and a large patio in the center" (Hammond and Rey 1928: 180). Ruiz echoed these same observations of town layout (Sauer 1932: 53).

The size of the towns described by the early Spaniards varied greatly. In the *Joint Report* of the journey of Cabeza de Vaca (Hedrick and Riley 1974: 62) there is mention of towns of some "twenty houses." In a letter to Viceroy Mendoza, Coronado reported that Melchior Diaz, who led the advance reconnaissance team into the region in 1539, came back with a report of "two or three poor villages, with twenty or thirty huts each" (Hammond and Rey 1940: 163). Obregon's account of the Ibarra venture (Hammond and Rey 1928) contains the most information about town sizes. He said that one unnamed town had 200 houses (p. 193), the town of Cumupa had 500 (p. 174), Guaraspi had 600 (p. 173), and Oera had 1,000 (p. 161). De Las Casas (1967, I: 281) even said that one town, in this case located specifically in the Valley of Sonora, had 3,000 houses! Such a claim seems a bit exaggerated. Nevertheless, the accounts of others, particularly Obregon, certainly suggest that sizeable towns did exist.

According to the Spaniards, the larger settlements appeared to have been regularly spaced at some distance apart, were near the centers of valley segments referred to as provinces, and were the dominant towns in the heartlands of landscapes containing numerous additional smaller settlements. Cabeza de Vaca and his companions were the first to relay information about settlement spacing and the role of towns as province centers. According to them: "they went more than eighty leagues, and every two or three days [for approximately eight months] they would arrive at towns and would rest a day or two" (Hedrick and Riley 1974: 61). In his own *Relacion*, Cabeza de Vaca later recalled that "the town where the emeralds were presented to us [Corazones] . . . is the entrance into many provinces" (Smith 1871: 172).

Obregon provided much more and somewhat better-detailed information, cited in Hammond and Rey (1928). In regard to spacing he specifically said that "towns were three or four leagues apart" (p. 163). His statement: "from town to town and from province to province" (p. 192) indicates not only that towns were distant but that they were also associated with larger regions as Cabeza de Vaca first noted. These towns, provinces, and the valleys in which they were located seem to have shared common names. In one place Obregon stated that the town of Cumupa "has a valley" (p. 175). Elsewhere he said: "these provinces . . . the valleys of Corazones, Señora, Guaraspi, Cumupa, Batuco, Chuparo, Caquaripa, Horeco, their surroundings, districts, and towns . . ." (pp. 170–171).

References to towns are clearly in regard to the larger settlements. Numerous smaller settlements also appear to have existed surrounding and between the larger places, but they received little attention and only slight and passing mention by the Spaniards. Castañeda, however, did note that "Around this province . . . there are large settlements forming separate small provinces. They are composed of ten or twelve pueblos," and "Round about this valley there are many pueblos" (Hammond and Rey 1940: 250). Obregon, using a new and previously unheard term for more diminutive settlements, said in one place that "hamlets" were "passed through" (Hammond and Rey 1928: 175), while in the "neighborhood"—province or valley—of previously mentioned Cumupa, there were also small towns.

In sum, and in contrast to the existing archaeological interpretations, ethnohistorical evidence from eastern Sonora includes numerous and detailed accounts of a variety of commonly used architectural forms, including three types of houses and public architecture, agglomerated rather than dispersed towns with plazas and planned streets, and a variety of settlement sizes ranging from small hamlets to large towns, comprising what might be considered central place systems (for example, see Christaller 1966). Each valley segment or province contained a population numbering in the thousands, numerous small settlements, and one large town that functioned as the social, economic, and political center of a statelet.

About the only point on which the archaeological and ethnohistorical materials are in total agreement is the physical location of the settlements themselves. That the towns were located along rivers seems obvious. Most were located on high ground overlooking the river, on the mesa tops or the ends of the interfluves between arroyos that converge with floodplains. Obregon reported such in the case of Caguaripa, whereby he noted: "It is surrounded on two sides by a rough and deep ravine" (Hammond and Rey 1928: 180). Castañeda provided further insight in terms of the nature and direction of the arroyos when he noted that: "In passing from one settlement to another [up and down river], there is always a ravine in the way" (Winship 1904: 86).

Although the Spanish reports, if accurate, portray conditions only at Contact, it is highly probable that people inhabited the region for a longer period of time than archaeologists accept. Relying principally on linguistic data, Riley (1979) once argued that the people encountered by the Spaniards in eastern Sonora were descendants of migrants from Casas Grandes. Such may be the case; however, a date of A.D. 1300 as he originally proposed (Riley 1982: 39) seems too short a time for changes of the noted magnitude to occur, even with diffusion. The patterns of occupance described by the Spaniards could only have been achieved by people who were in the region for several centuries. The perspective that the patterns of occupance found in eastern Sonora were developed indigenously and independently of migrations has been given little attention. For decades Sauer and Brand (1931: 116) were the only ones who suggested that developments in the region may have been the result of internal events, independent of other peoples. Today, however, even Riley (1987) himself has begun to question the influence of Casas Grandes on Sonora.

As might be expected, the Spanish descriptions have not gone without criticisms. For example, the archaeologist Kelley (1980: 65) stated emphatically that "KNOWN archaeological remains simply do not approach the cultural levels described in the ethnohistorical documents." Conflicts between the archaeological and the ethnohistorical evidence have long been recognized. Sauer (1935: 26–29), for example, found documentary evidence of a population much larger than that interpreted from the archaeological data he and Brand (Sauer and Brand 1931) recorded a few years earlier. For undetermined reasons, no one has attempted to resolve the discrepancies (Hinton 1983: 321). Archaeologists, for the most part, continue to accept the argument that the region was sparsely inhabited while the ethnohistorians still subscribe to the alternative point of view. In reality, neither group has conclusive evidence that supports their respective positions; inconsistencies not only continue to exist but they abound. This study should resolve the controversy. The purpose here is to provide an accurate picture of pre-Hispanic conditions in eastern Sonora.

THE ROLE OF OCCUPANCE RESEARCH

This study focuses on occupance, a metaphorical concept derived from the terms "occupy," to possess, control, dwell, or reside in a region, and "occupation," an activity that serves as one's regular source of livelihood. A commonly used concept in historical geography, occupance is defined simply as the combined efforts of inhabiting and utilizing a region. The human-environmental relationship is of the essence here. Interpretations of pre-Hispanic culture, including items typically of interest to archaeologists such as pottery, architecture, and social organization, are treated neither directly nor in detail. They are, however, discussed in the broader context of occupance. Theories of culture change, including those dealing with migration, contacts with other cultures, and trade are similarly treated.

The approach used here is necessarily archaeological. The ethnohistoric reports need to be tested and more detailed archaeological data are needed. Rather than attempting to resurvey the entire region in a manner similar to that used by early archaeologists, one of the five major valleys in eastern Sonora was systematically and intensively investigated. The 51 kilometer-long Valley of Sonora was chosen for several reasons. First, it has long been considered by both archaeologists and ethnohistorians as the core area of an eastern Sonora culture region (Amsden 1928: 44–45; Spicer 1967: 92–94). Second, prehistoric trade routes passed through this valley (Brand 1938; Riley 1976b), as did the Spanish explorers who were led by native guides (Sauer 1932). Third, it has been subjected to at least six extensive regional surveys that, by design, overlooked numerous sites (Wasley 1966).

In a sense, this study is more ecological than it is social or humanistic. The relationship between humans and the environment is the subject. People are treated as members of the human race, not as members of various cultures or ethnic and linguistic stocks. There is simply too little data available at this time to discuss with any degree of competency a topic as complex and with as many intangible nuances as "culture." However, sufficient data exist to discuss occupance.

Based on a combined Type III–IV survey as outlined by Ruppé (1966) and a Stage 3 survey as discussed by Schiffer, Sullivan, and Klinger (1978), this work reports the findings of a thorough local investigation rather than a regional reconnaissance. Such a methodology provides detailed evidence for identification, prevalence, distribution, and functions of relic settlements, especially where "relatively young sites are of primary interest" (Butzer 1982: 262). Evidence of prehistoric agriculture is also presented and discussed. The importance of analyzing settlements for understanding ancient occupance was stated appropriately by Willey (1956: 1), one of the pioneers of such studies: "In settlement, man inscribes upon the landscape certain modes of his existence. These settlement arrangements relate to the adjustments of man and culture to the environment and to the organization of society in the broadest sense."

Similar reasons can be advanced for the study of agricultural evidence. Such artifacts reflect adaptations to the physical environment, subsistence needs of the people, and the level of technology on which the population operated. Settlements and agricultural evidence are usually well-preserved manifestations of occupance. In concert, therefore, they are excellent items for study. Being to a large extent directly shaped by widely held cultural demands, they provide much insight into prehistoric occupance. Because both settlements and agriculture are simultaneously influenced by and modifiers of the environment, a thorough understanding of the physical conditions of the region is essential (Coe and Flannery 1964).

CHAPTER TWO

Physical Environs

Perhaps nowhere else in the New World have the environment, the prehistoric peoples, and the relationships between the two been so widely misunderstood as in northern Mexico. To be sure, the region is both a desert and sparsely populated. However, it is wrong to assume that the climate determines an area's patterns of occupance or that northern Mexico is environmentally homogeneous. High civilizations such as those of ancient Egypt and Peru, for example, developed in desert oases characterized by environmental diversity (Carniero 1970). The landscape of northern Mexico is markedly heterogeneous, involving elevations that range from sea level to over 3,000 m and vegetation differences that include pine forests in the higher elevations, riparian woodlands along the perennial rivers, and expanses of typical desert shrubs. If environmental diversity was essential for the emergence of such civilizations in deserts elsewhere, then areas in the desert of northern Mexico could facilitate occupance by people other than barbaric bands of nomads. Such an oasis is the Valley of Sonora. "Beautiful and fertile beyond anything else in this part of the country" (Sauer 1932: 35), the valley is one of several located in a region known as the *serrana* (Braniff C. 1978: 68) or foothills of the western flank of the Sierra Madre Occidental of eastern Sonora.

THE SERRANA

The serrana is characterized by considerable ecological diversity within broad environmental patterns. Overall, the nature of the region and its similarity to another area where agriculture and permanent settlements first appeared were most succinctly stated by Carl Sauer (1963: 123): "Perhaps no other area in the New World comes as close to the physical conditions of the Old World Fertile Crescent as does this one." The serrana is a semiarid ecological transition zone between the pine-covered Sierra Madres of Chihuahua and the coastal plain of the Gulf of California and the Sonoran Desert (Fig. 2.1).

Extending between 28°30′ and 31°0′ North latitude and 108°30′ and 111°0′ West longitude, the region forms the extreme southern end of the Basin and Range physiographic province of North America (Hunt 1974: 502–504). It is composed of a series of generally parallel ranges, of various ages, approximately 30 km apart with maximum elevations that increase from approximately 1,200 m in the west to over 2,600 m in the east. Partly controlled by structure, the valleys between these ranges are broken into discrete segments. Each segment is filled with thick Quaternary-age alluvial deposits that have coalesced to form extensive bajadas that range in elevation from approximately 600 m in the lower portion of the San Miguel Valley in the west to over 1,000 m in the upper segment of the Bavispe Valley in the east. These bajadas have been incised by rivers that have formed floodplains varying in width from 1 km to 4 km. Numerous arroyos of varying length and width have dissected the bajadas so as to form a series of elongated mesas that extend from the ranges of the floodplains. As they are today, the edges of these bajadas, overlooking the river floodplains and arroyos, were desired locales for permanent settlements in pre-

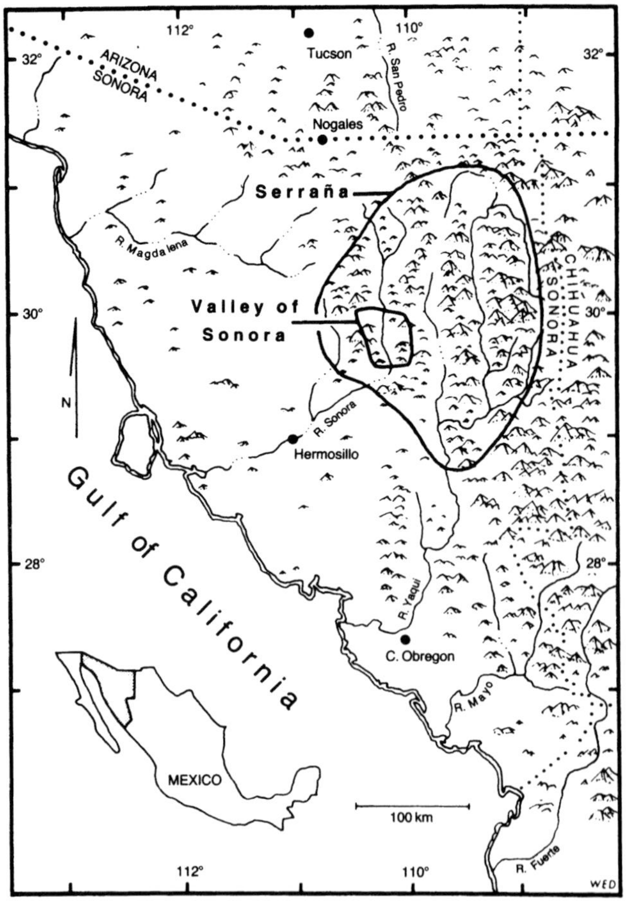

Figure 2.1. The serrana and the Valley of Sonora. (Reprinted from the *Journal of Field Archaeology*, Vol. 11, p. 14, 1984, with the permission of the Trustees of Boston University.)

historic times. Both the floodplains and the arroyos were farmed. Some arroyos still contain numerous relic agricultural features.

The region is characterized by a climate that has been considered subtropical steppe (Trewartha 1961: 271–275) but, because of extreme topographic variety, is more desert with an extremely wet summer (Garcia 1981: 14, 41–42). Average annual rainfall increases from approximately 250 mm in the extreme southwest to 500 mm in the northeast, and mean temperatures increase from approximately 20° Celsius (68° F) in the northeast to 23° C (73.4° F) in the southwest (S.A.R.H. 1961–1981). The index of aridity also decreases congruently with the regional increases in precipitation and decreases in temperature (Ives 1949: 150–151). Although some scholars disagree (Sykes 1931: 229), higher elevations appear to receive more rainfall than lower elevations. A seasonal dichotomy of winter and summer rains, the *equipatas* and *las aguas*, respectively, exists throughout the region (Ives 1949: 168–169); almost 60 percent of the average annual rainfall is generated by convectional thunderstorms in July and August. Another 20 percent falls in modest but steady amounts during December and January. Severe moisture deficits prevail during the late spring, and a more moderate dry period occurs in the fall. Snow is common in the higher elevations during the winter (Avila-Gonzales 1983), but rarely falls in the valleys. Indeed, the snowfall experienced in the valleys during the winter of 1984 to 1985 was reported by some elderly persons to be the first in their lifetimes. Summertime rainfall, as in most arid and semiarid regions, is marked by temporal, quantitative, and spatial variations (Turnage and Mallery 1941: 17–21). In any one year a locale might receive abundant rain while nearby none falls. Similarly, a given place might suffer severe drought conditions one year and receive abundant rainfall the next. Everywhere variations in annual precipitation totals are considerable. Although rainfall is unpredictable, the major valleys contain streams that provide abundant water for human use (Bell and Mackenzie 1923: 18; Dunbier 1968: 92).

Vegetation patterns tend to parallel elevation and precipitation patterns (Velazquez-Perez and Melo-Gallegos 1983). Three of the general Southwestern life zones are present: the Lower and Upper Sonoran Desert zones and the Transition Zone (Lowe and Brown 1982: 10–11). The lower elevations, especially the river valleys and the southwestern third of the serrana, fall within the vegetational subregion of the lower desert known generally as the "Foothills of Sonora" (Shreve and Wiggins 1964: 51–53), a true desert. Mesquite (*Prosopis* spp.), palo verde (*Cercidium sonorae*), and ironwood (*Olneya tesota*) are common trees. Shrubs include numerous species of acacia (*Acacia* spp.), ocotillo (*Fouquieria* spp.), yucca (*Yucca* spp.), agave (*Agave* spp.), and mimosa (*Mimosa laxiflora*). Cacti, including columnar species such as organpipe (*Stenocereus thurberi*), cholla (*Opuntia* spp.), and prickly pear (*Opuntia comonduensis*), are abundant. The upper desert extending between 1,400 m and 2,000 m above sea level (Little 1950) is characterized by junipers (*Juniperus monosperma*) and oaks (*Quercus* spp.). The Transition Zone includes the areas of highest elevation and rainfall (Little 1950) and is noted principally by stands of Ponderosa pine (*Pinus ponderosa*). Grasses, although now sparse because of overgrazing that began in Spanish times, are still found in some areas, particularly on the plains near the northern margin of the region (Johnson G. and Carrillo Michel 1977). Herbaceous species were probably more abundant in prehistoric times than they are now, especially on the bajadas (Hastings and Turner 1965: 285). Riparian woodlands, comprised of cottonwood (*Populus fremontii*) and willow (*Salix* spp.), are quite pronounced along the major streams.

THE VALLEY OF SONORA

Topography and Drainage

The Rio Sonora, like the other serrana valleys, is comprised of distinct sections. The river has three major reaches: upper, middle, and lower. The upper reach flows through extensive plains in the far north near the *ciudad* or city of Cananea and cuts through volcanic terrain between the pueblos or towns of Bacoachi and Sinoquipe in the south. The middle reach, the Valley of Sonora, has also been referred to as the Middle Rio Sonora Valley, the Valle de Sonora, the Valle de Señora, and even Señora. Providing the name by which the entire modern state is known, this valley extends southward from below Sinoquipe to the upstream end of a long and deep gorge that historically has been considered the gateway to Sonora (Sauer 1932: 17). This gorge begins near the *congregacion* or village of Mazocahui and ends at the edge of the serrana near the congregacion of Puerta del Sol or door of the sun (an appropriate name for a town located at the western end of a gorge through which light from the rising sun first breaks through the mountains). From there the river flows through the lower reach, across the Sonoran Desert Coastal Plain, emptying into the Sea of Cortez or Gulf of California.

Floodplain development is limited throughout the serrana. In the upper reach of the Rio Sonora, floodplains are found only in three areas: near Bacoachi, the pueblo of Chinapa, and the ciudad of Arizpe. The floodplains average only about 6 km in length and less than 1 km in width in these places. The single largest expanse of floodplain is that which extends throughout the entire length of the middle reach, the Valley of Sonora. Here the landscape is characterized by the river and its floodplain, cut through a broad basin situated between peripheral mountain ranges (Fig. 2.2). The lowest elevation in the valley, 520 m above sea level, is along the channel bottom at the southern end of the region. The highest point is atop the Sierra Aconchi, a Mesozoic batholith west of the river near the center of the region. This peak rises 2,185 m above sea level. The remainder of this western range averages about 1,200 m. Volcanic activity in upper Cenozoic times formed the range to the east. This range is slightly higher than the western range, averaging 1,600 m.

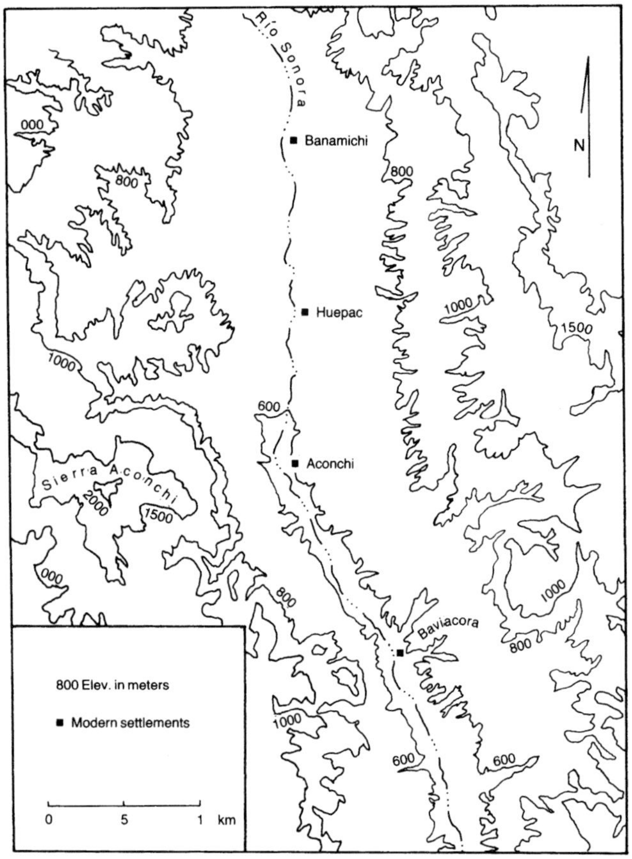

Figure 2.2. Topography of the Valley of Sonora.

The Valley of Sonora lies within the Mexican Transition Zone (King 1930; Nye 1972) of the Basin and Range province (Hunt 1974: 502–504). Here the structure changes strike from north-south to northwest-southeast, and the ranges become less parallel. The range to the east remains north-south trending, but the one to the west conforms generally with the direction of the Gulf of California coastline. The result is that the peripheral ranges are closer together in the southern end than in the northern end of the valley, with the river changing direction congruently with the change in strike.

The gradual southward taper to the ranges and the change in strike have affected the character of the basin structure, mainly by altering the stream configuration. In the northern part of the valley the river is much closer to the eastern than to the western range. It is through this section that the bajada development is areally larger west of the river. Southward, the river runs very close to the western range in the central part of the valley near the foot of the Sierra Aconchi. Through this stretch the bajada development is extensive to the east and absent to the west. Throughout the remaining southern portion of the area this configuration remains roughly the same. Some bajada development is noted on the west, but the preponderance of the bajada is to the east. The overall configuration of the valley can be viewed as one in which the river has cut its main channel diagonally between the adjacent mountain ranges. That is, rather than paralleling the ranges, which themselves are not parallel, the river enters the valley in the northeast corner and exits in the southwest corner (Fig. 2.3).

Figure. 2.3. Aerial view of the Valley of Sonora. Looking south, the pueblo of Huepac is in the lower left, Sierra Aconchi is at the far right.

The Rio Sonora is not a perennial stream today. Discharge is greatest in July and August and is nonexistent from March through June (Dunbier 1968: 89). Although the river as a whole is ephemeral, there are a few places, particularly in the middle of the valley, where springs provide a sufficient amount of water for constant streamflow over short distances. Hewes (1935: 288), for example, observed that: ". . . during the dry months of autumn and spring the Rio Sonora frequently is dry to the north of El Ojo de Agua, whereas southward, due to the welling up of water from below, there is always water in the river."

The springs, known as *nacimientos* or places where water is born, found throughout the Valley of Sonora, flow regularly. Indeed, this dependable ground water may possibly be the greatest single resource available to residents. It has been noted that in one arroyo near the Sierra Aconchi, bedrock is about 2.2 m below the arroyo floor, and that the basal 10.0 cm is saturated gravel (Schramm 1932: 42). This bedrock is not at a uniform depth throughout the valley, as attested by the various well depths. In many places wells for modern irrigation may be as deep as 3 or 4 m. In other places the water table is very shallow and can be tapped easily by hand-digging small wells (Fig. 2.4). Such features are similar to the sipping holes of the African Bushmen and the tamilas of the Middle East (Nir 1974: 63).

Figure 2.4. A shallow, hand-dug well used to obtain drinking water from an arroyo.

Basically, the locations where water is found in the channel during the height of the dry season are either at or a short distance downstream from springs such as that observed by Hewes at the congregacion of El Ojo de Agua, a few kilometers north of the pueblo of Huepac. The largest single stretch of uninterrupted flow occurs in the southern half of the valley (Fig. 2.5).

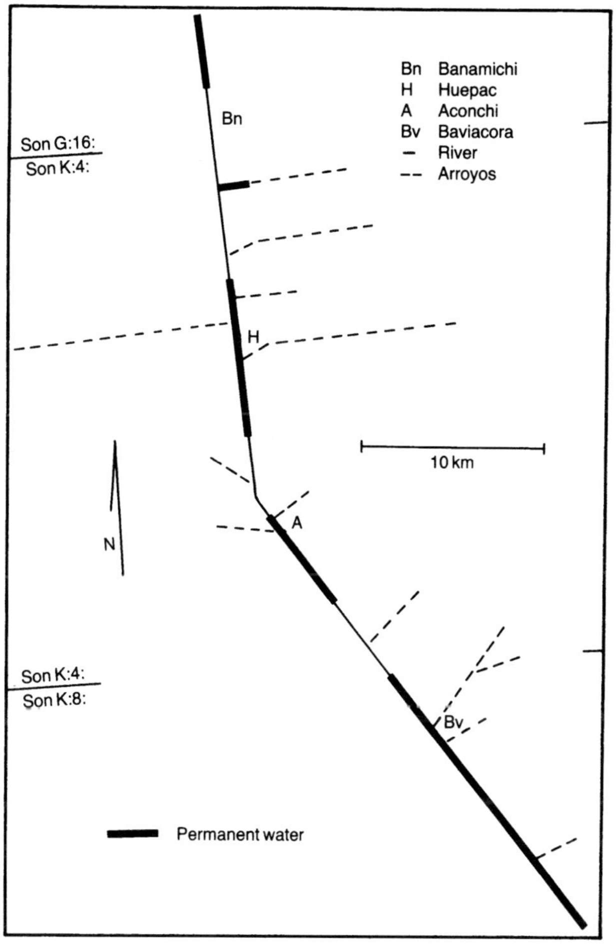

Figure 2.5. Dry season sources of water. (Observations made during June, 1977.)

The main river channel is also fed with water from a source other than springs and surface flow from the upper reach. This source is runoff from the peripheral mountain ranges flanking both sides of the valley. These ranges, which receive more rainfall than the valley proper during the summer and winter months, deposit water in the main channel through the numerous arroyos that dissect the bajada. Typically dry, these arroyos can have their floors covered with rapidly flowing water only minutes after the start of a thunderstorm in the mountains (Rahn 1967).

The overall drainage pattern of the valley is that of a trellis. The river, of course, is the most conspicuous water course. Arroyos extending from the mountains to the floodplain are numerous and vary in size. Because of several geological differences, the bajada is much more extensively dissected in some places than in others. As a result, a few long, wide arroyos separated by broad, flat interfluves characterize some places, while in others, often only a short distance away, short, V-shaped arroyos separated by narrow interfluves may be more common. In general, the former condition typifies the northern half of the valley, whereas the latter condition is characteristic of the southern half, especially on the west side of the river where bajada development is minimal.

In summary, the topography and drainage characteristics of the valley are conducive to locating permanent settlements along, or at least proximal to, major water courses. Although the water courses are typified by irregular flow, the discharge is of considerable size and, therefore, suitable for sustaining a large, agriculturally based population.

Climate

In the Valley of Sonora, as for the whole of the Greater Sonoran Desert region, there is a seasonal dichotomy of winter rains and summer rains, with a dry period occurring in the late spring and fall (Ives 1949: 168–169). A rainy day during the winter is commonly characterized by moderate but steady precipitation, whereas intensive early evening thunderstorms characterize the summer rainfall regime. As is typical of arid regions, rainfall is so marked by variations that generalizations are difficult. For example, the pueblo of Banamichi receives an annual average of 424.2 mm of precipitation (S.A.R.H. 1961–1981), whereas the pueblo of Baviacora receives only 278.0 mm (Hastings 1964: 16). In addition to quantitative variations, rainfall also varies in time and space. Temporal variability tends to be greatest when the amount of rain is low, decreasing as rainfall increases (Noy-Meir 1973: 28–33). Although the seasonality of the rainfall is predictable, the amount received is not. In Baviacora, for example, the average rainfall in July is 90.9 mm (Hastings 1964: 16). The total precipitation received during July was 24.2 mm in 1958 and 130.3 mm in 1959. Likewise, Baviacora received 3.2 mm and 109.6 mm of rainfall during August of 1953 and 1960, respectively. Both figures represent considerable departure from the 53.7 mm average. Probably the greatest temporal deviation in rainfall was the 290.0 mm experienced during November of 1946. Excluding that year, the average November rainfall for Baviacora was only 7.3 mm. It is difficult to discuss precipitation in terms of averages because of the extreme variabilities. Perhaps the most conclusive statement that can be made is that the months of July and August experience between 55 to 60 percent of the annual rainfall, and that December and January experience about 20 percent.

Although rainfall is greater in the summer, so is evapotranspiration. In contrast, lower evapotranspiration rates during the winter rainy season make the effectiveness of the rainfall greater than that of the summer season (Ives 1949: 171). This duality of rainfall seasons permits double cropping, today corn in the summer and wheat in the winter-spring (Doolittle 1983). Of course, the variability of precipitation can have disastrous effects on crop yields.

The spatial variability of Sonoran rainfall is as unpredictable as temporal variations. For example, the pueblo of Aconchi received 241.0 mm in August 1951, and Baviacora, only 14 km downstream, received only 87.3 mm (Hastings 1964: 1, 16). This spatial variation is largely the result of the stochastic processes involved in convective situations. It can result in a given place receiving excessive rainfall while another locale a short distance away might not receive any. In terms of crop production, dry farming or rainfall-dependent agriculture is precarious.

Although data are sparse for this region, examples from the neighboring Moctezuma Valley illustrate a correlation between mean precipitation and elevation. During a three-year period in which comparable data were collected from two stations only 8 km apart, the pueblo of Nacozari de Garcia, at an elevation of 1,082 m, received an annual rainfall average of 658.0 mm, and the pueblo of Pilares de Nacozari, at an elevation of 1,409 m, received 702.2 mm (Hastings 1964: 79, 95). The influence of the sierras is undoubtedly a factor affecting the regional climatic pattern.

In contrast to the variable rainfall figures, the average annual temperature, 22.8° C (73° F) in Baviacora (Hastings 1964: 16), varies little from year to year. During the summer season daytime highs in the Valley of Sonora can be well over 40° C (104° F) and sometimes over 45° C (113° F; S.A.R.H. 1961–1981). Summer nighttime low temperatures rarely go below 25° C (77° F), resulting in an average summer temperature of approximately 30° C (86° F). Winters in the valley are cool with a January average of 13.6° C (56.5° F; Hastings 1964: 16). Frosts are common but of short duration. Snow, which is rarely experienced in the valley, is common in the mountains during the winter seasons.

The rainfall and temperature regimes in the Valley of Sonora have cultural implications in that they are adequate for practicing agriculture. Although rainfall variability is a problem, it is partially offset by the dual rainfall regime that allows double cropping. The dependability of stream flow, and hence irrigation, is complementary crop-loss insurance.

Ecological Zones

In concert, the topographic and climatic conditions have resulted in the formation of seven distinctive, combined physiographic-vegetation or ecological zones in the Valley of Sonora: the riparian woodland-floodplain, monte-bajada, thorn forest-pediment, mixed scrub-slopes, piedmont transition, oak parklands, and pine-oak forest uplands (Fig. 2.6). These zones vary not only in size and physical composition, but also in the extent to which they have economic and cultural utility. Certain zones contain resources not available in other zones. In addition, some zones have, on the whole, more utilitarian value than others.

Although each of the ecological zones contains plants of economic utility, the distribution of these plants is by no means uniform. The productivity of such zones may be envisioned as a continuum representing a transect running from the river laterally across the valley to the mountain peaks. As in other places (Hastorf 1980), a distance decay function to the availability and exploitation of various plants in various zones appears to exist. For purposes of resource procurement, the pine-oak forest upland area, most distant from the river, was probably the ecological zone of the most limited utility. The riparian woodland-floodplain, conversely, was of the greatest attraction to the occupants.

Riparian Woodland-Floodplain

The riparian woodland-floodplain zone, the environmental center of the valley, ranges from only a few hundred meters in width in the extreme northern and southern ends of the valley to more than 2 km in width between Banamichi and Aconchi. From Aconchi to approximately 7 km south of Baviacora the average width of this zone is roughly 1 km. Approximately 25 percent of the 70 square kilometers in this region is occupied by the the active river channel and abandoned meanders. Like most semiarid land streams, the Rio Sonora with its 1.0 degree gradient maintains a typically low discharge that results in meandering (Butzer 1976: 151–154). Periodic flooding tends to aid in altering the stream flow by depositing additional materials (Kochel and Baker 1982). Torrential rains, however, often result in extensive degradation that tends to compensate for any previous aggredation.

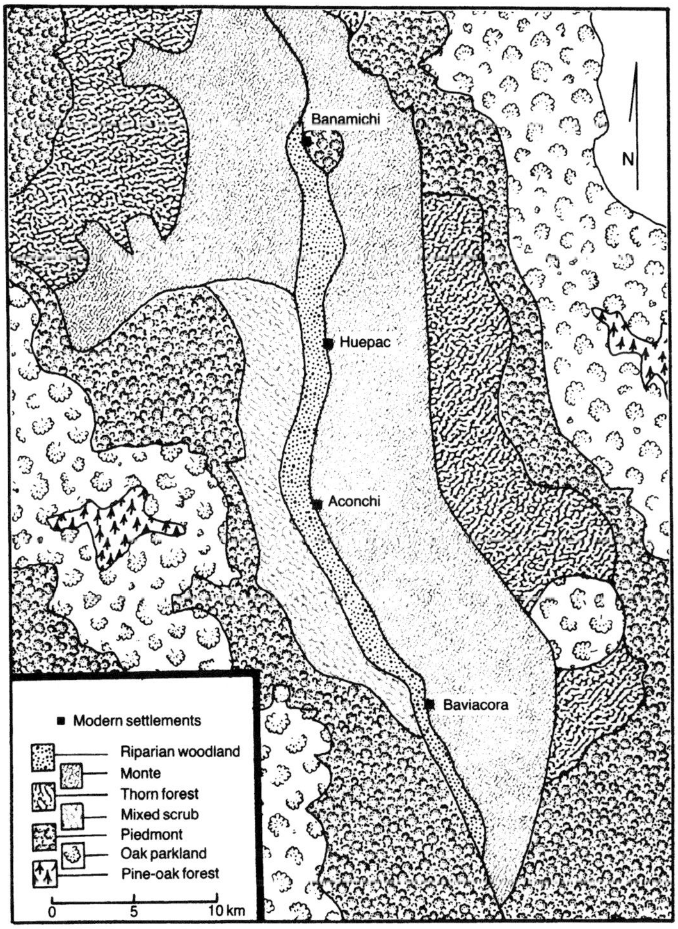

Figure 2.6. Ecological zones.

The soils of the floodplain are deep, fertile, and rock-free. They are typically brown (10YR 5/3), slightly alkaline (7.7 pH), young, and classified as Torripsamments (Soil Survey Staff 1975: 204–205). Their loamy sand texture is more efficient for retaining soil moisture in arid regions than are finer-grained soils (Buol, Hole, and McCracken 1980: 24–25; Walter 1973: 67–68, 100). This permeability also facilitates the recharge and flow of ground water.

The riparian woodland vegetation characteristic of the floodplain is predominantly mesquite (*Prosopis velutina*). The principal subordinate plants, willow (*Salix gooddingii*) and cottonwood (*Populus fremontii*), are both indicators of a high water table. Generally this area is classified as one of the Sonoran Riparian Deciduous Forest and Woodlands (Minckley and Brown 1982: 269–273). Vegetation is largely fast-growing and winter deciduous; phytogeographic affinities are with the north, or temperate North American (Felger, Nabhan, and Sheridan 1976). The relatively high degree of shade and shallow water table are conducive to heavy herbaceous ground cover. Many of the natural plants found along the riparian woodland have economic or utilitarian value (Table 2.1). The *quelites*, especially *Amaranthus palmeri*, that sprout and grow rapidly after the onset of the summer rains are particularly important (Meals for Millions Foundation 1980: 14–15). These greens are known to have been boiled and eaten much like spinach (Bye 1981). Indeed, it has been recorded that the neighboring Pimas relied heavily on gathered mesquite beans, even though 50 to 60 percent of their food was agriculturally produced (Castetter and Bell 1942: 56–57). The largest proportion of the floodplain is presently under cultivation, with only remnants of the woodland in the peripheral areas (Doolittle 1983). The most luxuriant stands of woodland are located in the southern end of the valley. It is highly probable that the shallow water table in this segment is conducive to this denser growth.

Monte-Bajada

The monte-bajada zone is the largest environmental zone in the Valley of Sonora. Covering 468 square kilometers, this zone is formed by alluvial and colluvial materials that have been poorly indurated into conglomerates and were overlain in Quaternary times by sediment eroded from the higher elevations (Salas 1976). Were it not for the presence of several arroyos of varying lengths and widths cutting traversely, the bajada would be a gently sloping but relief-free surface. Extending between 600 m and 800 m above sea level, the surface slopes an average of 2.0 degrees, and it is quite rocky.

Table 2.1. Common Plants of Major Economic Value by Ecological Zone in the Valley of Sonora

Plant	Main Usages	Riparian Woodland-Floodplain	Monte-Bajada	Thorn Forest-Pediment	Mixed Scrub Slope	Piedmont Transition	Oak Parkland and Pine-Oak Woodland	Large Arroyos
Agave spp.	Beverages, cordage, thatch		X	X	X			
Amaranthus palmeri	Greens	X						X
Bursera spp.	Medicine			X	X			
Capsicum sp.	Peppers					X		
Celtis pallida	Berries	X	X		X			X
Chenopodium sp.	Seeds	X						X
Dasylirion spp.	Baskets, cordage, thatch		X	X	X			
Juglans major	Walnuts, wood	X						
Juniperus monosperma	Fuel, seeds, wood					X		
Olneya tesota	Beans, fuel, wood		X		X			X
Opuntia spp.	Fruit		X	X	X			
Palmaceae spp.	Cordage, thatch	X						
Pinus edulis	Seeds						X	
Pinus spp.	Wood						X	
Populus sp.	Fuel, wood	X						
Prosopis spp.	Beans, fuel, wood	X	X		X			X
Quercus emoryi	Acorns						X	
Quercus spp.	Fuel, wood						X	
Salix sp.	Fuel, wood	X						
Stenocereus thurberi	Fruit		X	X	X			
Yucca spp.	Baskets, cordage, thatch			X	X			

Source: Castetter and Bell (1942); Pfefferkorn (1949); Felger, Nabhan, and Sheridan (1976); and Pennington (1980).

This zone includes two subregions, the main bajadas east and west of the river and the bajada edge along the east side of the river. The principal difference between the bajada subregions is the character of the soil. Soils of the bajada proper are slightly acid (6.2 pH), yellowish red (7.5YR 5/4), Haplargids (Soil Survey Staff 1975: 159–162) that are developed nearly enough to be classified as Aridic Haplustolls (Soil Survey Staff 1975: 303–304). The edge of the bajada has soils that are neutral (7.3 pH) and brown (7.5YR 5/3). Under normal conditions the soils of bajada edges are finer textured than the soils of higher elevations (Yang and Lowe 1956: 542). In the Valley of Sonora, however, this textural distribution is reversed. Although soils in both areas are technically sandy loams (Buol, Hole, and McCracken 1980: 24–25), those along the edge have an average of 4.7 percent more sand and 2.8 percent less clay than the other bajada soils. The differences in the soils are probably the result of intensive human occupation along the bajada edge. Accordingly, soils in this area are classified as Arents (Soil Survey Staff 1975: 187).

The vegetation of this zone is characterized by a proliferation of small trees and thorny shrubs. In addition to being known locally as the *monte* (Hewes 1935: 284), this type of vegetation has been referred to as an arborescent desert (Shreve and Wiggins 1964: 52) and as Sonoran Desertscrub (Turner and Brown 1982: 181–182, 218–220). This vegetation zone is dominated by mimosa (*Mimosa laxiflora*), which accounts for approximately 40 percent of all vegetation. Trees, especially palo verde (*Cercidium* spp.) and mesquite (*Prosopis* spp.), are common. Grasses and other ephemerals, common in the riparian woodland, are thin and nearly nonexistent on the bajada. In contrast, cacti, which are largely absent in the riparian woodland, are common in the desert scrub zone. The distribution of cacti, however, is not uniform. Along the bajada edge east of the river, cacti account for nearly 20 percent of all vegetation. In the central portion of the zone, cacti comprise only about 6.5 percent of all plants. Organpipe (*Stenocereus thurberi*) is characteristic and common in all parts of the bajada, but jumping cholla (*Opuntia fulgida*) is most common in all parts of the bajada edge. The formidability of this plant to archaeological surveys was noted by Amsden (1928: 39), who claimed "it is the awfullest cactus I ever saw." The proliferation of cholla and other *Opuntia* spp. along the bajada edge is largely the result of edaphic conditions resulting from extensive human intervention.

The vegetation of the monte differs significantly from that of the riparian woodland. Mesquite (*Prosopis* spp.) is less dense than on the floodplain and was probably even less dense in pre-Hispanic times (see section on paleoenvironments). Accordingly, the species was probably not exploited on a major scale in this zone. Cordage plants and a number of wild food plants, however, are more numerous in the monte than in the riparian woodlands (Table 2.1). The fruit of the organpipe cactus (*Stenocereus thurberi*), known as tuna, is most plentiful. Buds of *Opuntia* spp. are also abundant, but they are not used by present-day inhabitants and might not have been used to any great extent prehistorically.

Thorn Forest-Pediment

The thorn forest-pediment zone, extending from 800 m to 1,100 m in elevation, is named after a similar vegetation zone found along the Rio Mayo in southern Sonora (Gentry 1942) and a geologic feature common in basin and range country (Tuan 1959). A pediment is an erosional surface formed by headward erosion of the mountain slope. These relief-free and gently sloping surfaces usually have thin deposits overlying planed bedrock. In the Valley of Sonora, however, pediments are highly dissected by the arroyos originating in the mountains. This dissection is so advanced that little true pediment surface remains. Theoretically, the surface slopes should be approximately 3.0 degrees, but because of dissection they often approach 25 degrees. Because they are formed on steep bedrock slopes, soils on the pediment are much thinner and less well-developed than the alluvial soils of the bajadas. Sandy loam in texture (Buol, Hole, and McCracken 1980: 24–25), these soils are classified as Lithic Torriorthents (Soil Survey Staff 1975: 196–198). They range from brown to dark brown in color (7.5YR 4/3 to 10YR 4/3) and are slightly acid (6.1 pH).

Covering 260 square kilometers, the thorn forest, which is similar to the Sinaloan Thornscrub (Shreve and Wiggins 1964: 71; Brown 1982b: 101–105), is distinctive, characterized principally by the boat thorn acacia (*Acacia cymbispina*) with its stiff, curved, silvery thorns. Palo blanco (*Lysiloma candida*), with its smooth light-colored bark, and ocotillo (*Fouquieria splendens*) are also prolific. Many varieties of cacti are common in the zone. Grass cover is somewhat more dense than that of the monte, but it is by no means luxuriant. Other contrasts between this zone and the monte are fewer shrubs, more trees and cacti, less dense vegetation by number but increased plant diversity, and increased height.

As distinct as it is, the thorn forest-pediment zone is less productive than the monte-bajada zone in terms of useful vegetation. Although the number of species found in this zone is larger than in the monte-bajada zone, useful plants are not as numerous (Table 2.1).

Mixed Scrub-Slope

The mixed scrub-slope zone is a relatively small area, 80 square kilometers, on the west side of the river overlooking the floodplain from north of Huepac to south of Baviacora. The physiography of this area is undifferentiated and botanically it is a mixed scrub zone. The amorphous name applied to this zone is the result of the numerous, complex elements that defy mapping. Although the elevation ranges only from 600 m to 700 m, this zone is noted for extreme variation in slope angles and in the composition of the underlying materials. This zone is comprised of pediments in some places and bajadas in others. The average slope for this zone, approximately 12 degrees, is intermediate between that of the pediment and that of the bajada. The short distance from the mountain peaks to the river explains the lack of substantial bajada development. The mountains to the east are younger and higher than those of the west, thereby determining the westward location of the river. As will be recalled, the river runs asymmetrically through the valley, and it is this westward offset that results in a mixed pediment-bajada slope.

Many of the soils in this zone are extensively disturbed by human activity, taking on latent characteristics of Arents (Soil Survey Staff 1975: 187). In most places, however, they have the appearance of Aridic Haplustolls but are actually Camborthids (Soil Survey Staff 1975: 303–304, 170–173). As with the bajada, soils are slightly alkaline (7.4 pH) and have a sandy loam texture (Buol, Hole, and McCracken 1980: 24–25). Unlike the bajada, however, these vary enormously in color, including grays (2.5YR 7/2), browns (10YR 5/3), and reds (2.5YR 4/6).

The vegetation of the mixed scrub zone has affinities to both the monte and the thorn forest (Gentry 1942; Shreve and Wiggins 1964: 51–53). Canopy cover is similar to that of the monte, but the density of plants is more like that of the thorn forest. The frequency of cacti and grass is more like the thorn forest than the monte, and the frequency of trees is less than in the thorn forest. This zone is quite varied both physiographically and biotically, and is proximal to the river. It has significant exploitative potential (Table 2.1).

While most of the vegetation in the Valley of Sonora is drought resistent, that of the monte, thorn forest, and mixed scrub zones is more so than that of the other zones. This vegetation is intimately linked to the summer monsoon precipitation and is almost totally leafless in late spring and early summer prior to the summer rains. Although vegetation of these zones has a subtropical element, it appears not to be vulnerable to temporary freezes (Felger, Nabhan, and Sheridan 1976).

Piedmont Transition

The piedmont transition, covering approximately a 500 square-kilometer area with slopes averaging greater than 20 degrees, is characterized by the rolling to rugged terrain between the pediment surface and the higher elevations or by the numerous intrusive stocks. Rugged dissected volcanics, including flows and intrusions, abound. Elevations throughout the area range between 800 m and 1,200 m above sea level. Soil characteristics in this zone vary due to the diversity in geology and, hence, parent material. Lithic Torriorthents, Camborthids, and perhaps some Lithic Haplustolls (Soil Survey Staff 1975: 196–198, 170–173, 303–305) are all found here. On the average, these soils are coarser and darker brown (10YR 4/3) than those downslope on the pediments, but they still have a sandy loam texture (Buol, Hole, and McCracken 1980: 24–25) and are slightly acidic (6.3 pH).

The vegetation of the piedmont transition zone may be equated to the Desert Woodland Ecotone of other parts of Sonora (Felger, Nabhan, and Sheridan 1976) or the Sinaloan

Deciduous Forest (Gentry 1982). The transition zone includes species from other vegetation types, yet also may contain a different array of dominants; kapok (*Ceiba acuminata*) is characteristic in the southern portion of the valley and mesquites (*Prosopis* spp.) are common in the north. Competition between shrub and tree species may be intense, yet there are seldom pure stands of one tree or shrub species. At any site, the plant assemblage may be peculiar to itself; the zone includes a large expanse of diverse territory and vegetation. Grass cover ranges from light to heavy, the latter being more common. Much like the riparian woodlands, trees can reach great heights, often more than 8.0 m. Juniper (*Juniperus monosperma*) is found in some locales in the higher elevations, especially toward the north end of the valley. This zone was probably little-utilized in pre-Hispanic times, other than for hunting and gathering. Deer are plentiful, and chiltepin (*Capsicum* sp.), a spice, is still gathered seasonally (Table 2.1).

Oak Parklands and Pine-Oak Forest Uplands

Oak parklands and pine-oak forest uplands cover the majority of the higher elevations. Including all lands between 1,100 m above sea level to the mountain peaks, these zones cover approximately 450 square kilometers. The rolling terrain, with slopes averaging 16 degrees, is similar to that of the piedmont zone. Soils have a loam texture (Buol, Hole, and McCracken 1980: 24–25) that is much finer than any other zone, but they are quite thin and rocky. Lithic Torriorthents and Camborthids prevail. Some areas may have Lithic Haplustolls (Soil Survey Staff 1975: 196–198, 170–173, 303–305). These upland soils are both more yellowish brown (10YR 5/4) and more acidic (5.1 pH) than elsewhere.

Vegetation in the oak parkland, as the name implies, is dominated by oaks (*Quercus* spp.). The distribution and density of trees, however, are not uniform. The relative paucity of trees produces a parkland characteristic similar to the Oak Forest described in other parts of Sonora (Gentry 1942) and the Oak Woodland of Arizona (Hastings and Turner 1965: 49–108). The oaks found within the Rio Sonora drainage are largely deciduous, lacking leaves in the late spring and early summer. Their presence is dependent on slope exposure and edaphic conditions (Felger, Nabhan, and Sheridan 1976), although temperatures and probably moisture are also important. *Quercus* spp. produce acorns in early summer. In favorable years acorns, primarily from the emory oak (*Q. emoryi*) are harvested and consumed in nearby towns (Table 2.1).

The dominant oaks are often integrated with pines (*Pinus* spp.) in the higher elevations. This zone, covering only about 20 square kilometers and limited to those elevations over 1,800 m above sea level, is part of the Madrean Evergreen Woodlands (Brown 1982a: 59–65).

The general aspect of the pine-oak forests is evergreen with maximum renewal of growth occurring in late spring and again with the onset of the summer rains. During drought years, however, the oaks (*Quercus* spp.) and certain other broadleaf trees and shrubs become deciduous toward the end of the late spring and early summer season. The Sierra Aconchi is the southwestern limit for montane vegetation in the Basin and Range Province of Sonora.

All of the ecological zones in the higher elevations, the oak parkland, and the pine-oak forest uplands, have been subjected to a great deal of human activity in historic times. Minerals, associated with brecciation (Sawkins and Scherkenbach 1981), especially gold, silver, tungsten, lead, and particularly copper were of economic concern to both the Spaniards and the present-day occupants (Daco 1976). Whether or not the aboriginal inhabitants mined any of these minerals is unknown; however, they had the technology (Ross 1968) and they did utilize copper (Pailes 1980: 35). Pinyon (*Pinus edulis*) is common in the higher elevations. Because seeds of this species were consumed by prehistoric peoples throughout the Southwest, it is highly likely they were gathered here as well.

Arroyos

Although the seven ecological zones are regionally identifiable, they are not all internally homogeneous or areally continuous. With the exception of the riparian woodland-floodplain, these zones, especially the monte-bajada zone, are dissected by numerous disjunct arroyos that in many respects may be collectively considered as a discrete ecological zone. Though these arroyos are treated here as a separate environmental entity, it is realized that they are actually only subregions of larger zones. Generalizations may be made about these features, although their discontinuous nature and extreme variations in size make them nearly impossible to map on a small scale.

The large arroyos are in many ways similar to the riparian woodland-floodplain zone. Soils, classified as Torripsamments (Soil Survey Staff 1975: 204–205) are pale brown (10YR 6/3) to brown (10YR 5/3) with a sandy loam to loamy sand texture (Buol, Hole, and McCracken 1980: 24–25). Although they are thin, these soils are rock-free, permeable, and retain moisture for long periods of time (see Fig. 2.5). Gradients are slight, varying up to 1.3 degrees, thereby further facilitating slow stream velocities and high infiltration rates. The vegetation of the large arroyos is similar to the natural vegetation of the riparian woodlands; it is dominated by large trees, especially mesquite (*Prosopis* spp.).

Small arroyos have slopes that are somewhat steeper than the large arroyos (1.4 degrees), especially in their upper reaches. Another difference is that soils in the smaller arroyos contain fewer nutrients and minerals than do their larger counterparts. The soils are also thinner and rockier, and therefore support little plant life. High stream velocities also contribute to the paucity of vegetation (Wertz 1966). Such disastrous floods occur less frequently in the large arroyos and accordingly do not hinder plant growth.

Paleoenvironment

The degree to which current environmental conditions reflect prehistoric conditions in any region is speculative. However, convention dictates that a thorough understanding of the contemporary environment, such as that just presented, is necessary for comparative purposes (for example, Coe and Flannery 1964; Sanders 1976). Although the Valley of Sonora lies in a region known to have violent earthquakes (Bennett 1977) and a long history of volcanic activity (Sillitoe 1976), it is assumed that such geological events probably had little, if any, impact on pre-Hispanic occupance. No such assumption can be made for either the climatic or biotic conditions, however. Both the climate (Smith 1956) and the vegetation (Harris 1966) of the Greater Southwest are known to have changed significantly in the past millennium. The degree to which these changes have occurred in the Valley of Sonora is therefore assessed using accepted approaches. Paleoclimatic conditions are estimated by reviewing the results of dendroclimatological research and by estimating the extent of aggradation and degradation relative to relic settlement and agricultural features in the valley. Vegetation differences are estimated by reviewing the results of palynological research and by soil analysis.

Dendroclimatic research conducted in northwestern Mexico has been extremely limited compared to that performed in the western United States. Only recently have scientists gone into the region specifically to obtain dendroclimatic data (Wiseman 1976). Unfortunately, this work remains unfinished and the results unpublished, so that inferences must be drawn largely from conclusions obtained in the United States. Schulman (1942) provided the first tree-ring documentation of prehistoric climatic changes in the Southwest. In a later work he identified major periods of drought, as well as periods of sufficient rainfall (Schulman 1956). His data describe a 200 year period of rainfall and runoff in the Colorado River Basin; the 1200s were extraordinarily dry, the 1300s extraordinarily wet. Martin (1963) later substantiated that this period experienced abnormally low amounts of winter precipitation, but tempered his comments not to include a decrease in annual rainfall. The drought of the first interval and the floods of the second appear to have far exceeded in duration and intensity those recorded during the 1940s and 1950s (Schulman 1956: 69). Recent work has shown that climatic conditions in the Southwest today are drier than in the 1940s (Dean and Robinson 1977). These conclusions tend to suggest that conditions today might be approaching those of the 1200s. Indeed, Schulman (1956: 69) even states that precipitation highs in the decades prior to the 1950s broke a drought rivaling that of the 1200s.

Evidence indicates that the present fluctuation represents, in terms of secular dendroclimatic data, a major disturbance in the general circulation pattern over the western United States (Kalnicky 1974). A similar regionalization of such activity is noted by the decrease in the intensity of the 13th-century drought found in dendrological data from the Rio Grande Valley (Smiley, Stubbs, and Bannister 1953). This drought extended south into Mexico, at least as far as Casas Grandes, Chihuahua (Scott 1966). That the intensity was as high in Mexico as it was farther north is doubtful, due to the general circulation pattern in this part of the continent. The climate of the four-corners region is influenced by polar continental upper atmospheric conditions (Euler and others 1979). That factors controlling the climate of Sonora are predominantly tropical and maritime (Ives 1949: 150–151) suggests that the relative effects of the 13th-century drought were less severe in this region.

That the extended period of drought did not affect the pre-Hispanic population of the Valley of Sonora and did not produce an environment much different from that of today is borne out by the location of pre-Hispanic features in relation to aggradation and degradation evidence. The relative abundance of relic foundations (Chapter 3) found along the bajada edge and of terraces (Chapter 4) found in arroyos suggest that severe entrenchment has not occurred since the time in which such structures were utilized. If such were the case, these features probably would have washed away. Periods of degradation are well documented as occurring simultaneously with drought conditions (Bryan 1928, 1940), or at least with periods of secular rainfall changes (Leopold 1951; Cooke and Reeves 1976). Of course, it could be that moderate degradation has occurred, as many of these features are in a dilapidated condition. Such destruction is probably more a function of age. That such features may have been buried during a period of aggradation (higher rainfall period?) and later exposed by degradation is possible. However, such an elaborate sequence is unlikely to have occurred at each site in the valley simultaneously. It can be concluded, therefore, that pre-Hispanic climatic conditions were probably not too different from those of today. Substantial short-term climatic changes since pre-Hispanic times have not occurred to the extent that vegetation has been permanently affected (Bahre and Bradbury 1978).

Recent comparisons of fossil and modern pollen data from sites along the edge of the bajada indicate that the pre-Hispanic vegetation, although similar to the modern vegetation, was ". . . of a more open form both during and subsequent to occupation" (Rankin 1977). Two problems exist with this conclusion. First, because she was looking mainly at spores from plants of known economic value, no pollen from *Mimosa laxiflora* was listed from the excavated or surface collections. It is possible that this pollen was collectively listed in the *Leguminosae* family, in which case differences between genera and species are obliterated. That 43 percent of all modern vegetation on the bajada is *M. laxiflora* should be requirement enough for separating *Leguminosae* pollen by species. It is also possible that *M. laxiflora* is a very recent introduction on the bajada and would not be found in the fossil pollen. This situation is highly likely since it and other *Leguminosae* species are notorious invaders of disturbed grasslands (Walter 1973: 19). Overgrazing is common in the Valley of Sonora today (Aguirre M. and Johnson G. 1983: 25). The second problem with the pollen data is the lack of emphasis placed on *Gramineae*. A pollen core from one site demonstrated a slow decline in *Gramineae* pollen through time, with a rapid disappearance near the surface of the core.

Table 2.2. Profile of a Haplargid Bajada Soil

Depth	Color	pH	% Sand	% Silt	% Clay	Texture	Structure
0–20 cm	Reddish brown, 5YR 5/4	7.0	35.2	39.6	25.2	Loam	Medium angular blocky
20–35 cm	Light brown, 7.5YR 6/4	7.6	29.2	39.6	31.2	Clay Loam	Medium angular blocky
35–50 cm	Pale brown, 10YR 6/3	7.7	33.2	41.6	25.2	Loam	Coarse angular blocky
50–70 cm	Very pale brown, 10YR 7/3	7.7	43.2	45.6	11.2	Loam	Coarse angular blocky
70–100 cm	Very pale brown, 10YR 7/3	7.2	61.2	33.6	5.2	Sandy Loam	Very coarse angular blocky

This decline in grasses is also noted in the morphological characteristics of the bajada soils. As will be recalled, the soils of the bajada are classified as Haplargids that are developed nearly enough to be classified as Aridic Haplustolls. Aridisols are quite young and, by definition, are found in arid and sparsely vegetated regions. Mollisols, typically found in subhumid and semiarid regions, are associated with grasslands and savanna vegetation. The modern vegetation of the desert scrub zone in the Valley of Sonora can hardly be considered grassland today. Nevertheless, evidence tends to indicate that soils in this zone were developed under conditions somewhat grassier than today. These soils (Fig. 2.7 and Table 2.2) show the beginning stages of argillic (clay) illuviation (increases in the 20–35 cm horizon), displaying Haplargid characteristics. The epipedon is actually too dark for the soil to be classified as a Typic Aridisol. It is also too thin for a true Mollisol; however, the abundance of rocks on the surface as compared with the paucity below the surface suggests that much of the epipedon has been eroded, and denudation is evident. These features probably indicate that the soil once had a grass cover, albeit not dense, producing organic matter resulting in the dark epipedon, however thin, characteristic of Mollisols. Drying by increased solar exposure resulted in the loss of organic matter and lightening of the soil color. Removal of the grass not only facilitated denudation but it also promoted clay illuviation.

Under conditions of more dense grass one would expect to find fewer *Leguminosae* (pollen) than under overgrazed conditions. Indeed, such were the findings of Hastings and Turner (1965: 152) and Bahre and Bradbury (1978: 158) for other overgrazed grasslands in parts of Sonora and southern Arizona. In the Valley of Sonora, *Leguminosae* pollen shows no continual increases through time (Rankin 1977). The *Gramineae* pollen, however, shows a noted decline in very recent times. It is therefore suggested that in pre-Hispanic times the monte zone probably had fewer trees and shrubs and more grass than is found today. Possible grass species may have been *Hilaria mutica, Muhlenbergia perteri*, and *Sporobulub airoides*. These species are found in what appear to be a few undisturbed stands in parts of eastern Sonora today (Johnson G. and Carrillo Michel 1977).

Figure 2.7. Profile of a Haplargid bajada soil.

The pollen analysis was limited solely to archaeological sites along the edge of the bajada. As was noted earlier, this zone has vegetation and soil characteristics different from the whole of the bajada. There is a proliferation of *Opuntia fulgida* and *Prosopis* sp. along the mesas. These plants, which are the result of vegetation destruction by intensive occupation, have been documented as species that not only invade but also proliferate in heavily disturbed areas, according to Fred Wiseman. The relationship between soil formation and vegetation changes has long been recognized by soil scientists (Jenny 1958). For reasons not clearly known, however, it has not been widely employed as a key to understanding paleoenvironments (Butzer 1976: 149). The dynamic nature of soils is exemplified on the bajada as a function of positive feedback or deviation amplification processes (Flannery 1971). Vegetation was first removed from the mesas or bajada edges through the development of pre-Hispanic settlements. Abandonment was followed by the invasion of these areas by *Prosopis* sp., not grasses that were common prior to occupation. As is the case today, these mesquite-infested sites probably provided shade that was attractive to cattle responsible for overgrazing the remainder of the bajada grasses. The congregation of cattle in these shaded locales resulted in changes in soil structure and texture due to pulverization by hooves, changes in organic matter, and chemical properties, and pH due to feces accumulation contributed to the formation of the previously discussed Arents. Changes in soils then promoted the growth of *Prosopis* while the presence of cattle further hindered the growth of grasses on what were once ancient settlements.

Environmental change was not limited solely to the monte, of course. Under pristine conditions the riparian woodland would have covered the entire floodplain except the river channel. Accordingly, mesquite (*Prosopis* spp.) would not only have been dominant but ubiquitous throughout this zone. The degree to which this woodland area was destroyed can be seen only as a function of the amount of land under irrigation during the period in question. Suffice it to say that the riparian woodland currently covers significantly less area than it would have under nonagrarian conditions.

The higher elevations also have been subjected to environmental degradation, especially during the 20th century. Marshall (1957), who provided the first description of the vegetation atop the Sierra Aconchi, noted that pine (*Pinus* spp.) had been extensively logged by the early 1950s. Reports from local informants indicate that oaks (*Quercus* spp.) were extensively depleted throughout the early and middle decades of the 20th century. These species were not cut for timber, but rather for fuel for nearby grain mills. Large open areas are currently intermixed with groves in the oak park. The extent and cultural impact of this degradation were not measured for this study, but it is certain that exploitation of acorns would have been greater before the cutting.

In summary, it is doubtful that the climate in the Valley of Sonora during pre-Hispanic times was much different than it is today. It is probable, however, that minor climatic fluctuations occurred periodically. That these fluctuations affected vegetation or human occupance to any great extent is questionable. It is also unlikely that the "Great North American Drought" of the 13th century had much, if any, effect in the valley. These findings not withstanding, the evidence for or against major climatic change in the valley during the periods in question is tenuous and all conclusions must be viewed with extreme caution. Unlike climatic conditions, vegetation patterns were quite different in late pre-Hispanic times than they are today. The riparian woodland, the oak park, and the pine-oak woodland are much less wooded today than in the past. Increased agriculture near the river, with wood and timber exploitation in the mountains, account for this vegetation decline. The monte was probably more like a desert grassland in the past.

These changes had minimal effects on the pre-Hispanic inhabitants of the valley, although environmental changes are most important for interpreting pre-Hispanic occupance patterns from modern data. Modern conditions are noted by a ubiquitous distribution of leguminous species. Such plants, of course, have utilitarian value in their edible seed pods. In pre-Hispanic times such species would not have been numerous enough to exploit in substantial quantities from most ecological zones. The most exploited species were more abundant in the riparian woodland and in the large arroyos. Both of these areas were also important for agriculture.

Ecological Factors of Agriculture

The physical environs of the Valley of Sonora are so sufficiently varied that a number of different agricultural techniques, each suited to particular conditions, could have been practiced in pre-Hispanic times. For example, a modified form of swidden or slash and burn (Geertz 1963: 15–28) farming referred to as burn-plot agriculture perhaps was used in the pine-oak woodlands. Such a system recently has been proposed as possibly the method used prehistorically in the pine forests of the Mogollon region, eastern Arizona (Sullivan 1982), an area not too unlike the pine-oak woodlands of Sonora. Relying on nutrients provided by burning litter (needles and cones) rather than felled trees, this form of agriculture would have been ecologically feasible (Sullivan 1982: 5–7). Similarly, a truer form of slash and burn agriculture such as that currently being practiced in the dry forests of southern Sonora (Fish 1980) was also suitable. In terms of vegetation, the monte and the thorn forests in the Valley of Sonora are purported by Alfonso Daco to be comparable to the environs where swidden is being practiced in other parts of Sonora.

It is unlikely, however, that either form of dry farming was practiced to any great extent prehistorically, or that any of the mentioned ecological zones were heavily used for agricultural purposes in the Valley of Sonora. Although ecologically feasible, it is highly improbable that burn-plot farming was economically practical on anything other than a very small scale. There is simply too little suitable forest for such agriculture to have been practiced extensively in pre-Hispanic times. While the monte and the thorn forests may be similar to environs where swidden is practiced elsewhere, the amount of rainfall is not. Rainfall in southern Sonora is much greater, averaging more than 700 mm annually

Figure 2.8. Floodplain irrigation.

Figure 2.9. Living fencerow. Main channel is on the left, an irrigated field is to the right. Note the differences in turbulence and, hence, velocities on either side of the fencerow.

(S.A.R.H. 1961–1981), and less variable than in the Valley of Sonora. Furthermore, the soils of the bajada and the pediments are too thin and rocky for cultivation. In some places the soils are also too acidic and infertile; in others, steep slopes facilitate rapid runoff and increased soil erosion.

In spite of the environmental diversity, the floodplain and the floors of the large arroyos are the only places suitable for agriculture today, and they were probably the only sites suitable in pre-Hispanic times. In addition to the attributes discussed previously, these soils are fertile. The levels of phosphorous, at an average of 41.7 ppm, and potassium, at an average of 100.0 ppm, are more than sufficient for good plant growth and crop production on the floodplain (Brady 1974). The levels of organic matter, at an average of 1.3 percent (Thompson and Troeh 1978), and nitrate nitrogen (13.4 ppm) are low; however, these deficiencies are more illusionary

Figure 2.10. *Temporales* fields. Arroyo Rancho, north of Baviacora.

than real. At certain times of the year the amount of litter is relatively low. This condition is typically the case during the growing season. For short periods during the year, especially when the numerous mesquites (*Prosopis* spp.) produce and disperse their beans, the level of organic matter is quite high, and soil nitrogen is fixated (Richardson 1946). In turn, the nutrients are rapidly absorbed by the plants, resulting in a soil with apparent low levels of organic nutrients (Nye 1961). Rapid absorption of organic matter is typical of hot environs whether arid or humid.

Floodplain farming is the most common and widespread form of agriculture practiced in the Valley of Sonora today (Doolittle 1983). The relatively simple techniques involved are certainly not beyond the technical ability of ancient inhabitants. Most fields are irrigated from acequias or canals leading from diversion weirs constructed across the river channel (Fig. 2.8). In some cases, seedlings are cut, trimmed, and planted in a row adjacent to and paralleling the river channel (Fig. 2.9). These living fencerows (Nabhan and Sheridan 1977) promote silt deposition, extending the size of the *milpas*. These fixtures also help retard flood damage.

During the dry season and periods of drought, cultivation is dependent entirely on permanent springs that flow from the riverbed. In some places a spring provides water, but the valley is too constricted to permit farming to take place; in others, arable land exists, but the riverbed is dry during most of the year. On the whole, however, springs provide a dependable source of water relative to the variability of rainfall and surface water.

In summary, the riparian woodland floodplain is an optimal zone for plant populations. Regularly available water and porous, fertile soils facilitate luxuriant vegetation growth. The same conditions that are favorable for the growth of natural plants also provide for the growth of domesticated plants. To this end the riparian woodland-floodplain has been the focus of human occupance in the valley. This situation was as true in pre-Hispanic times as it is today.

In addition to the floodplain, large arroyos are also suitable agricultural environs. The levels of soil phosphorous (45.9 ppm), potassium (124.0 ppm), nitrate nitrogen (11.6 ppm), and organic matter (1.2 percent), and a slightly alkaline condition (7.6 pH) are comparable to the floodplain, and, therefore, are sufficient for good plant growth and crop production (Brady 1974). There is, however, one major difference between the floodplain and arroyos that is critical for agriculture—arroyos do not experience consistent or predictable flows of water. Some soil moisture, of course, is provided by direct precipitation; most of the necessary water, however, comes from runoff produced by summer rains in the mountains. Summertime thunderstorms, as discussed earlier, often produce massive amounts of rainfall in periods of time so short that much of the water cannot be absorbed by either the vegetation or the soil. Excess water first runs into rivulets, then into gullies, and eventually into arroyos. While the chances of the arroyo-bottom fields dependent on direct precipitation or runoff, known as *temporales* (Fig. 2.10), receiving sufficient amounts of direct precipitation to produce a good crop are low, the probability of the fields receiving runoff in sufficient quantities is high. Because arroyos with large drainage areas collect much runoff, the effects of rainfall variability there are reduced in comparison with arroyos that have small catchment areas. Although the most productive *temporales* are located in large arroyos, arroyo agriculture wherever practiced is still precarious.

Farmers have developed numerous ways to use runoff in arid lands (Lawton and Wilke 1979: 3–5). Among the simplest techniques used is "floodwater farming" (Bryan 1929; Nabhan 1979). Floodwater fields are located in usually dry low-lying areas that are inundated by flash floods when arroyos overflow their banks. The selection of a site for locating "fields on low flood terraces of large arroyos" (Hack 1942: 30) involves an intimate knowledge of local conditions. The field must be flood-prone, but the sheet of water must not attain a velocity that will wash out a crop or bury it with sediment. A more elaborate technique is appropriately called "runoff farming" (Nabhan 1981) because agriculture is practiced in areas where crops receive water that runs off adjacent unprepared slopes. In many cases runoff fields have low rock terraces that trap silt, conserve moisture, and distribute water evenly across the area (Fogel 1975: 134–139). A third technique, "water harvesting" (Frazier 1975), relies on runoff collected from prepared catchment areas and diverts this runoff onto the fields. In many ways, this form of agriculture is a rudimentary form of canal irrigation. Stake and brush diversion weirs and canals not unlike those associated with floodplain irrigation are employed (Fig. 2.11).

Figure 2.11. A *temporal* diversion weir and canal.

Each of these agricultural ecosystems has been viewed as a specific adaptation to a localized environ (Woosley 1980). However, present-day *temporales* rarely fit neatly into one of these categories. In fact, they actually represent stages on a continuum of agrotechnological development (Glassow 1980; Doolittle 1984b). Through time floodwater farming evolves first into runoff farming and then into water harvesting.

In summary, the Valley of Sonora has been categorized in terms of seven ecological zones. Of these, the floodplain and the large arroyos with their recent alluvial soils have the best agricultural soils. Although some of the other zones have soil nutrient levels adequate for agriculture, steep slopes, rocky soils, and deficient water impede agriculture.

Two general types of agricultural ecosystems, canal irrigation and *temporales*, are found in the Valley of Sonora today. Each of these systems represents a different environmental adaptation. *Temporales* depend on direct rainfall to supply part of the soil moisture and runoff to supply both moisture and nutrient-laden silt. These fields are found away from the river channel in large arroyo beds. Floodplain farming involves the utilization of water from the main river channel. This form of agriculture relies on regular flows of surface water.

The availability of water in proximity to arable land is the central geographical factor limiting agriculture in the Valley of Sonora. Water, however, is largely a function of rainfall and is not always dependable, with drought years that occur in a frequent but unpredictable fashion. Drought conditions undoubtedly would have a greater effect in the arroyos than on the floodplain. Under extensive environmental degradation, neither soils nor moisture would be deposited adequately enough to sustain even marginal crop yields. Floodplain agriculture would be less affected under drought conditions. Short-term droughts (one to perhaps two or three consecutive years) may be partially alleviated on the floodplain. Extended droughts, however, probably would result in a significant lowering of the water table, thereby increasing crop losses.

Flooding is another threat to crop production in certain sections of the valley. Floods are capable of destroying fields along the floodplain and in large arroyos, but usually do not affect both zones simultaneously. In addition, flooding is rarely a threat to both winter and summer crops in the same year. In contrast, a severe long-term drought could prove disastrous to all forms of agriculture in all ecological-land use zones.

The riparian woodland-floodplain and the large arroyos are the best agricultural and resource procurement zones in the valley. As such, they probably were utilized ever since the first inhabitants entered the valley and continually have served, especially as agriculture was developed, as the economic core for subsistence.

Ecological Factors of Settlement

"The first principal of settlement geography is that the group chose its living site where water and shelter were at hand and," said Sauer, "about which food, fuel and other primary needs could be collected within a convenient radius" (Sauer 1969: 12). Accepting that people could build houses, they would only have to locate near water, food, and fuel. The ecological zone that produces these commodities most abundantly and with the greatest regularity in the Valley of Sonora is the riparian woodland-floodplain; second would be the large arroyos. Other zones do possess these resources, but in lesser amounts and often less regularly. Small populations might subsist quite well in areas such as the oak parkland and pine-oak woodland, but a population of any significant size could be concentrated only near the river. Not surprisingly, most of the permanent pre-Hispanic settlements are located proximal to the river and its immediate environs.

As is the case with present-day towns, most of the permanently inhabited pre-Hispanic settlements were located on the interfluves separating the arroyos, at the edge of the bajada overlooking the floodplain (Figs. 2.12, 2.13). Such locales are known locally as mesas. That settlements were located on these mesas overlooking the river and not on the

Figure 2.12. Typical pre-Hispanic settlement location. Site Son K:8:34 OU is indicated by the arrow. The present-day pueblo of Suaqui is on the right.

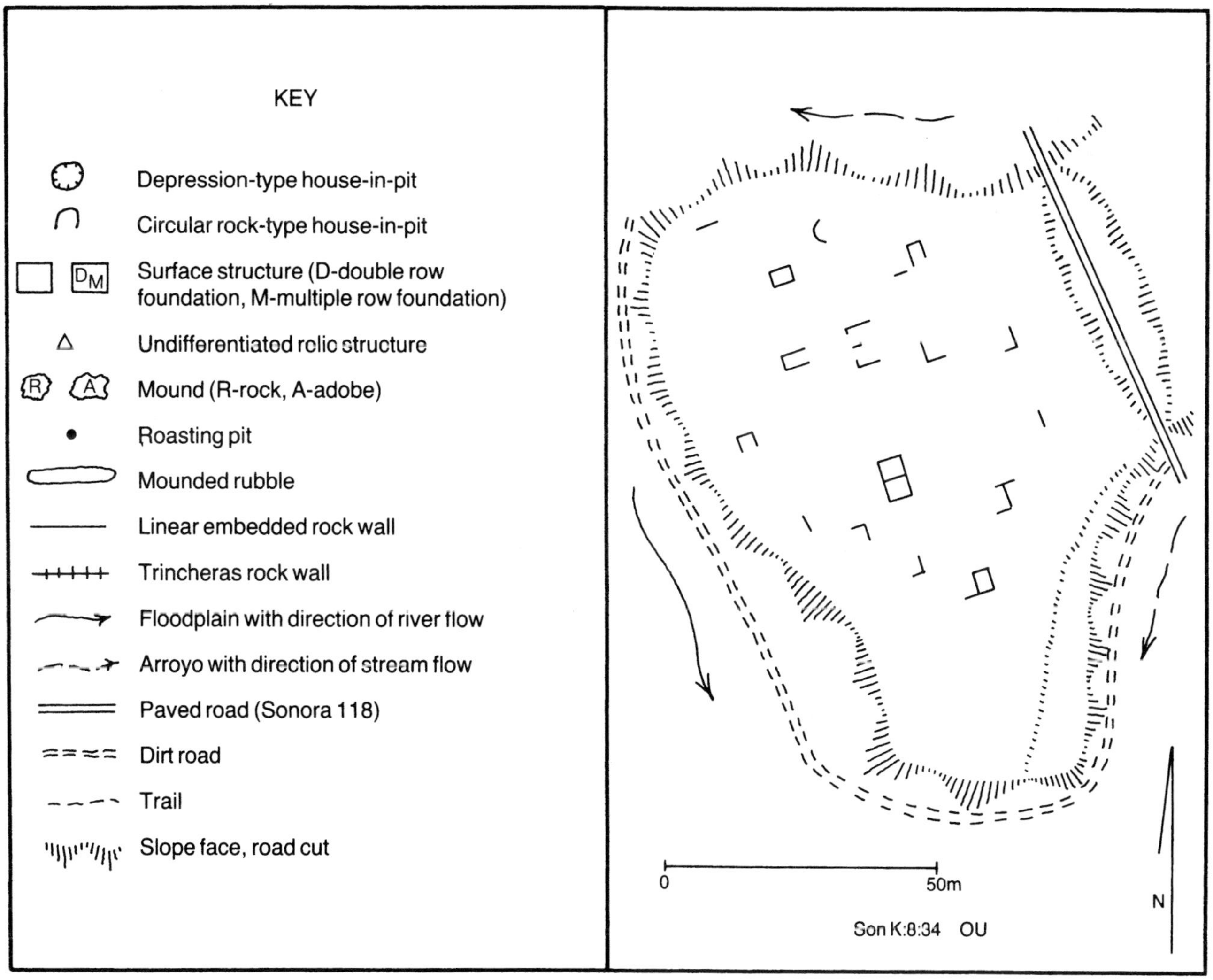

Figure 2.13. Site Son K:8:34 OU.

Figure 2.14. Slopes unsuitable for the placement of permanent settlements.

floodplain is a curiosity. Safety from flooding is the most obvious explanation; another is the annoyance created by mosquitos and other insects. Mesas above the lower, wetter areas are relatively insect-free, probably because of breezes not felt in low-lying areas. These breezes occur throughout the day and also have the effect of cooling body temperatures, even during the hottest summer hours. Furthermore it is possible that mesas provided freedom from cold air drainage, especially during summer nights.

Under homogeneous conditions, one would expect to find settlements uniformly distributed along the bajada edge throughout the entire region. The region is not homogeneous, however, and sites are not uniformly spaced. Although sites are located with a high degree of regularity, there are places in which pre-Hispanic settlements are situated with great irregularity and infrequency. Three such areas are on the west side of the river from Baviacora to the south end of the valley, between Aconchi and the pueblo of San Felipe, and west of Banamichi. Another area is on the east side of the river between El Ojo de Agua and the *ejido* or community of La Mora a few kilometers south of Banamichi. These four areas are physiographically different, each with its unique physical qualities that discourage site location. Two of the west side areas do not have extensive bajada development due to the proximity of mountains to floodplain. The area south from Baviacora is rugged hill lands covered largely by recent volcanic materials. The area from Aconchi to San Felipe shows limited bajada development. The type, proximity to point of origin, and amount of formative materials have implications limiting settlement location here. The formative materials of which this area is composed are predominantly Cretaceous-age intrusive granites. Part of the area is made up of pediments created by erosion on the face of the Sierra Aconchi batholith. The limited bajada portion of the area is alluvium and colluvium created by the erosional forces that formed the pediment. The granitic materials of which this bajada is composed are so well-cemented and erosion has been so extensive that the arroyos are V-shaped and unsuitable for the placement of permanent structures (Fig. 2.14).

The area west of Banamichi has an exactly opposite orogeny to the area just discussed. Here, the bajada is well developed but the underlying material is granitic conglomerates with interbedded tuffs. This relatively hard material results in numerous deeply incised arroyos forming a typical "badlands" topography. Between El Ojo de Agua and La Mora on the east side of the river the bajada development is quite extensive with some of the longest and widest arroyos found in the Valley of Sonora. So wide are these arroyos that in some cases the interfluves are very thin with tops too narrow to be suitable for settlements; in others, they are large and the only suitable settlement locales for considerable distances. The remaining mesas in the valley are flat-topped, rather uniform in size, and evenly spaced. They are ideal locations for the settlements.

CHAPTER THREE

Settlements

The importance of mesa tops as settlement locations was first recognized by Bandelier when he made the pioneer survey of the Valley of Sonora in 1884. Following his lead, archaeologists who carried out surveys through the 1960s investigated only a sample of the several mesas in the valley. In attempts to collect as much data as they could with limited time and finances, these scholars bypassed most mesas. Although they were all familiar with the documentary accounts, the archaeologists either inadvertently overlooked or, for reasons now unknown, intentionally chose not to survey mesas that were the possible locations of the large sites the Spaniards claimed to have seen. The archaeological studies resulted in some mesas being resurveyed by different scholars on as many as three occasions whereas the potentially important contents of others remained virtually unknown. Some settlement information, of course, was recovered through these endeavors; much, however, was not. Especially deficient is knowledge of the types, functions, and ages of relic structures; community organization or the relationship between structures and settlement hierarchies; and prevalence and spatial distribution of ancient settlements.

STRUCTURES

The principal indications of structures noted by the early archaeologists who surveyed the Valley of Sonora were the embedded rock foundations similar to those of pueblos in other parts of the Greater Southwest (for example, Tuthill 1947: 18–19; LeBlanc and Nelson 1976: 76). These features have long been accepted as being remains of structures that once functioned as houses (Hrdlička 1904: 59). In part, the discovery of only these kinds of features led investigators to conclude the region was occupied but briefly in late pre-Hispanic times. New evidence indicates that a variety of structural types existed and that occupance was much longer than previously thought.

Determining the functions, ages or periods of use, and number of structures by means of surface evidence, even when supported by collaborating excavations, is a practice that requires a great deal of caution. Difficulties with contemporaneity (Patterson 1963; Schacht 1984), superposition (Thompson 1971), and disturbance (Roper 1976) are frequently encountered during archaeological investigations. These problems, however, appear to be relatively minimal in eastern Sonora because of the shallowness of artifact deposition (Tolstoy and Fish 1975), the limited amount of denudation (Kirkby and Kirkby 1976), the durability of artifacts under consideration, like structures (Gifford 1978), and the paucity of postoccupational activity on the sites (Hughes and Lampert 1977). For example, of the 59 structures that were excavated in the valley between 1976 and 1978, only two earlier structures were obscured by more recent ones (Pailes 1980: 29). Therefore, given the areal limitation of the survey, it is assumed that most, if not all, visible relic structures were located and that evidence from each phase of occupation was found in representative amounts on the surface (Sauer and Brand 1930: 417–418; Redman and Watson 1970; Flannery 1976a: 51–62).

The number of structures indicated by surface remains, of course, is fewer than the number actually occupied during pre-Hispanic times. Subsequent historic and modern constructions and erosion have contributed to the destruction of some houses. Although these problems frequently restrict research endeavors, in this case they actually pose few difficulties. At worst, house counts may be considered as conservative estimates.

Three types of habitation structures are identified by their relic foundations or constructional characteristics: surface structures, of which there are four variations; houses-in-pits, of which there are two subtypes; and stone mounds (Appendix A; maps of all pre-Hispanic settlements located in the Valley of Sonora are in Doolittle 1979).

Surface structures are indicated by rows of vertical rocks embedded in adobe footings (Drake 1954) measuring 20 cm to 30 cm in width (Figs. 3.1, 3.2) or by mounds of deteriorated or "melted" adobe (Fig. 3.3). Typically, foundations or cimientos are either square or rectangular in shape and average 23.2 m in area. The most common surface foundations measure approximately 4 m by 5 m. The similarity between currently occupied adobe houses in the Valley of Sonora and pre-Hispanic houses is striking. The difficulty in distinguishing between prehistoric and historic surface structure foundations was noted as early as the first survey (Bandlier 1892: 498). Differentiating criteria were established in this study in an attempt to insure that relic foundations of historic houses were not included. Relic surface structures with currently standing walls or portions of walls were found through excavation not to have been occupied pre-Hispanically, and therefore they were excluded from consideration. Similarly excluded were house sites lacking associated prehistoric ceramics and lithics but containing abundant historic and recent artifacts.

Figure 3.1. Pre-Hispanic surface structure foundation, site Son K:4:94 OU. (Reprinted from the *Journal of Field Archaeology*, Vol. 11, p. 16, 1984, with permission of the Trustees of Boston University.)

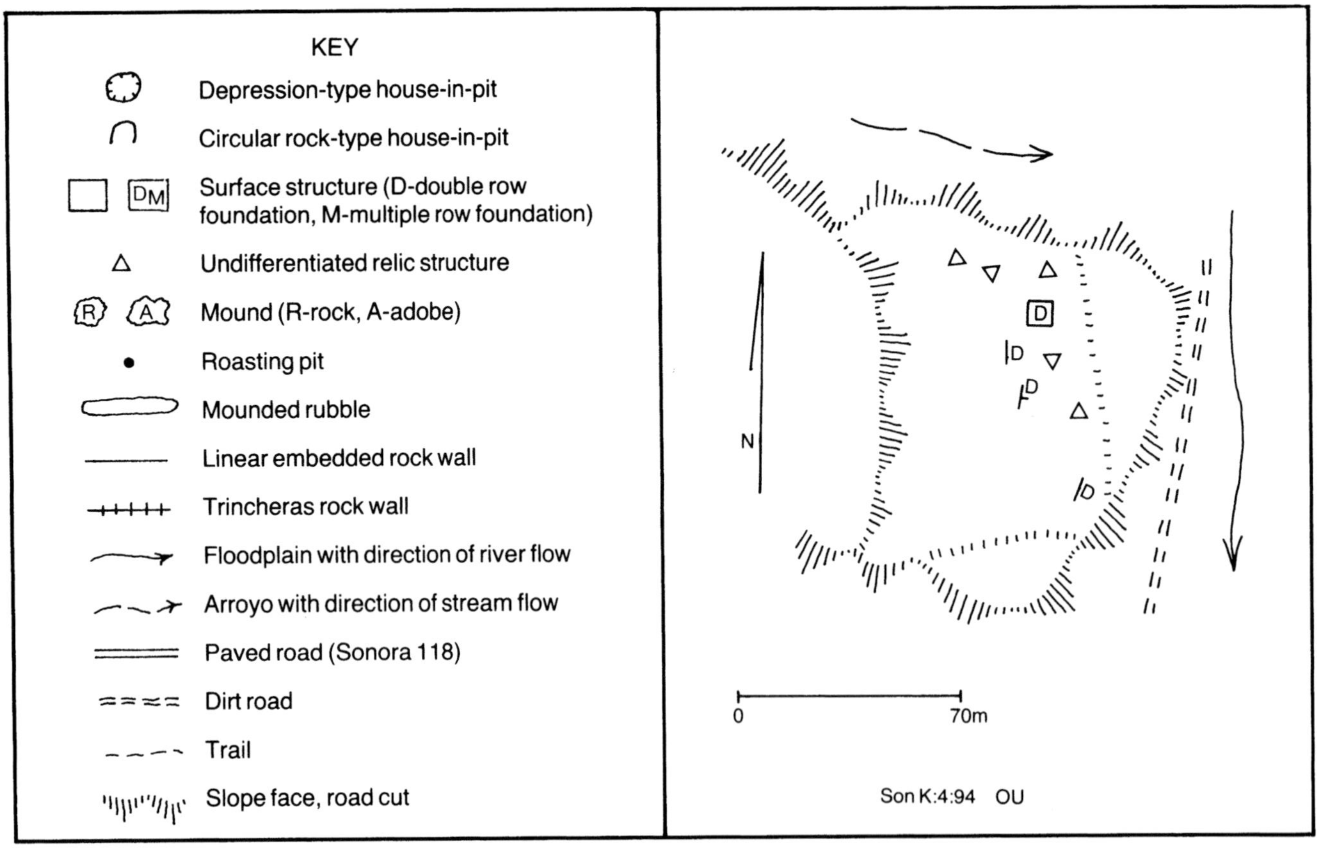

Figure 3.2. Site Son K:4:94 OU.

Figure 3.3. Deteriorated adobe surface structure, site Son G:16:27 OU (see Fig. 3.33).

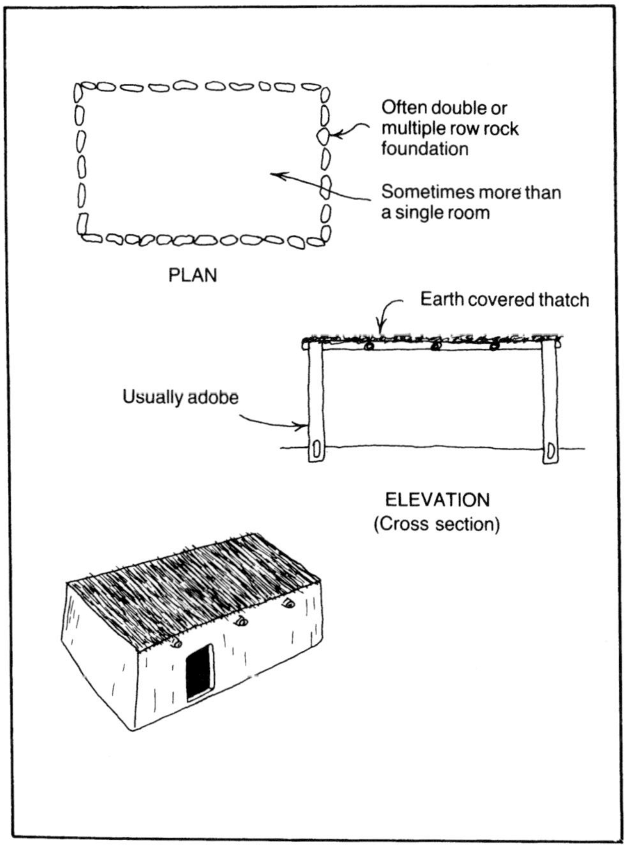

Figure 3.4. Schematic of a typical surface structure.

Perhaps the greatest distinguishing characteristic between ancient and modern structures is the use of brick, a Spanish-introduced trait. There is no evidence to indicate that pre-Hispanic surface structures were made of bricks; instead they appear to have been made of puddled adobe. Although stakes-and-brush and wattle-and-daub may have been used, adobe was probably the most common material, as evidenced by vast amounts of melt found on archaeological sites (see also Bandelier 1892: 487; Amsden 1928: 37).

Other architectural features uncovered during recent excavations include adobe floors (Pailes 1980: 32) and mesquite (*Prosopis* spp.) roof timbers (Gasser 1977). Although no other roofing materials have been recovered, it is most likely that thatch covered with earthen materials was utilized (Fig. 3.4).

Pre-Hispanic surface structures are divided into four subtypes. Most typical are the single-room structures with a single row of rocks constituting the foundation. One variation of this design is a single room, with double rock-row foundation. The significance of the double row is not completely understood. Amsden (1928: 45, 47) postulated that a double row provided a tight joint for walls reinforced with poles. That the two rows are often in contact verifies the tight fit but casts doubt on the reinforcing capabilities of an infinitely thin pole.

In addition to the single-room structures are multiple-room variations that usually have double row foundations and possibly may be the result of expanded single-room structures. The size of individual rooms in such features is comparable to the size of single-room houses.

It has long been assumed that residents of the serrana lived only in single-story surface structures because there was no known archaeological evidence of multiple-story houses. This assumption is especially curious because some mid-16th century Spanish explorers did note the existence of such features (see Hammond and Rey 1928: 197). Although no multiple-room, multistory structure walls have stood for some time in Sonora, some archaeological evidence, albeit tentative, for their previous existence does exist (Howard and Griffiths 1966: 56). Most of the surface structures just described have foundations of single and double rows of rocks. Adobe walls were constructed on top of these foundations in a manner somewhat similar to that used in the construction of present-day single-story houses. Because of their relative narrowness, these foundations could not have footed walls of sufficient thickness to support a second, much less a third story. There are, however, a number of relic foundations of multiple-room houses that have three, four, and even five rows of rocks (Fig. 3.5). Presumably these larger foundations supported the multiple-story structures observed by the Spanish. An archaeological parallel supporting this conclusion can be found at the Los Muertos site in Arizona (Haury 1945: 17) and an ethnohistorical one throughout present-day Sonora (Drake 1954). Interestingly, the prehistoric Sonoran foundations are wide enough to meet current building codes for multiple-story adobe structures in several Southwestern United States locales (Hinrichs 1981). Many sites containing large foundations are also characterized by an inordinate amount of melted adobe. Although conjectural, it seems logical that melted adobe would be abundant on sites that had large structures.

Surface structures, like many archaeological features, deteriorate with age. Accordingly, evidence of these features is often fragmentary at best and sometimes no more than speculative. Many of the surface structures recorded from the Valley of Sonora are indicated solely by a few linearly arranged rocks. In other cases the location of prehistoric structures is suggested by a clustering of surface rocks in an otherwise rock-free area. Excavation has substantiated that such features are indeed house remains. Furthermore, most sites with suspicious rock clusters also contain a few distinctive structures.

Pailes (1980: 29) has evidence of surface structures occurring in the later phases of occupance that has been confirmed by radiocarbon dates and obsidian hydration analysis (Doolit-

Figure 3.5. Rectangular triple rows of rocks that are typical surface evidence of probable multiple-story structures, site Son K:4:20 OU (see Fig. 3.32). (Reprinted from the *Journal of Field Archaeology*, Vol. 11, p. 17, 1984, with permission of the Trustees of Boston University.)

tle 1981). In addition, excavations revealed that polychrome ceramics from the Chihuahuan cultural province were associated with surface structures. Typical polychrome ceramics include Carretas, Huerigos, Ramos, Dublan, Villa Ahumada, and Babicora types, which were produced in greatest quantities during the Paquime and Diablo phases at Casas Grandes (Di Peso 1974, Vol. 6: 183–300). Although the exact ages of these phases are in dispute (Lekson 1984), they date sometime between A.D. 1205 and the early 1400s, thereby verifying the mid to late age of surface structures.

In addition to surface structures, numerous houses-in-pits were used prehistorically in the Valley of Sonora. These structures vary in size, depth, shape, and constructional features. Although the specifics of their architecture are beyond the scope of this study, they were generally rectangular with rounded corners and rarely more than 1 m deep. The visible evidence of this kind of building is usually a circular depression averaging 6.6 m in diameter. The exact size and shape of the buried features, however, cannot be ascertained from surface evidence. Houses-in-pits quite often are filled with debris from later occupations or are filled with sediment as the result of natural erosion processes. Such features appear either as circular depressions in an otherwise flat landscape (Figs. 3.6, 3.7) or as horseshoe-shaped piles of rubble with a slight central depression (Figs.

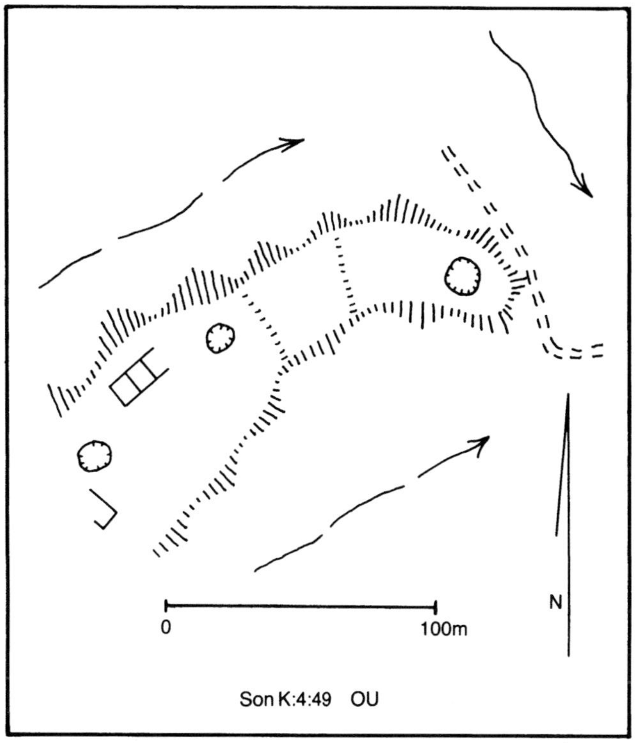

Figure 3.7. Site Son K:4:49 OU. (See Fig. 3.2 for Key.)

Figure 3.6. Surface depression indicative of a house-in-pit, site Son K:4:49 OU. (Reprinted from the *Journal of Field Archaeology*, Vol. 11, p. 16, 1984, with permission of the Trustees of Boston University.)

Figure 3.8. Rock ring indicative of a house-in-pit, site Son K:4:130 OU. Ascending arrows point to ring, descending arrow to center of pit.

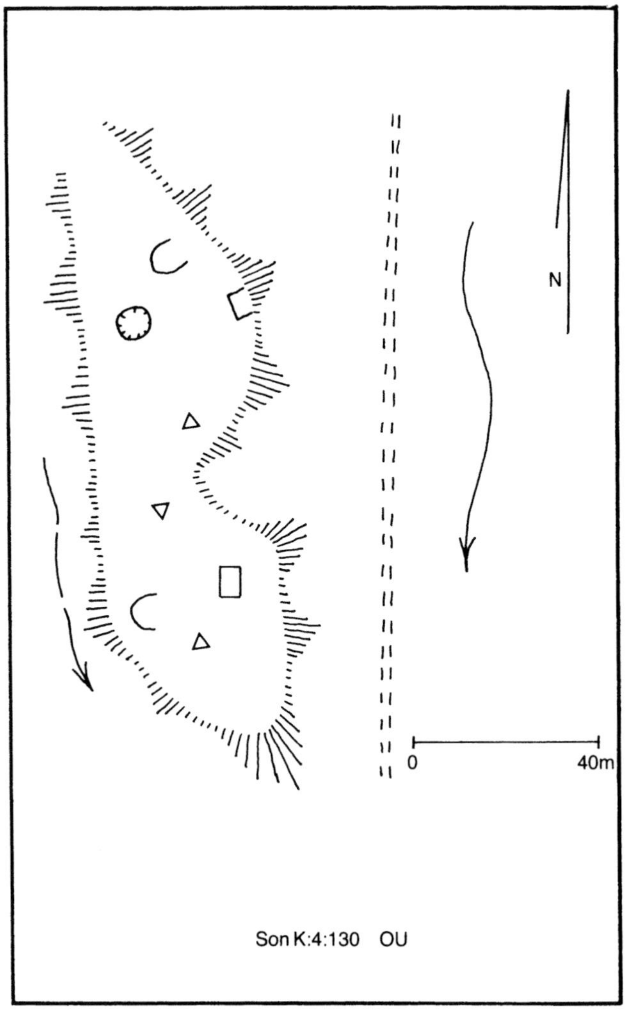

Figure 3.9. Site Son K:4:130 OU. (See Fig. 3.2 for Key.)

3.8, 3.9), perhaps indicative of subsurface constructional differences. Recent excavations have shown a tendency for the horseshoe variety to have raised floors and adobe block entrances. There appears to be a lack of contemporaneity between the types, but as of yet this idea has not been fully substantiated (Pailes 1980: 29–31).

Architecturally, houses-in-pits are semisubterranean structures of varying depths in which the sides of the pit are not integral parts of the structural wall (Fig. 3.10). Floors are either adobe or raised on mesquite (*Prosopis* spp.) piers and beams. Determining the wall material is more speculative for houses-in-pits than for surface structures. Sauer and Brand (1931: 114–115) did note that cobbles set in adobe mortar were used in some cases to prevent caving below the surface. It is most probable, however, given the reports of the early Spanish explorers, that mats and wattle-and-daub were utilized as the principal superstructure materials. Burned structural timbers have been identified by R. C. Koeppen as mesquite (*Prosopis* spp.). Like the surface structures, it is most probable that roofs were made of thatch. A few houses-in-pits are currently occupied in the serrana (Hinton 1959: 17). Much of what is known concerning houses-in-pits comes from the work at Snaketown (Haury 1976) and San Cayetano del Tumacacori (Di Peso 1956), both in Arizona.

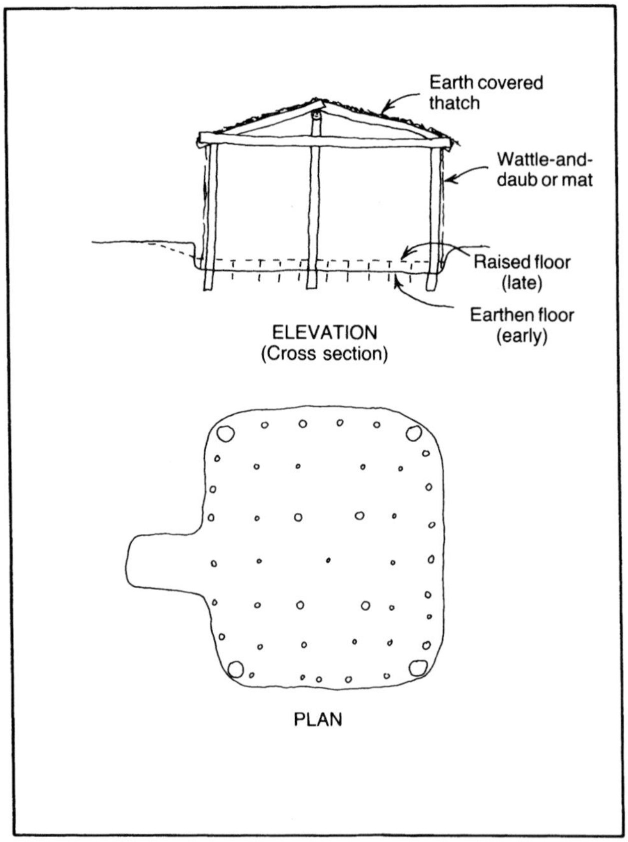

Figure 3.10. Schematic of a typical house-in-pit.

Without question, houses-in-pits were the earliest form of permanent architecture recorded in the Valley of Sonora and throughout the American Southwest. Obsidian hydration and radiocarbon analyses provided the basis for ascertaining the early dates of such houses in Sonora (Doolittle 1981). In addition, excavations revealed that polychrome pottery was associated largely with the structural back-fill of many houses-in-pits. The relatively late age of this pottery and its use as fill support the earlier dating of the back-filled structures. That polychrome pottery was found in association with surface remains of all structural types also verifies that houses-in-pits were not only early but were utilized throughout the occupance sequence (Pailes 1978; 1980: 29). Indeed, houses-in-pits have a long history of use throughout the Southwest (for example, Bullard 1962).

Figure 3.11. Rock mound that may have served as a house platform, site Son K:4:72 OU.

Remnants of another type of structure probably representing dwellings are also found in the Valley of Sonora. These features are rock mounds (Fig. 3.11) that vary considerably in size but average approximately 20 m in surface area and that resemble mounds noted for the Trincheras culture of far northern Sonora (Johnson 1963: 176 177). It is likely that these mounds functioned as platforms on which houses were built, but the probability of determining superstructure characteristics is low. Given the lack of foundation stones necessary for adobe, it is likely that jacales, mat, or wattle-and-daub houses were elevated for some reason, possibly in order to keep runoff from flowing through the structure. Such construction techniques are also noted among the Tepehuan in extreme southwestern Chihuahua (Riley 1969: 817). These mounds may have an earthen core, as do those of the Trincheras area, but so far none have been excavated. As is the case with other surface structures found in the valley, mounds have associated ceramics from relatively late pre-Hispanic times.

In addition to the numerous relic dwellings there exist several other structural remnants that served various purposes. Some of these features, because of their size, must have involved communal labor during construction and probably served the entire community and often the entire valley population.

At sites Son K:4:24 OU and Son K:4:72 OU (Fig. 3.12, Appendix A) are large features not found at other sites in the Valley of Sonora. These structures, because of their size, most probably involved communal and possibly societal labor during construction. Briefly, these features are two parallel mounds of rubble (Fig. 3.13) approximately 3.0 m wide, 0.5 m high, 45.0 m long, and 28.0 m apart. One of these features had an adobe wall of now undeterminable height built between the mounds at each end (Fig. 3.14). The other had surface structures on the ends.

The similarity of these features to both Southwestern and Mesoamerican ballcourts suggests that their function was probably of a ballcourt nature, according to Arturo Oliveras M. Although they are crude by Mesoamerican standards (for example, Smith 1961), they are elaborate in comparison to similar features found in other parts of the Southwest (for example, Wasley and Johnson 1965). The same polychrome ceramics associated with surface structures are common in the rubble fill utilized for construction of the mounds. Accordingly, these structures appear to be relatively late cultural features.

Two sites, Son K:4:16 OU (Figs. 3.15, 3.16), and Son K:4:127 OU (Fig. 3.17) have enclosure features that in many ways resemble ballcourts but are much smaller, averaging 18.0 m by 31.0 m (Fig. 3.18). In addition, the walls themselves are somewhat smaller, approximately 0.25 m high and 2.0 m thick. Both of these structures have a break in one longitudinal wall. While erosion may have contributed to the size of these openings, it is possible these gaps were deliberately planned to serve as doors. Although the wall is smaller, its construction is similar to that of the ballcourts. Unlike ballcourts, however, these enclosures have mounded rubble along all four sides. It is not likely that these features were roofed as no post holes were found. Certainly a roofed structure of such dimensions would have required numerous supports. Their exact function remains unknown but these structures at the very least filled some communal purpose and may have served significant portions of the valley's population.

SPECIAL SITES AND STRUCTURES

In addition to the structures that are located with permanent habitation sites or settlements, two other types of structures—small, usually single, rock rings and large rock enclosures—occur in isolation on prominent hills and mesas and each, by itself, constitutes a site. Although distinctive and not found together on sites in the Valley of Sonora, these two types of structures actually may have interrelated functions (Fontana, Greenleaf, and Cassidy 1959). On the peaks

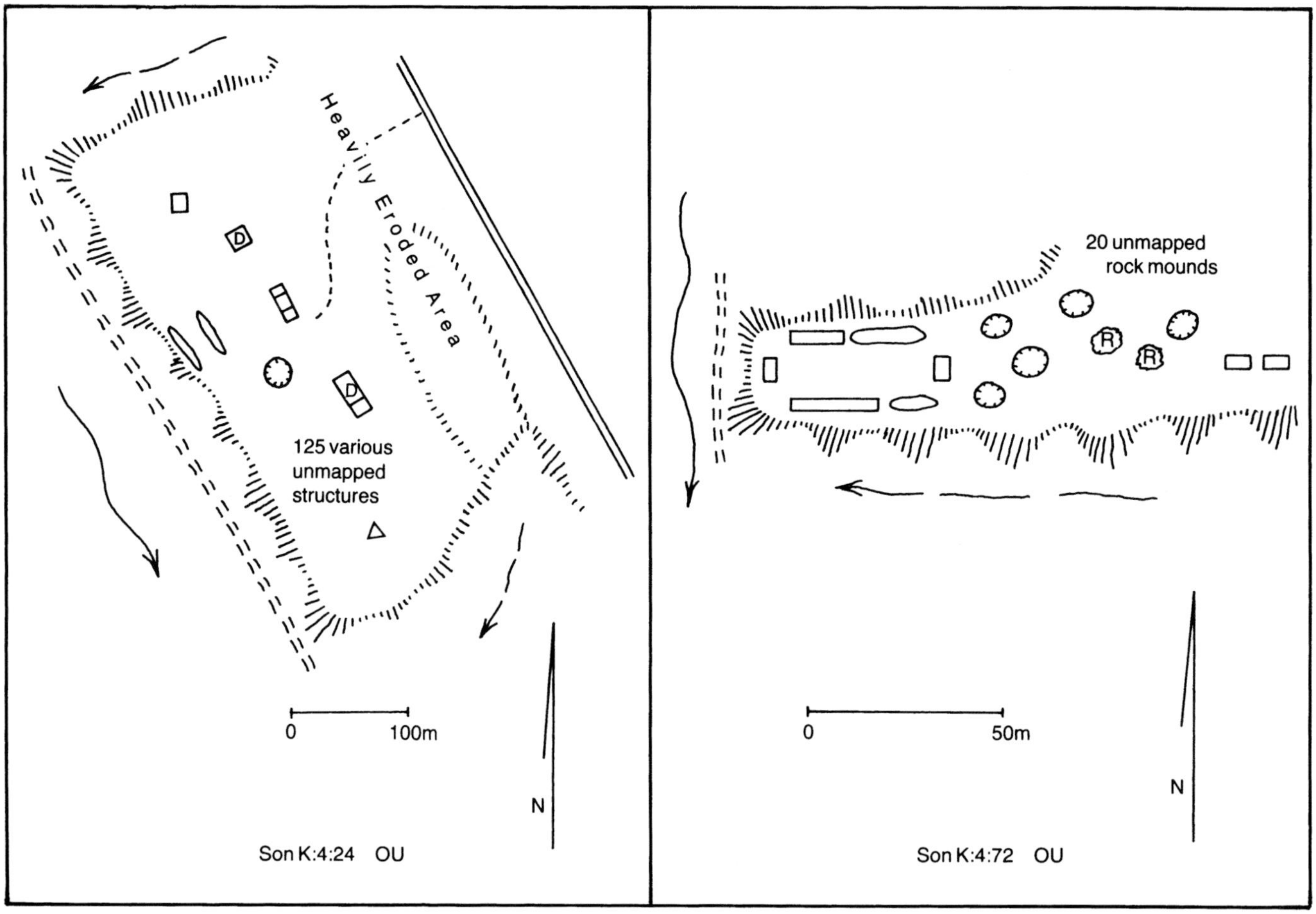

Figure 3.12. Sites Son K:4:24 OU and Son K:4:72 OU. (See Fig. 3.2 for Key.)

Figure 3.13. Mounded rubble forming one side of a possible ballcourt, site Son K:4:24 OU.

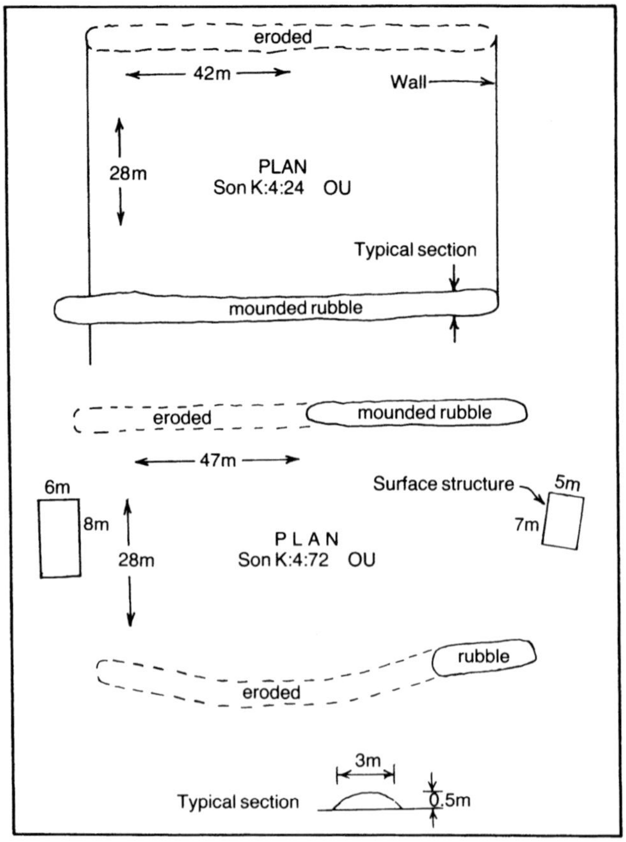

Figure 3.14. Schematic of possible ballcourts.

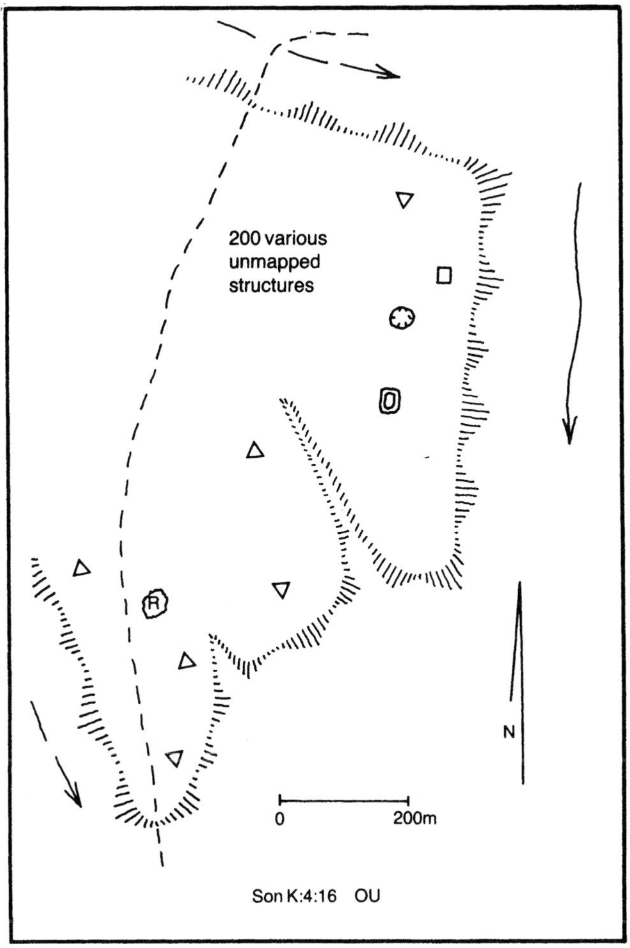

Figure 3.15. Site Son K:4:16 OU. (See Fig. 3.2 for Key.)

Figure 3.16. Surface remains of a pre-Hispanic enclosure, site Son K:4:16 OU. Arrow indicates rubble delimiting one side and the pack is approximately in the center.

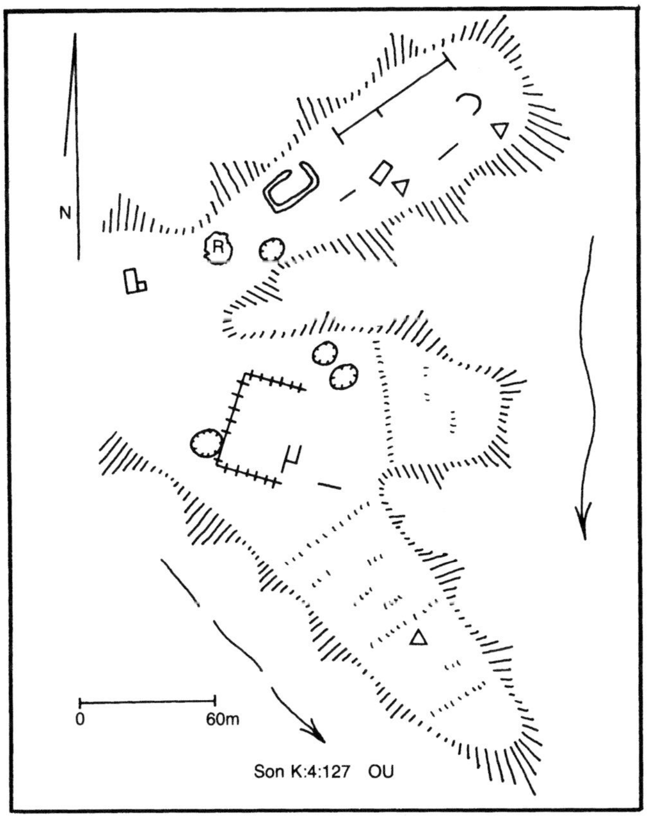

Figure 3.17. Site Son K:4:127 OU.

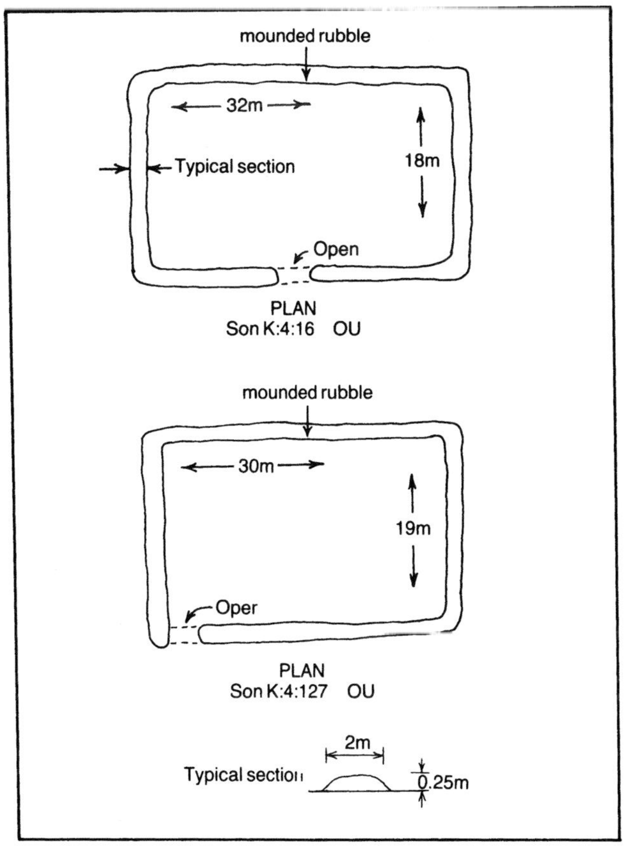

Figure 3.18. Schematic of pre-Hispanic enclosures.

Figure 3.19. Possible pre-Hispanic signal site; Son K:4:141 OU, Appendix B.

of seven hills in the valley are circular rock rubble features. Each ring has an inside diameter of approximately 1 m, an outside diameter of 3 m, and a height of approximately 0.3 m (Fig. 3.19). All of these features are eroded to some extent, with the side farthest downslope the most heavily damaged. Excavation of them revealed only burned earth, and it is likely these locales were components of a pyrosignal complex similar to that found near Casas Grandes (Di Peso 1974, Vol. 6: 183–300). Such a system might have served as a communication device in the valley. Each site has a panoramic view of a large portion of the valley and is clearly visible from the next similar location (Fig. 3.20). Furthermore, the site at each end of the valley and the one located 11 km west of Huepac along an arroyo also could have functioned as look-out stations to warn of intruders. Similar arrangements are noted in the ethnohistorical literature about the Valley of Sonora. Fray Marcos, for example, reported seeing several "smokes" that could have been from signal fires (Hallenbeck 1949: 35). Obregon, the chronicler for the 1565 Ibarra expedition, was more specific, noting: "Through war signals . . . they signaled one another from the different towns and provinces. According to their military custom, they called one another by means of smoke columns . . .

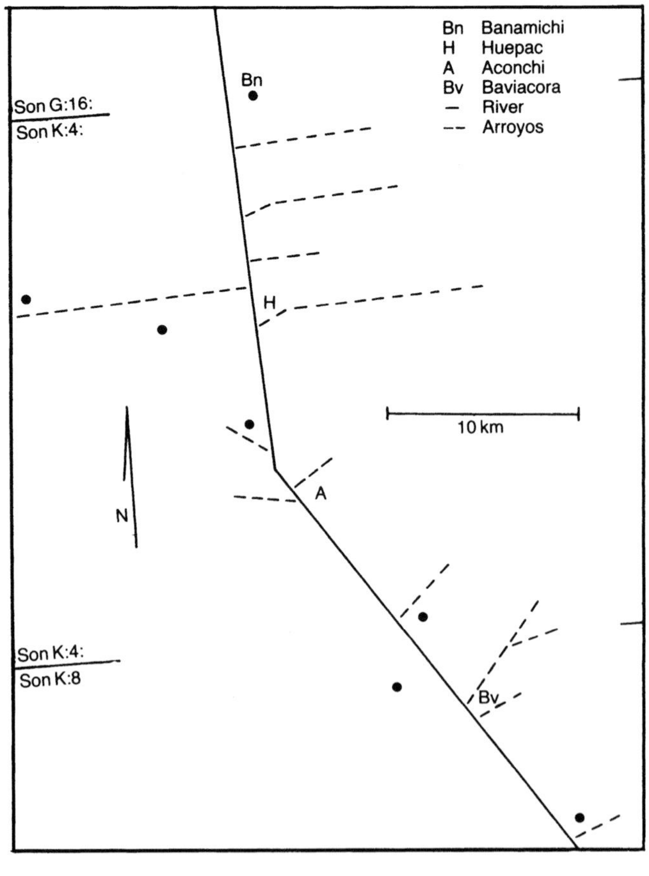

Figure 3.20. Distribution of possible signal sites in the Valley of Sonora.

By means of these fires they communicate with and understand one another easily" (Hammond and Rey 1928: 178, also 155, 177, 192). Until recently, however, these reports had not been confirmed archaeologically.

The large boulder enclosures are undoubtedly parts of cerros de trincheras or terraced hills, the most well-known of all pre-Hispanic constructions in northwestern Mexico (Sauer and Brand 1931). Cerros de trincheras are usually conical hills that were terraced and fortified presumably for defensive purposes during pre-Hispanic times. They are most common northwest of the serrana in the Sonoran desert (Hinton 1955). Fortified hills are also found in regions peripheral to the Trincheras culture area (Johnson 1963), which has its core near the pueblo of Altar (for example, Hoover 1941). Those in the Valley of Sonora are a variation of the true cerros de trincheras. According to Sauer and Brand (1931: 69): "Dissected, lava-capped terraces in the valleys were also utilized prehistorically. . . . Where a smooth summit exists, partly surrounded by cliffs, the prehistoric occupation may have been restricted to such a buttressed flat mesa, its weakest points reenforced by rock walls or corrals."

Mesa-top trincheras enclosures in the Valley of Sonora vary in size and shape from a 15 m square to a 60 m by 28 m rectangle. They are dry work consisting of vesicular basalt boulders averaging approximately 20 cm in diameter. The original height, thickness, and shape of the walls are unknown. They may have had straight sides that have since collapsed. Today the walls are approximately 1 m high and 2 m thick at the base (Fig. 3.21).

Figure 3.21. Enclosure walls of a cerro de trinchera, Cerro Batonapa, site Son K:4:22 OU.

All of these enclosures are located on high mesas, most overlooking the floodplain. They are found at four and possibly six places in the valley. The largest and best-known is atop Cerro Batonapa (Son K:4:22 OU, Figs. 3.22, 3.23), 2 km southeast of Banamichi. The other three confirmed sites are all in the northern section of the valley (Fig. 3.24). One of the possible hill sites is also in this general vicinity. Site Son K:4:105 OU (Fig. 3.25) is 1 km south of Huepac. This location, which has been heavily disturbed by a historic mining mill, is probably the long-lost cerro de trinchera noted by Bandelier (1892: 449) in the 1880s. The mill was constructed in the early 1900s and, according to Alfonso Daco, was destroyed by fire in 1943, which might explain why Bandelier knew of this site and other surveyors did not record it and why present-day residents have no knowledge of it. The other possible site is approximately 13 km northeast of Baviacora, far from the river. It overlooks a large arroyo that begins in a pass through the mountains between the Rio Sonora and Rio Moctezuma drainages. This possible cerro de trinchera was spotted from an airplane in 1981; it has not been investigated on the ground and remains unconfirmed.

Although no house remnants were found on most cerros de trincheras, it is suspected that at least a few pre-Hispanic people resided at such places. Evidence of houses on Cerro Batonapa was noted by Bandelier in 1884 (Lange and Riley 1970: 235–236). It is possible that these features were obliterated during the past century. Permanent habitation structures were also found at site Son K:4:127 OU (Fig. 3.17), suggesting occupation at least on that same mesa top. Whether or not the features are contemporaneous, however, has yet to be determined.

Although there is no conclusive evidence, it is highly probable that the cerros de trincheras served as gathering places during times of war. During the Mexican revolution one terraced hill in another part of Sonora was a battle site (Harlem 1964: 345). Earlier, in historic times, Bandelier noted that people gathered on such hills to defend themselves against the Apache (Lange and Riley 1970: 242). Both of these accounts parallel observations made by Obregon, the only 16th century Spaniard to relay information about defensive structures. He noted that near the town of Caguaripa (probably not in the Valley of Sonora) "at the end of and above this gorge there is a fortress" (Hammond and Rey 1928: 180), and the residents "fortified themselves in their fortress" (p. 181). That this particular structure was on a promontory is evident from his statement that combatants were "fatigued and out of breath from the hardship of ascent" (p. 180). These accounts are admittedly fragmentary. Nevertheless, they tend to support each other and an acceptable interpretation other than defense has not been proffered.

In a defensive capacity, an intravalley and perhaps an intervalley communication system would prove to be most advantageous. It is in this regard that the previously discussed signal sites may have functioned (Wilcox 1979: 17). Interestingly, the locations of the possible cerros de trincheras along the arroyo in the southeastern part of the valley is not unlike

Figure 3.22. Aerial view of Cerro Batonapa, site Son K:4:22 OU.

the locations of the possible pyrosignals along the arroyo in the northwestern section. Both sites overlook natural corridors between serrana valleys. Apparently, the small rock rings are signal sites that functioned in concert with the large rock enclosures that are cerros de trincheras.

Determining the ages of periods of use for each of the two types of structures is difficult because of the paucity of cultural debris on them. Some Trincheras Purple-on-red pottery was found on Batonapa. On the basis of this ceramic type, cerros de trincheras were in one case thought to have been used between A.D. 800 and 1100 (Johnson 1963: 183). However, it also has been suggested, on the basis of other ceramic evidence, that cerros de trincheras were used between A.D. 1100 and 1300 (Fontana, Greenleaf, and Cassidy 1959: 47; Wilcox 1979: 29). The remnants of surface structures on site Son K:4:127 OU (Fig. 3.17) tend to confirm this later date. Of course, the houses and the enclosure may not be directly associated and therefore not contemporaneous.

COMMUNITIES

Structures are the prinicipal components of settlements. As such, their number, density, and orientation on each site

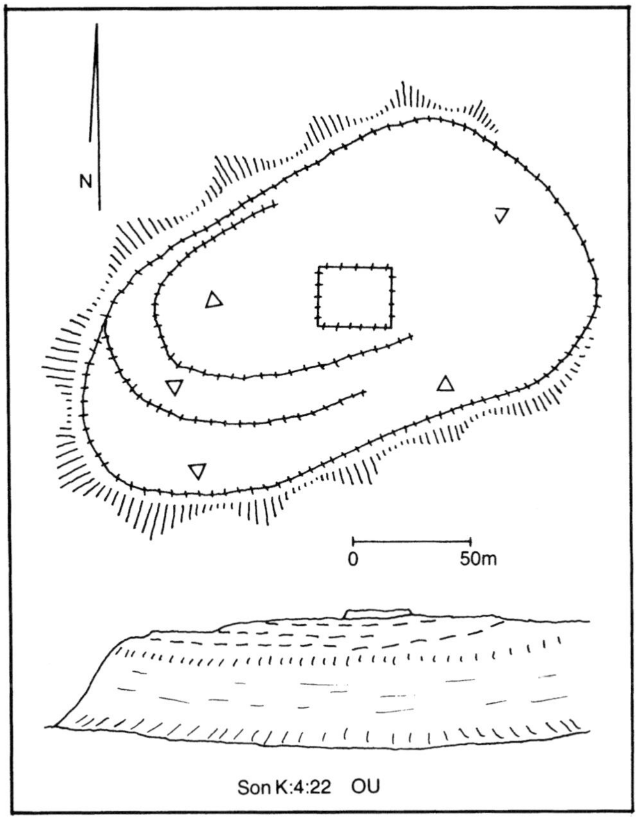

Figure 3.23. Site Son K:4:22 OU. (See Fig. 3.2 for Key.)

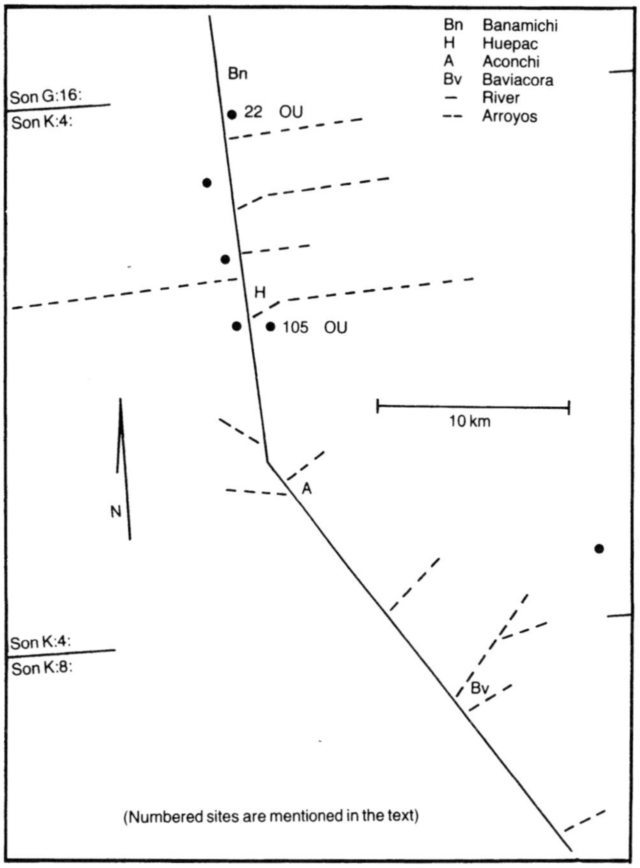

Figure 3.24. Distribution of cerros de trincheras in the Valley of Sonora.

often can be used to infer community organization (Beardsley and others 1956). For example, small sites comprised principally of houses have been interpreted in several cases as agricultural settlements (Chang 1958: 303–304; Trigger 1968: 60–66), while large sites with public architecture have been envisioned as religious (Hammond 1974), political (Blanton 1977), and economic (Millon 1967) centers. Taking the level of investigation one step further, the relationship between sites frequently can be inferred from differences in the individual communities or settlements (Flannery 1972: 418). Settlement patterns characterized by a few, scattered, small sites, for example, have been considered to be indicative of limited intraregional interaction (Grove and others 1976). Conversely, formal and structured intersite interaction has been deducted from patterns in which there is one large, a few intermediate-sized, and several small settlements, all uniformly spaced (Johnson 1972). Any study of occupance based on settlements therefore requires the development of a site typology, a classification that reflects the differences in size, function, features, and other attributes of sites dating to the same period. The need for establishing such a typology is especially important in the case of the Valley of Sonora during pre-Hispanic times in light of the Spanish claims that sites varied considerably in size, function, and importance.

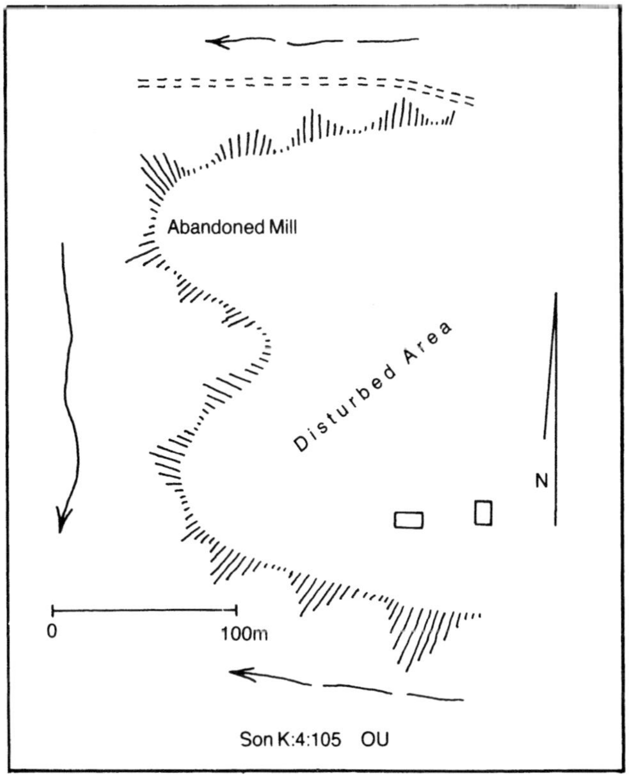

Figure 3.25. Site Son K:4:105 OU. (See Fig. 3.2 for Key.)

Classification

As discussed earlier, problems frequently exist in the use of surface remains as evidence of past conditions. In many cases, however, such data may be used in producing site typologies if caution is exercised. Most notable in this regard are the studies conducted in the Valley of Mexico (Parsons 1971; Parsons and others 1982; Blanton 1972; Sanders, Parsons, and Santley 1979). That area is both optimal and similar to the Valley of Sonora in terms of its geoarchaeological conditions or factors affecting sites and their preservation (Butzer 1982: 35–42). The typology used for settlements in the Valley of Sonora follows the example set by these works. It is based principally on size as measured by the number of houses and secondly on surface area as measured in hectares; on occupational intensity as determined by the density and spatial distribution of other cultural materials, especially ceramics; and on architectural complexity. A four tier community or settlement hierarchy is evident from the data collected in the Valley of Sonora.

Regional Centers

Large, nucleated, and architecturally complex with large-scale public architecture are criteria for classification of a site as a regional center (Parsons and others 1982: 71). Regional centers in the Valley of Sonora are similar to those of the "secondary" subcategory defined by Parsons (1971: 22) and Blanton (1972: 20) for highland Mexico. Parsons's scheme requires a population, estimated from surface area and occupational intensity, of several hundred to a few thousand. Blanton puts the population estimate between 1,000 and 2,000 inhabitants.

Villages

Sites comprised principally of houses, with little architectural complexity, usually lacking large-scale public architecture, and with a minimum population of 100 are classified as villages. Blanton (1972: 20) uses 1,000 persons as a maximum population for such sites, while Parsons (1971: 22) uses 1,500, with villages over 500 persons classified as "large." Being rather densely occupied, villages in the Valley of Sonora are more like the "nucleated villages" than the "dispersed villages" in the Valley of Mexico (Parsons 1971: 22; Parsons and others 1982: 70).

Hamlets

Parsons (1971: 22) defined a hamlet as any community of under 100 persons, and Blanton (1972: 20) placed sites with populations between 10 and 100 in this category. Both concur that such sites lack public architecture and are solely residential sites. In some cases, hamlets have been distinguished from villages by the latter's arrangement around a plaza (Sanders 1956: 117), with hamlets composed solely of small house groups. Such a distinction, however, is not evident in the Valley of Sonora.

Rancherias

The term rancheria is only sometimes used in reference to settlements in highland Mexico (Sanders 1965: 50) but is common among southwestern ethnographers and archaeologists (Spicer 1967: 12–13). It is applied to small, scattered, and riverine-oriented permanent habitation sites. The dispersed nature of these settlements is often noted as a contrast to the densely populated pueblos of the northern Southwest. Typically, rancherias have only a few houses, and frequently they are isolated residences. Blanton (1972: 20) considers such sites distinct from sites with two or more houses, but here the inclusive term "rancheria" is used in reference to all small sites.

Chronology

The paucity of archaeological work conducted in the Valley of Sonora prior to this project made the dating of sites a difficult task. Although a ceramic typology and sequence have yet to be established, a settlement chronology based on architectural differences has been developed. From excavations on 34 sites, including intensive excavations at Son K:4:24 OU (Fig. 3.12), a seriation of house types and an occupation sequence have been outlined for the Valley of Sonora (Pailes 1980: 29). Based principally on architectural superposition, the sequence begins with houses-in-pits about A.D. 1000 and terminates with public architecture in late pre-Hispanic times (Fig. 3.26). The archaeological remains, including one component (Son K:4:25 OU, lithic scatter, Appendix B) radiocarbon dated at 450 B.C., pit-and-groove petroglyphs (Fig. 3.27) that have been dated in other areas at 5000 B.C. (Heizer and Baumhoff 1962:234; Greenwood 1969: 52, 58), a one-hand Cochise-type metate (Fig. 3.28) possibly dating as early as 6000 B.C. (McGregor 1965: 127), and Clovis points dating to roughly 11,000 B.C. but found in other serrana valleys (Robles Ortiz and Manzo Taylor 1972), indicate very early but poorly defined periods of occupance. The sequence becomes much clearer with the development of permanent dwellings.

The earliest phase, noted by houses-in-pits, existed from about A.D.1000 through most of the 1100s. This phase was identified by a large house-in-pit measuring 8.5 m in diameter and 90 cm in depth. A plastered, sloping entry and plastered floor characterize this house. Burned timbers from this structure, which apparently was destroyed by fire, provided dates of about A.D. 1100. Pailes (1980) reported uncalibrated dates of A.D. 1075 and 1085, measured in radiocarbon years. Based on the MASCA correction factor (Ralph, Michael, and Han 1974) and a high-precision calibration method (Stuiver 1982), these dates could read anywhere between A.D. 1080 and 1200. The second phase, which included the 13th and early 14th centuries, is a transitional phase in which the relative importance of houses-in-pits declined as adobe surface structures increased in number. Datable material for this phase came from a reoccupation of the house-in-pit described for the first phase. This structure was rebuilt with a raised floor, indicated by numerous postholes, and a new entry flanked by two massive adobe blocks. Like its predecessor, this house also burned, providing calibrated radiocarbon dates of about A.D. 1320. The third phase, extending through the later half of the 14th century into the 15th century, is represented predominantly by rectangular surface structures. Although the use of houses-in-pits never completely ceased, relative frequency of these houses declined substantially in the later phases. The fourth phase extended through the 15th century until the arrival of the Spanish. This phase also includes single and multiple-storied surface buildings.

Even though there is considerable contemporaneity between houses-in-pits and surface structures, especially during the second phase, a seriation of house types is identifiable and can be used to date sites on the basis of surface evidence. In addition to the obsidian hydration, radiocarbon, and ceramic analyses, two clear cases of superposition have

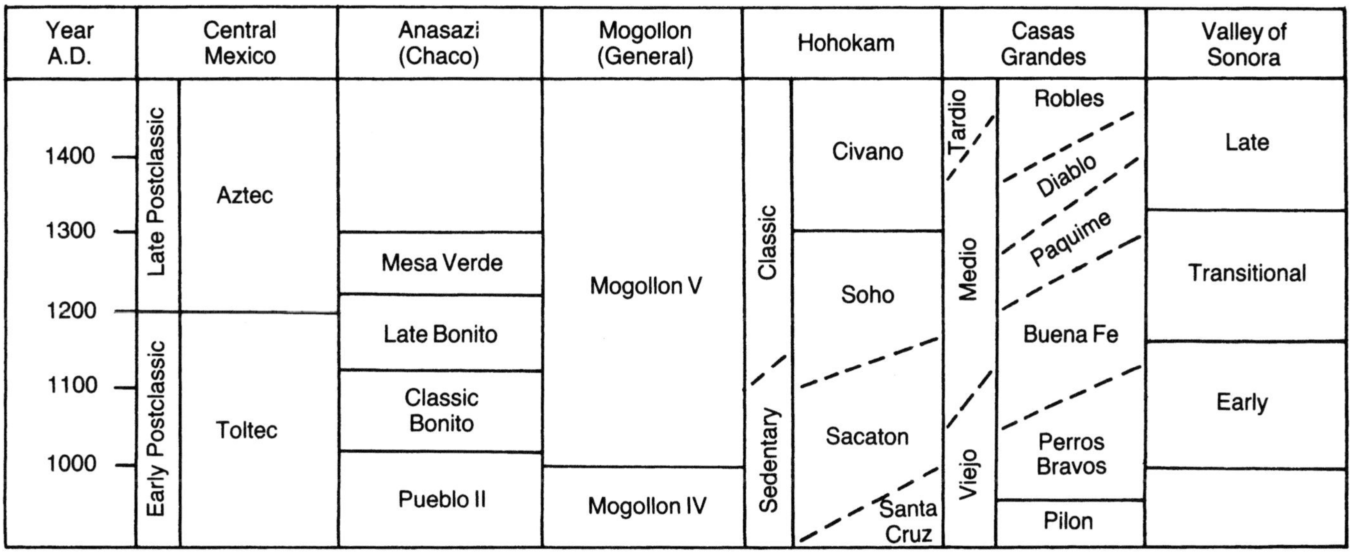

Figure 3.26. Comparative regional chronology. Dashed lines separating phases reflect current disputes over dates. Sources: Central Mexico (Sanders and Price 1968), Anasazi (Hayes, Brugge, and Judge 1981; Cordell 1984), Mogollon (Wheat 1955; Cordell 1984), Hokokam (Haury 1976; Plog 1980; Schiffer 1982), Casas Grandes (Di Peso 1974, Vol. 4; Wilcox and Shenk 1977; LeBlanc 1980; Lekson 1984).

Figure 3.27. Pit-and-groove petroglyphs. Depressions are filled with dark soil for delineation. (Reprinted from the *Journal of Field Archaeology*, Vol. 11, p. 17, 1984, with the permission of the Trustees of Boston University.)

Figure 3.28. A one-hand Cochise-type metate.

been found in which surface structures overlie houses-in-pits. There are no known cases where surface structures were built prior to houses-in-pits or where houses-in-pits overlie surface structures. Houses-in-pits were apparently not constructed during late pre-Hispanic times, but many earlier ones were rebuilt and used, in some cases continuously, even past Contact. It appears that those houses-in-pits that were used contemporaneously with surface structures were both built and occupied during the earlier times. Similar architectural changes dating to this same half-millennium have been documented archaeologically in other parts of the Southwest. This change may indeed by a pan-Southwestern phenomenon (for example, Doyel and Haury 1976; Whalen 1981a, b; Tuthill 1947).

On the basis of data collected during excavations, it is assured that surface structures were occupied only during late pre-Hispanic times. Houses-in-pits, except those overlain by surface structures, were probably occupied throughout the sequence. In this study, all qualifying relic houses are considered to date to a late pre-Hispanic phase (about A.D. 1350 to 1550), while all relic houses-in-pits are considered to date to both the late phase and an earlier phase (about A.D. 1000 to 1200). Unfortunately, houses occupied during intervening times are not clearly distinguishable from those of the earlier or later phases at this time. However, enough evidence does exist to suggest that architectural and, hence, settlement changes between the two phases were regular and continuous and not discrete and abrupt.

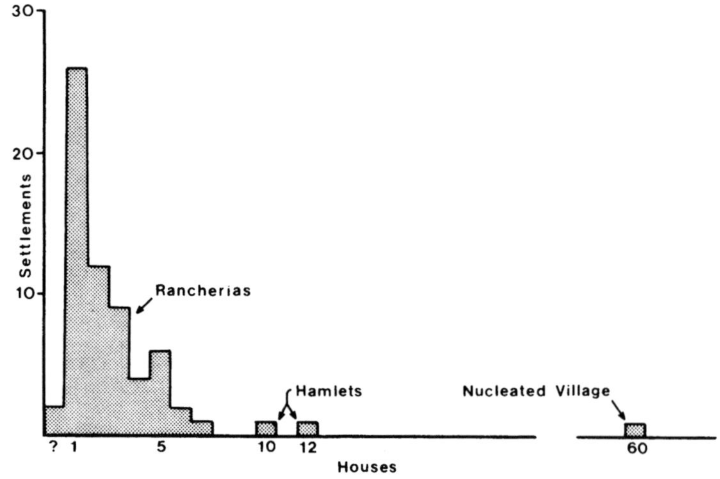

Figure 3.29. Early phase settlement sizes.

Hierarchies

A total of 65 settlements involving 224 houses was identified for the early phase of occupation. Sixty-two (95.5 percent) of the settlements were rancherias, and of these 26 (40.0 percent of all early phase sites) were isolated residences (Fig. 3.29). Two sites (3.0 percent) with 10 and 12 houses respectively are identified as hamlets (Son K:4:32 OU and Son K:4:110 OU; Fig. 3.30; Appendix A). Only one site (Son K:4:24 OU; Fig. 3.12; Appendix A), San Jose, with

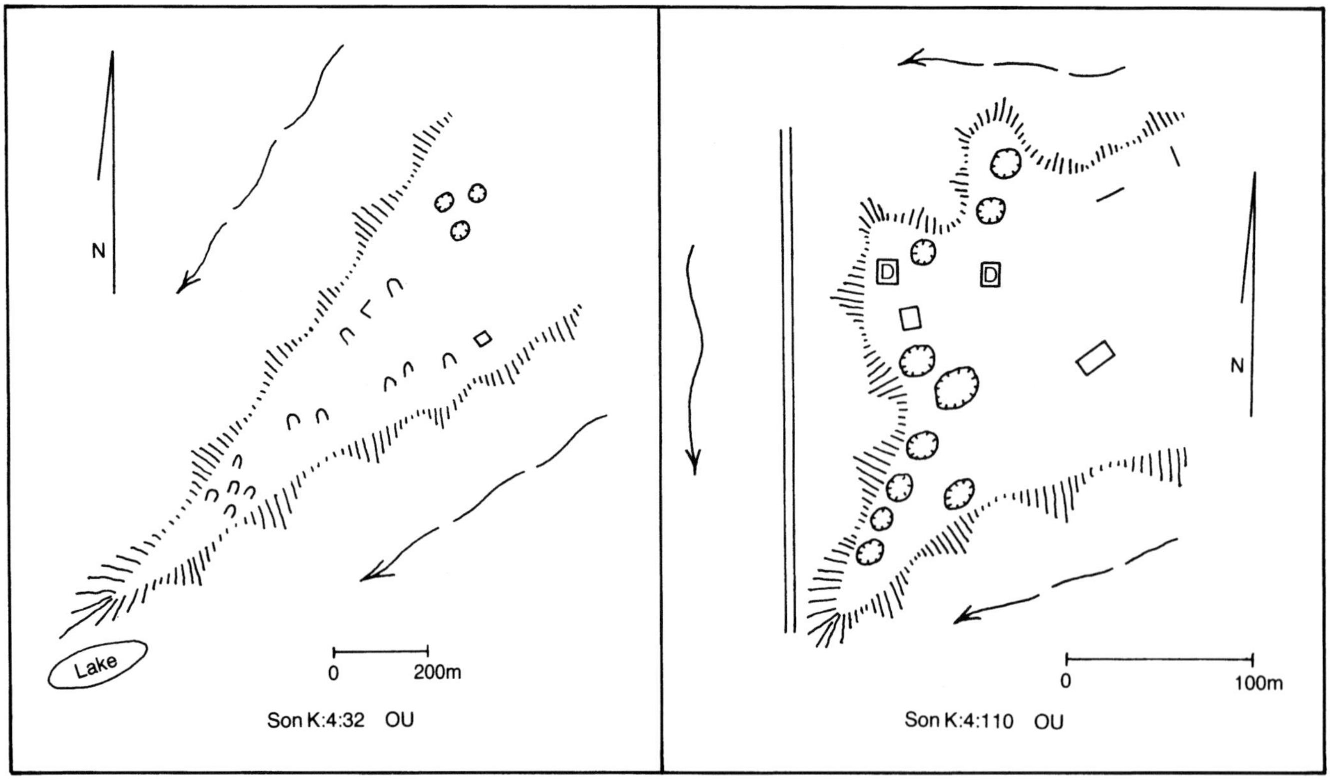

Figure 3.30. Sites Son K:4:32 OU and Son K:4:110 OU. (See Fig. 3.2 for Key.)

more than 60 houses-in-pits, is classified as a village. There were no early phase regional centers in the Valley of Sonora.

Between the early and late phases the number of settlements increased approximately 150 percent and the number of houses increased nearly 450 percent. Most of this change involved rancherias and, to a lesser extent, hamlets. Late phase occupation involved 162 settlements and 1,289 houses (Fig. 3.31). There were 130 (80.2 percent) settlements that had 8 or fewer houses at this time. Twenty of these contained only fragmentary evidence of late occupation but were classified as rancherias because they were located on small mesas that could not have contained many houses. Although the actual number of rancherias increased by two-fold, the percentage of these settlements actually decreased. The greatest decrease was in isolated residences; only 15 (11.5 percent) existed in the late phase. This drop in number but increase in size suggests population agglomeration and a trend toward nucleation. During the late phase 26 (16.0 percent) settlements were of sufficient size to be classified as hamlets. The smallest had evidence of 9 houses, the largest had 21 houses. The two early phase hamlets did not grow into villages. Their architecture was predominantly houses-in-pits, thereby indicating little growth.

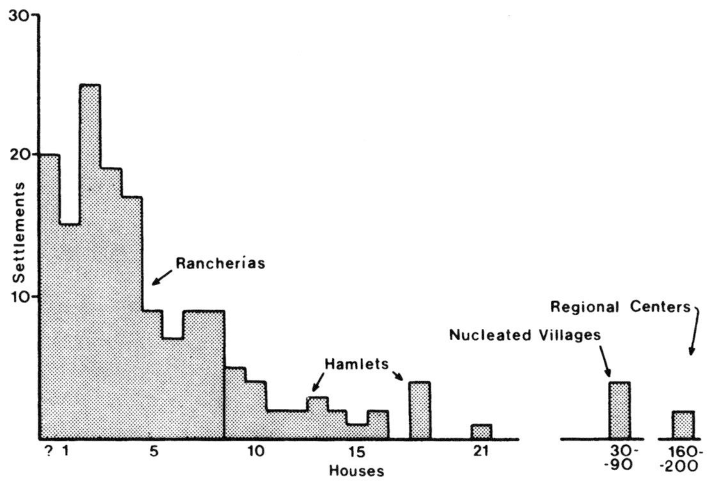

Figure 3.31. Late phase settlement sizes.

Four (2.5 percent) of the late phase settlements were villages: Son K:4:20 OU and Son K:4:120 OU (Fig. 3.32), Son K:4:72 OU (Fig. 3.12), and Son G:16:27 OU (Fig. 3.33; Appendix A). Some of these settlements may have served some extracommunity functions. Indeed, Son K:4:72 OU contains

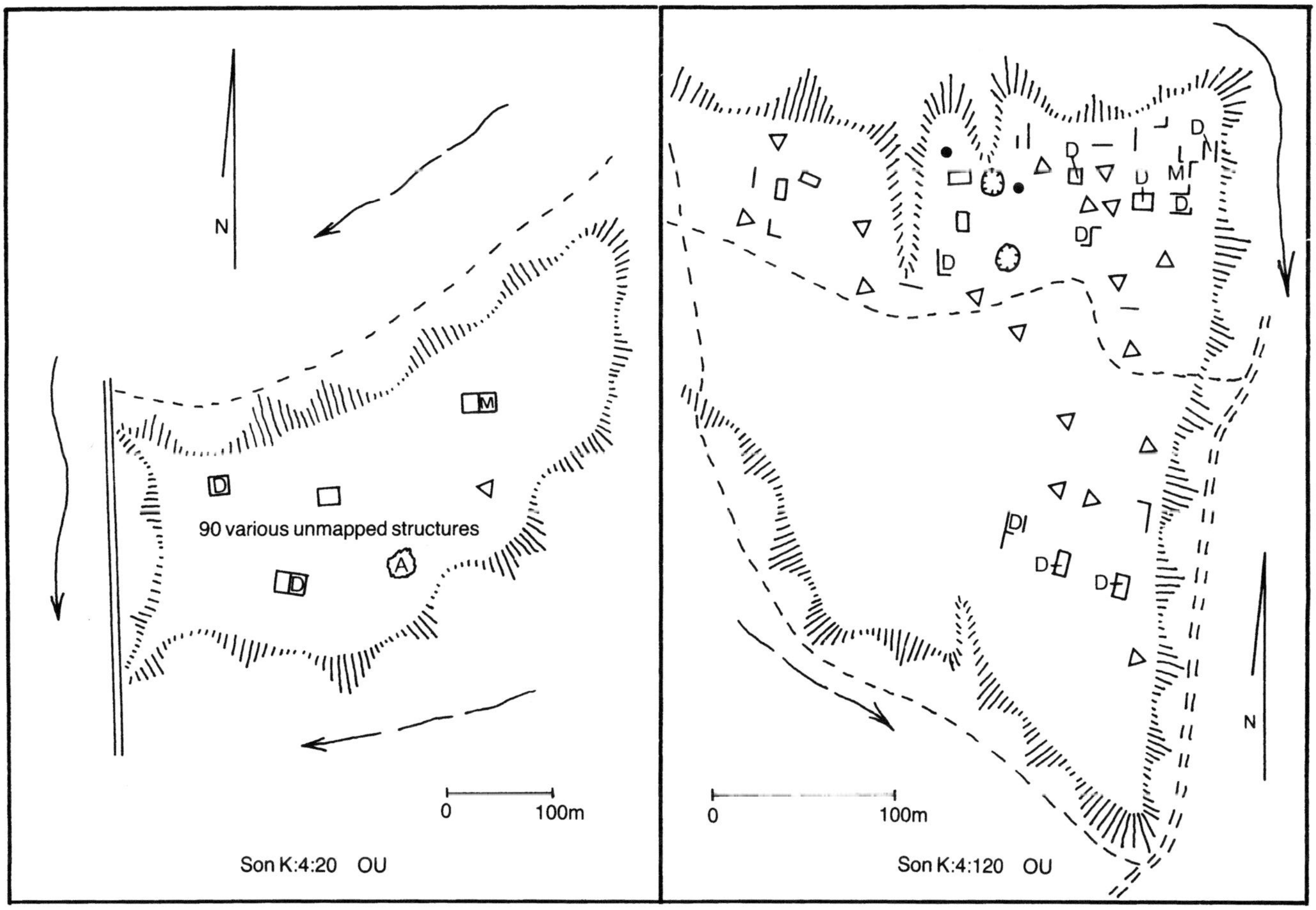

Figure 3.32. Sites Son K:4:20 OU and Son K:4:120 OU. (See Fig. 3.2 for Key.)

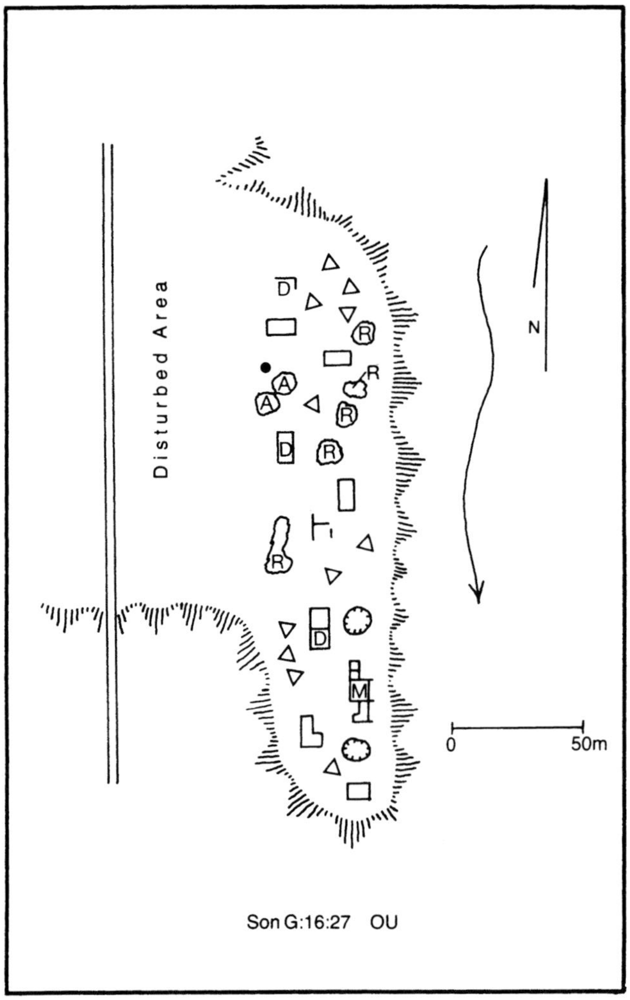

Figure 3.33. Site Son G:16:27 OU. (See Fig. 3.2 for Key.)

a possible ballcourt that suggests considerable intersite interaction. Although no settlements were large enough to be classified as regional centers during the early phase, two (1.2 percent) had attained such status by the late phase. Site Son K:4:24 OU (Fig. 3.12), which is the sole early phase village, has nearly 100 clearly identifiable house remains and well over 60 tentatively identified houses. The settlement at Son K:4:16 OU (Fig. 3.15) had grown from an early phase rancheria to over 200 houses by the late phase. In addition to being large, both sites contain public architecture. The former has a possible ballcourt, the latter an enclosure. These features tend to confirm that these settlements served as focal points for some intravalley interaction. The regional centers also fit the descriptions of the large towns reported by the Spaniards.

SETTLEMENT PATTERNS

It is a common practice in settlement studies to describe regional patterns as being either clustered, random, or dispersed—uniformly spaced across a given area (Haggett, Cliff, and Frey 1977: 99). Although settlement patterns may be envisioned as lying anywhere on a continuum from clustered to dispersed, it is probably inappropriate and perhaps totally incorrect to refer to any pattern as random (Graham 1980: 106), because human activities are rarely random. In order to satisfy their specific needs, people tend to respond deliberately and rationally to identifiable conditions or factors. Settlement patterns often reflect these factors, which can be dichotomized as either environmental or social. Factors associated with the physical environment typically involve subsistence, particularly water, wild foods, and land suitable for agriculture (for example, Beardsley and others 1956). Social factors involve interactions such as economic exchanges and political control (Johnson 1972). In most cases, individual settlement locations and, hence, settlement patterns are influenced by a combination of both environmental and social factors (Flannery 1972). Settlements occupied in the Valley of Sonora during pre-Hispanic times are no exception. During the early phase, however, environmental factors were more important than social factors.

Of the 65 early phase settlements, 58 were located on mesas overlooking the river and floodplain (Fig. 3.34). Al-

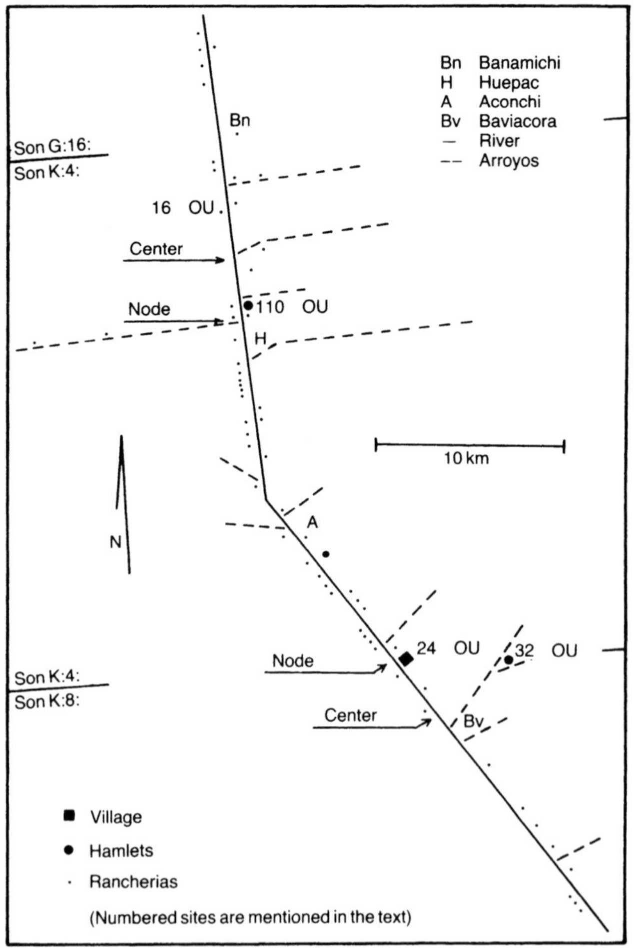

Figure 3.34. Distribution of early phase settlements in the Valley of Sonora.

though they were nearly equally divided between the northern (30; 51.8 percent) and the southern (28; 48.2 percent) segments of the valley, these settlements were not dispersed or uniformly spaced. Instead, they tended to be clustered, albeit only slightly. Most of the settlements (39; 67.2 percent) were located near permanent water sources (see Fig. 2.5 for comparative purposes). The importance of water for settlement is indicated not only by the number of sites located near permanent water but also by the size of such sites. Two of the largest early phase settlements were located near major springs that ensured a constant flow of water through much of the valley. One of the two hamlets (Son K:4:110 OU, Fig. 3.30) was located near previously discussed El Ojo de Agua in the northern segment, and the village (Son K:4:24 OU, Fig. 3.12) was located near a spring that today provides abundant water for irrigation as well as contributes to regular stream flow in much of the southern segment.

In addition to being located near water, many settlements were also located wthin an area of diverse wild plant resources. Twenty-six (40.0 percent) of the early phase settlements were situated in the mixed scrub-slope ecological zone. As was noted earlier, this zone shows the most promise for natural resource utilization because of the dense and varied vegetation within a relatively restricted area.

Virtually all early phase settlements were located near lands that are cultivated today. The seven settlements not situated along the bajada edge overlooking the river and floodplain were positioned on mesas overlooking large arroyos. One of these settlements (Son K:4:32 OU, Fig. 3.30), at the confluence of two arroyos 3 km from the floodplain, was large enough to be classified as a hamlet.

It is apparent from their locations that early phase settlements in the Valley of Sonora in large part were positioned based on environmental factors, especially water for consumption and probably incipient irrigation, agricultural lands, and wild plant resources. However, there is evidence that social factors also might have influenced this settlement pattern. In addition to being proximal to major springs, the village and one hamlet were located near the physical centers of discrete physiographic segments of the valley. Perhaps more significantly, however, each of these settlements was located exactly at the node, or point of minimum aggregate distance to all other settlements in their respective valley segments (Fig. 3.34).

Calculation of the node in a one-dimensional region, such as a river valley, first involved drawing a line through the sites from one end of the region to the other. This line was then scaled and the numerical value of each site location was determined. Because the measure involves aggregates, a weighting factor for each site (here the number of houses) was multiplied by the locational value of the site. The mean of all weighted site values was calculated and then mapped on the original scaled line. The location of the mean is the node.

Although there has been much debate over the applicability of some locational models (see Crumley 1979), simulation studies (White 1977) and numerous empirical studies (for example, Burghardt 1959; Flannery 1976b) have demonstrated that such conditions are typical of cases where one settlement (the large one) serves as a central place or as a settlement that provides goods or services to numerous other settlements (the small ones) in a surrounding market area. Currently there are no data that indicate exactly what kinds of social activities might have been centered at those two sites. Certainly some type of intravalley interaction, perhaps local redistribution of wild resources and agricultural products, contributed to the development of large settlements at these nodal locations.

The settlement pattern of the late phase is in many ways similar to that of the early phase. There is, however, one major difference: the locations of the very large settlements, the regional centers, were influenced largely by social factors. The locations of the smaller settlements, for the most part, continued to be influenced predominantly by environmental factors.

Of the 162 settlements occupied during the late phase, 142 were located overlooking the river (Fig. 3.35) and tended to be dispersed rather than clustered as during the early phase.

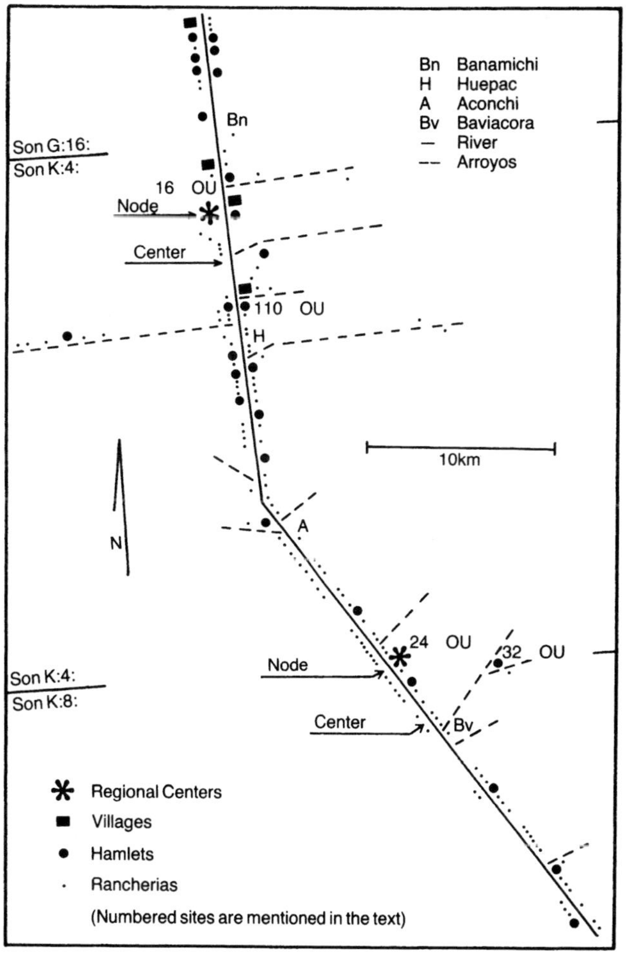

Figure 3.35. Distribution of late phase settlements in the Valley of Sonora.

Most settlements (100; 70.4 percent) continued to be located in areas with permanent water close at hand. Although the number of settlements increased in both segments of the valley, the better-watered southern segment, especially the upper reach on both sides of the river and the lower reach on the east side, experienced the largest increases. Slightly more than half of the late phase river-oriented settlements (76; 53.5 percent) were located in the southern segment, and 45 (31.7 percent) were on the east side. Here mesas are both numerous and uniformly spaced, but only moderate in size. Accordingly, there was space available for the addition of several small settlements in this portion of the valley.

Perhaps more striking than the increase in the number of settlements, especially small ones, are the characteristics of the large settlement locations. Of the 26 hamlets, 19 (73.1 percent) are found in the northern segment of the valley as are all four villages and the largest regional center. This situation is largely a function of two environmental factors. First, unlike the mesas in the south, those in the northern segment are few but large. Three of the villages are located on the only mesas that overlook the floodplain for considerable distances. For example, site Son K:4:120 OU (Fig. 3.32) southwest of Banamichi is situated on the inhabitable mesa nearest to a broad expanse of floodplain. Most of the terrain in this area is heavily dissected and is not suitable for settlements. Second, although it is not as well-watered, there is approximately twice as much floodplain land available for agriculture in the north as in the south.

As in the early phase, all late phase sites are located near lands that are cultivated today. Although the number of arroyo-oriented settlements increased from 7 to 20, the proportion of arroyo to river locales changed only slightly by the late phase (from 10.7 to 12.3 percent). Significant, however, is that arroyo settlements were small and overall decreased through time in their hierarchical importance. Indeed, one early phase hamlet (Son K:4:32 OU, Fig. 3.30) did not increase greatly in size even though it was located on a very large mesa.

The relative importance of locating near a diversity of wild plant resources seems to have been less in the late phase than during earlier times. Although the number of sites in the mixed scrub-slope zone increased to 51, the proportion of these sites to the total dropped to 31.5 percent.

Although environmental factors continued to play a major role in the locating of settlements, social factors also increased in importance during the late phase. Nowhere is the significance of social factors more evident than in the positioning of some large settlements, especially regional centers. Both regional centers are located at the nodes of their respective valley centers (Fig. 3.35). The early phase village grew large enough to be classified as a regional center by the late phase. Paralleling the growth of this center was an increase in the number of small settlements in the southern segment of the valley. Together these increases resulted in the node remaining in the same location throughout the sequence of occupance. Such was not the case in the northern segment of the valley.

The early phase hamlet in the northern segment did increase by the late phase. However, unlike the early phase village in the south, it did not grow large enough to be classified as a regional center. The relatively moderate size of the mesa on which this settlement was located severely restricted the extent of its growth. The emergence of other large settlements on large mesas in this valley segment resulted in the node shifting north by approximately 6 km, very near the largest mesa in the northern segment. It is on this mesa that the largest regional center (Son K:4:16 OU, Fig. 3.15), was located.

The two late phase regional centers undoubtedly served as hubs for much intravalley interaction. Not only do their nodal locations suggest such was the case, but the public architecture in the form of a possible ballcourt at one and a large enclosure at the other tend to confirm that intersite activities were centered at these two settlements.

Social factors may also have played a role in the development of other late phase sites. One of the late phase villages (Son K:4:72 OU, Fig. 3.12), was located on the east side of the river opposite the northern regional center. This settlement, which was also near the node of the northern valley segment, contained the other possible ballcourt. Considering the presence of this public architecture and the nodal location, it can be surmised that social factors probably played a role equally as important as environmental factors in the location of this settlement.

It is evident that both environmental and social factors were important in determining the locations of late phase settlements. The proximity to permanent water sources was as crucial as it was during the early phase. However, settlement locations seem to have been influenced less by proximity to diverse wild plant resources than during earlier times and more by the availability of land that could be cultivated. Furthermore, the development of large settlements, especially regional centers, characterized by public architecture and nodal locations indicates that a great deal of intravalley social interaction, as originally reported by the Spaniards, was occurring in the Valley of Sonora by the late phase.

In summary, pre-Hispanic settlements in the Valley of Sonora are characterized by a number of different types of structures. The early archaeological surveyors reported mainly surface structures and rock enclosures associated with cerros de trincheras. However, houses-in-pits were also inhabited and the occupants used pyrosignal structures, large enclosures, and possibly ballcourts. Many of these structures were reported by the Spanish explorers, and remnants of all currently exist. Datable evidence uncovered during recent excavations was sufficient for the establishment of a settlement chronology. Two distinct phases of occupance have been outlined, an early phase based principally on the presence of houses-in-pits extending from A.D. 1000 to 1200 and a late phase based on the existence of all types of structures extending from A.D. 1350 to 1550. An intervening phase characterized by a shift from houses-in-pits to surface structures was also noted but sites dating to this time are not clearly discernible. The two phases used in this study are disjunct but data indicate that settlement changes were gradual and continuous.

A three-tiered community hierarchy consisting of several rancherias, a few hamlets, and one village existed during the early phase. Settlements tended to be clustered and located principally in relation to environmental factors, especially permanent sources of water, agricultural land, and wild plant resources. Two of the larger sites occupied nodal locations in their respective segments of the valley, suggesting that at least some intersite social interaction was occurring at this time, perhaps local redistribution of subsistence goods.

Late phase settlements were larger and more numerous than those of the early phase. They were also more dispersed. The large growth of two settlements resulted in the emergence of a fourth tier in the community hierarchy—regional centers. The location of most settlements continued to be determined by environmental factors, but proportionally fewer of them were situated near abundant wild plant resources. The two regional centers were positioned largely on the basis of social factors. Their size, nodal locations, and the presence of public architecture are indicative of extensive intra-valley interaction.

The settlement data presented here contradict the popular archaeological interpretations that are based almost entirely on the work of the early surveyors. In general, the evidence, especially for the late phase, tends to support the Spanish reports. The existence of a few, widely spaced, large settlements with public architecture surrounded by numerous small sites was described by the explorers.

Although the site hierarchy outlined here is more complex than that recorded in the ethnohistorical documents, a pattern in which one settlement was considerably larger and more nodally located than the others did exist in late pre-Hispanic times. Anomalies in the community hierarchy seem to reflect environmental rather than cultural factors. Such an interpretation is not inconsistent with descriptions provided by the Spanish chroniclers. These early reporters were more interested in identifying sites of cultural significance than they were in assessing settlement patterns. In all likelihood they ignored many larger-than-average settlements that were not distinctive centers of regional activity.

The Spanish reports are often terse and incomplete. Nevertheless, they give a fairly accurate description of aboriginal settlements at Contact in the Valley of Sonora. By extension, as indicated by Woodrow Borah, it seems highly probable that their descriptions of other phenomena, such as agriculture and population, are also accurate. Such items, however, must be subjected to further investigation.

CHAPTER FOUR

Agriculture

Ethnohistorical evidence indicates that the serrana was the only region in northern Mexico and the southern part of the Greater American Southwest in which an abundance of agricultural goods was produced at the time of Spanish Contact (Riley 1982). After experiencing great hunger while traveling through the sparsely populated deserts to the north and east, Cabeza de Vaca reached the serrana where he found an "abundance of maize . . . grain and flour, pumpkins, and beans" (Smith 1871: 167). Similarly, on arriving from the south and west, Coronado reported that he "found extensive planted fields and more people than anywhere in the country which we had left behind" (Hammond and Rey 1940: 164). Although there have been some arguments to the contrary, the most favorable descriptions of the region's productivity were probably based on observations made in the Valley of Sonora (Sauer 1932). Furthermore, these reports constitute much of the currently available knowledge on agriculture in the area.

Data pertaining to pre-Hispanic agriculture in the region are sparse. Nevertheless, information from a variety of sources is sufficient to piece together a reconstruction of agriculture as it existed in the Valley of Sonora prior to the arrival of the Spanish. Here information pertaining to pre-Hispanic agriculture is synthesized from three sources—historical documentations, archaeological remains, and ethnographic parallels based on traditional practices and techniques employed in the region today. The partial reliance on historical sources is not ideal. Given the accuracy of the Spaniards' accounts of settlements, however, it seems logical that their descriptions of agriculture would be correct also.

CROPS

The early Spanish reports provide little more than a cursory catalog of crops. Maize, beans, squash, cotton, and "other seeds," which might have been grain amaranth (*Amaranthus hypocondriacus*), were first observed by Cabeza de Vaca (Theisen 1972: 253; Hedrick and Riley 1974: 61, 145). Reports of the later explorers and missionaries add nothing to this list, but they do confirm the presence of the four explicitly identified crops (de Benavides 1653; Hammond and Rey 1940: 384).

Two archaeological projects have provided some additional information about crops grown prehistorically in parts of the serrana and crops available to the ancient inhabitants of the Valley of Sonora. These projects not only confirm the crops identified in the Spanish reports, but they also add specificity by revealing varieties. Mangelsdorf (1958) identified five types of maize (*Zea mays* L.) that were discovered by Lister in caves in the Bavispe Valley. These include two early forms of *chapalote*, a type of *chapalote* with *teosinte* (*Zea mays mexicana*) introgression, *harinoso de ocho*, and *maiz cristalino de Chihuahua*, also known as *maiz blando*. Vegetal materials collected during the same excavations and identified by Cutler include pinto beans (*Phaseolus vulgaris*), gourds (*Lagenaria* sp.), and "cultivated" squash, possibly either *Cucurbita pepo* or *C. mixta* (Lister 1958: 67–68). Beans, amaranth seeds, and unspecified maize kernels also have been excavated by Pailes in the Valley of Sonora and identified by Gasser (1977).

The archaeological data are more specific than the early Spanish reports, and the contemporary ethnographic data provide even greater detail. During the late 1940s and early 1950s, Wellhausen and his colleagues (1952) discovered several varieties of pre-Hispanic maize growing in eastern Sonora. These included the "Ancient Indigenous," *chapalote*; the "Pre-Columbian Exotic," *harinoso de ocho*; and the "Prehistoric Mestizos," *reventador, tabloncillo*, and *tuxpeño*. In addition, the "Poorly Defined" varieties, *maiz blando, onaveño* or *maiz amarillo*, and *maiz dulce* were also found. Later, in the 1970s, Felger, Nabhan, and Sheridan (1976) observed the cultivation of several varieties of maize, beans, squash, and a chile (*Capsicum annuum*) in fields in the San Miguel Valley. Pennington (1980: 123–141) found many of these same crops, together with several other varieties of maize, cultivated by present-day Pima Bajo in the far southern end of the serrana. The crops found by Felger and his colleagues and by Pennington include all the previously identified races of maize, several types of squash (*Cucurbita moschata*, *C. mixta*, and *C. pepo*), the gourd (*Lagenaria siceraria*), the common bean (*Phaseolus vulgaris*), the tepary bean (*Ph. acutifolius* var. *latifolius*; Kaplan 1965; Nabhan and Felger 1978; Bouscaren, Waines, and Boykin-Bouscaren 1983), and the chile (*Capsicum annuum*).

Ethnographic parallels, of course, can be misleading in some cases (Cordell and Plog 1979). It is probable, however, that all New World crops found during these studies also were used in the Valley of Sonora during late pre-Hispanic times. The archaeological evidence verifies the prehistoric use of some of these crops in the region. The lack of archaeological evidence for the others might well be a function of the paucity of excavations and searches for them to date.

CROPPING PRACTICES

The diversity of cultivars known to have been used in the serrana and undoubtedly grown in the Valley of Sonora, although not impressive in terms of numbers, has important ecological and cultural implications. With the exception of chili and cotton (*Gossypium* sp.), a nonfood crop that is reported in the documents but has not been confirmed archaeologically, the crops listed above are beneficial in three ways: when consumed together, maize, beans, and squash satisfy basic nutritional requirements; when grown together (intercropped), they facilitate each other's growth; when cultivated two times a year (multicropped), they can result in a high yield per unit area.

Maize, the staple crop of much of the New World, is a poor source of the amino acids ("building blocks" of protein) threonine, tryptophane, and especially lysine (Nabhan, Weber, and Berry 1979). Beans, particularly teparies, are rich in these amino acids, but they are deficient in the sulphur amino acids that are abundant in maize. Together these cultivars provide a well-balanced, protein rich, high calorie diet, especially when prepared in a traditional manner (Katz, Hediger, and Valleroy 1974).

Grown in concert with squash, maize and beans are also advantageous in terms of promoting each other's growth (Harwood 1979: 86). These cultivars have intercropping qualities that, in effect, make them mutually symbiotic (Isom and Worker 1979). By growing earliest, maize stalks facilitate the climbing of beans planted later. In turn, the beans are beneficial to the maintenance of soil fertility because their roots support colonies of essential nitrogen-fixing bacteria (Thorne 1979: 93–94). The squashes, with their long vines and especially their broad leaves, complete the complex (Gliessman 1984: 166). They cover the ground, thereby reducing splash erosion and evaporation of soil moisture. Furthermore, the dense shade provided by squash leaves inhibits weed growth (Ewel and others 1982), and chemicals they produce are washed into the soil by rainfall and act as natural herbicides, thereby eliminating competing wild species (Gliessman 1983).

The nutritional and ecological characteristics of the maize-bean-squash complex have been understood for some time, as has the knowledge that these crops were grown in the Valley of Sonora during pre-Hispanic times. However, new knowledge has developed concerning the seasonal growth characteristics of certain varieties. Most of the varieties of maize that are found in eastern Sonora today are grown during the period of summer rains known as las aguas. In past times, however, *reventador, maiz blando, maiz amarillo,* and *chapalote* have been planted during the period of winter rains, las equipatas, after the danger from frost has passed (Pennington 1980: 148). Similarly, certain varieties of one squash, *Cucurbita mixta*, are currently cultivated during the winter and spring while other squashes are grown only during the summer (Pennington 1980: 140). Reports from the Valley of Sonora also indicate that tepary beans are grown today in both seasons (Bouscaren, Waines, and Boykin-Bouscaren 1983).

Unfortunately, direct evidence of early multicropping is sparse. In fact, there are no archaeological data and the only known specific ethnohistoric report of the practice is a claim that may have been exaggerated. Cabeza de Vaca wrote that: "three times the year it [the land] is planted with maize and beans" (Smith 1871: 172; also see Bandelier 1905: 161; Nuñez Cabeza de Vaca 1942: 84). This statement did not come from the "Joint Report," written for the Viceroy shortly after Cabeza de Vaca's return, but rather from his "Relation," written six years after the observation. The original joint report was lost, and none of the numerous copies and translations (see Davenport 1924–1925; Theisen 1972; Hedrick and Riley 1974) mention or even allude to multicropping. Furthermore, Cabeza de Vaca was not in the region long enough to witness three crops, and it is unlikely that the environmental conditions of eastern Sonora could have facilitated triple cropping. Double cropping is possible, and Cabeza de Vaca was in the region at a time when he would have been able to witness the growing of a winter-spring crop.

Additional ethnohistoric documentation of double cropping in the region is indirect and must be viewed with caution. During his search for the fabled seven cities of gold in 1539, Fray Marcos de Niza described the Valley of Sonora as being "like a garden" (Hallenbeck 1949: 25). This account, if accurate, was based on direct observations made during April and early May (Hallenbeck 1949: 51). Therefore, the friar was describing a winter-spring crop; another crop could and probably was grown during las aguas.

Another indirect reference to double cropping is a comment made by one of the first missionaries in the area, who, on his initial reconnaissance in the early 17th century, noted that people living in the neighboring lower Moctezuma Valley "are never hungry no matter whether the season be wet or dry" because their fields "seem like gardens" (de Azpilcueta 1630). This statement is unquestionably a reference to the climatically distinctive wet and dry periods (summer and winter, spring and autumn, respectively) within each calendar year; de Azpilcueta was in the region for six months when his report was made (Bannon 1955: 46). He was clearly referring to double cropping.

Pennington (1980: 148–149), who is familiar with the archival material dealing with subsistence in northwestern Mexico, has found only three other references to double cropping in the entire region and none from the Valley of Sonora directly. Nevertheless, statements by both the explorers and the missionaries in light of ethnographic studies of agriculture conducted by Hewes (1935) in the valley and by Castetter and Bell (1942: 144–153) and Pennington (1980: 140) for the Pima strongly suggest that double cropping was common prehistorically in the Valley of Sonora. Although some of the interpretations presented here are based on assumptions, the pre-Hispanic occupants of the Valley of Sonora had the ability and the knowledge to engage in double cropping.

AGRICULTURAL ECOSYSTEMS

Successful double cropping in the Valley of Sonora cannot be practiced today and could not have been carried out in pre-Hispanic times without irrigation. Crops planted during the winter rainy season must be irrigated during the spring in order to insure fruition. In spite of rains that do occur during the early part of the winter-spring growing season, a second crop could not be produced without irrigation because of the severe moisture deficit experienced late in the spring.

Because water can be diverted from the rivers, the floodplain historically has been irrigated and, hence, is considered the most important agricultural land in the valley (Dunbier 1968: 279–288). Evidence of floodplain irrigation in protohistoric times and probably late pre-Hispanic times comes mainly from historical observations made by explorers, their chroniclers, and the early missionaries. Fray Marcos de Niza remarked, for example, that the valley was "all irrigated" (Hallenbeck 1949: 25). Also, Juan Jaramillo, a chronicler of Coronado's 1540 expedition (Pacheco and de Cardenas 1870: 304–317; Hammond and Rey 1940: 296), and Obregon (Hammond and Rey 1928: 162; Cuevas 1924: 148) both reported irrigation. Later, in the early 1600s, a Spanish missionary (Mendez 1628) indicated that "there are streams of fine water which the Indians employ with no little ingenuity for irrigating their fields," commenting presumably on the valley of the Rio Sahuaripa (Bannon 1955: 46). Also de Azpilcueta (1630) noted that inhabitants of the lower Moctezuma Valley were "expert in the use of irrigation . . . with numerous ditches." By the middle of the 17th century, irrigation systems throughout eastern Sonora, including the Valley of Sonora, were reported by the Jesuits as contributing greatly to the food supply of the mission Indians (de Benavides 1653; Pérez de Ribas 1944, Vol. 2: 186).

Most of these floodplain lands (with the exception of those areas distant from the river channel and close to the arroyo mouths) are today under irrigation (Hewes 1935; Doolittle 1983: 302). From descriptions provided by the Jesuits (for example, Pfefferkorn 1949; Nentvig 1980) who worked in the region, it has been inferred that present-day irrigation technology, involving gravity-flow and a network of distribution canals, is similar to that used under the mission system and probably not much different from technologies used prehistorically (Beals 1932: 100, 141; Johnson 1950).

Speculation such as this was deemed essential because virtually no archaeological evidence for prehistoric irrigation was thought to have survived on lands continuously cultivated for 450 years. New evidence presented here supports the inference that aboriginal, Spanish, and present-day irrigation systems are similar. The elaborate network of irrigation canals and ditches currently in use in all probability was constructed prehistorically (Dunbier 1968: 288), just as many of the canals currently in use in southern Arizona were built by the ancient Hohokam (Masse 1981). At the very least, ancient canal routes were followed or paralleled during the construction of later canals.

Figure 4.1. Glyph map depicting a portion of a pre-Hispanic canal irrigation system; site Son G:16:24 OU, Appendix B. Scale atop rock is 0.3 meters long. Pecked depressions were chalked for delineation. (Reprinted from the *Journal of Historical Geography*, Vol. 10, p. 253, 1984, with the permission of Academic Press.)

The new archaeological evidence for irrigation consists of what might well be one of only a few maps known to have been made prehistorically in the New World. Overlooked since it was first reported in an obscure Mexican publication in the early 1950s (Sandomingo 1953: 352–355), the "map," carved on the flat side of a large boulder (Fig. 4.1), was found on the edge of the floodplain in the extreme northern end of the Valley of Sonora, a few kilometers north of Banamichi. The glyph appears cluttered and is composed of "abstract" or "meandering rectilinear" designs (Heizer and Baumhoff 1962: 83; Grant 1967: 27). Nevertheless, it does bear a strikingly similar likeness to the portion of the valley immediately surrounding the location of the glyph as seen from above (Fig. 4.2). Especially evident are the accurate locations of the main river channel, the *acequia madre* or principal irrigation ditch, fields, and the adjacent permanent habitation sites. The actual locations of fields are indicated on the glyph by the dots within circles. This particular iconographic motif has been interpreted as maize, beans, or squash plants in another part of Mexico (Mountjoy 1982: 119). Settlements are depicted by the concentric circles, a motif commonly used by many cultures to represent areas of habitation (for example, Munn 1973: 119).

The interpretation of this glyph as a map is admittedly speculative. Similar glyphs found in various parts of the world (Raisz 1948: 1–7; Lugli 1967; Thrower 1972: 8–14; Wilford 1981: 8–11; Blakemore 1981), including the New World (Heizer 1958; Grant 1965, Plate 3), have been identified as aboriginal maps, some of agricultural lands. One such work portrays physical and cultural features along the lower Colorado River in a fashion similar to features noted on the glyph described here (Schroeder 1952: 44). In addi-

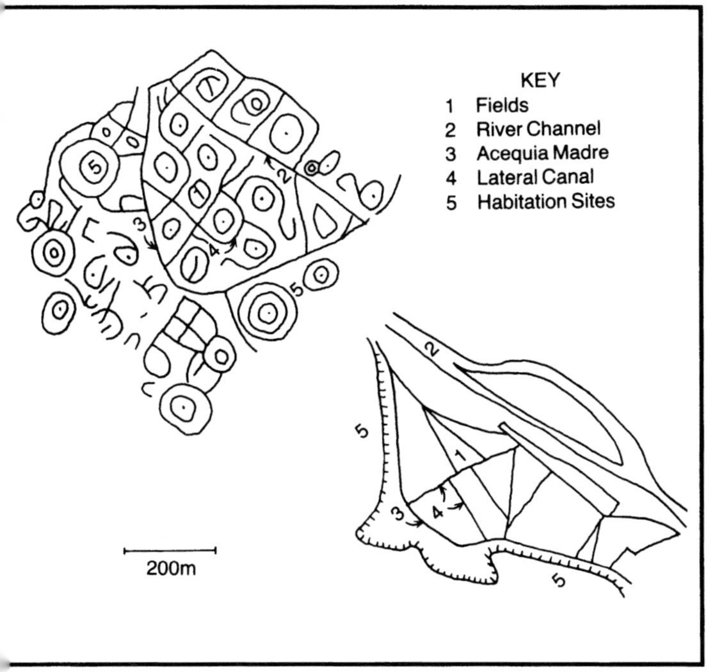

Figure 4.2. Comparison of the glyph map with a map of the actual floodplain and irrigation system made from aerial photographs. (Reprinted from the *Journal of Historical Geography,* Vol. 10, p. 254, 1984, with the permission of Academic Press.)

tion, numerous pre-Hispanic people not only made maps on a variety of materials (Glass 1975: 33–36), but also maintained cartographic records of agricultural lands that were more detailed than European records of the time (Coe 1964: 93, 96; Harvey and Williams 1980).

Arguments could be made against the map interpretation on the basis of fluvial geomorphology. That the river might have changed course is certainly a possibility, but since it was under constant human control meandering would have been minimized (Nabhan and Sheridan 1977). A similarity exists between the location of modern and suspected prehistoric canals that is not accidental. Irrigation ditches are located so as to tap water sources in the most efficient manner. The conditions promoting efficiency were the same in prehistoric times as they are today. In addition, constant utilization and maintenance of canals is preferable to building totally new canals. It is feasible, therefore, to interpret the Sonoran glyph as a map of irrigated fields.

Although the exact agricultural procedures used prehistorically in the Valley of Sonora are not known, analogs drawn from present-day inhabitants who use traditional techniques and ethnohistoric comparisons with people from neighboring areas offer probable parallels. Stone axes that were found during the survey and were uncovered during excavations probably were used to clear the riparian woodlands (Pennington 1980: 143). As mentioned in Chapter 3, fields were irrigated by canals leading from diversion weirs constructed across the river channel (Fig. 4.3). Weirs probably were built by driving short stakes into the riverbed to form a diagonal barrier across the flow of the river (Bahre 1984: 62). Branches were woven among the stakes, and low earth was mounded atop and downstream of the brush. Because gaps were left in these structures to allow excess water to escape,

Figure 4.3. Diversion weir for floodplain irrigation.

they must be considered weirs and not dams. The weirs did not create reservoirs and water was never impounded (Felger, Nabhan, and Sheridan 1976). Instead, water was channeled directly into canals.

The diversion weirs were not durable structures and must have been replaced periodically, especially after floods (Hewes 1935: 292). The canals were more permanent but still had to be repaired and cleaned (Castetter and Bell 1942: 158–161). Regulation of the amount of water to each field probably was accomplished by the opening and closing of canals. Canals were closed by back-filling dirt at the appropriate point. Removal of this fill opened the canal to resume the flow. The technology needed to carry out this intensive form of agriculture required the construction of permanent canals and large diversion weirs. Annual maintenance involved cleaning and some reconstruction (Felger, Nabhan, and Sheridan 1976). Planting was done by deep tillage, and weeding was essential (Castetter and Bell 1942: 152, 136).

Manure was probably not used as the valley occupants did not have large animals until the 18th century (Pfefferkorn 1949: 46). The natural soil fertility was replenished partially with mineral and organic materials deposited by the rivers during occasional floods (Castetter and Bell 1942: 172). Fallowing was possible (Hewes 1935: 290) during pre-Hispanic times but has no analogous ethnohistoric parallels. Historically, many southwestern Indians planted in randomly spaced mounds rather than regular rows. The soil between the mounds was not worked at planting time, and no attempt was made to locate mounds in the same spots year after year. These procedures helped to maintain soil fertility and to compensate for nutrient depletion (Castetter and Bell 1942: 153). Although the individual pieces of evidence are fragmentary, the documentary data, the archaeological data, and the comparative ethnographic data confirm that the prehistoric inhabitants of the Valley of Sonora, especially during late pre-Hispanic times, were sophisticated floodplain irrigators.

The practice of cultivating arroyos in the past as well as at present involved the use of techniques that differed considerably from those used to farm the floodplain. As discussed in Chapter 2, the differences between the two practices were a function of moisture utilization. Floodplain fields depended on water diverted from the perennial rivers, and arroyo fields relied on seasonal runoff. Double cropping is not possible in the arroyos because of seasonality. There is currently no known direct ethnohistorical account of arroyo cultivation in protohistoric times in the Valley of Sonora. The use of these environs for agricultural purposes in later historic times, however, is confirmed by a document stating that in the early 1700s Indians were forced to cultivate an arroyo near the town of Aconchi after being evicted from their floodplain fields by Spanish colonists (Pineli 1709) and by reports provided by informants in 1884 (Bandelier 1892: 17). Evidence for the use of arroyos for agriculture in prehistoric times is found in the form of numerous relic trincheras in the smaller arroyos of the higher elevations in other parts of the serrana (Lumholtz 1902: 20–22; Donkin 1979: 58–61;

Figure 4.4. Remnant channel-botton weir terrace; site Son K:8:63 OU, Appendix B.

Howard and Griffiths 1966: 53–57) and of channel-bottom weir terraces (Fig. 4.4) in the downstream ends of the large arroyos (Doolittle 1980: 333–335). Six of these agricultural sites have been identified in the Valley of Sonora. Trinchera fields are not used today; arroyo fields that use channel-bottom weir terraces, however, are common and they are currently increasing in number (Doolittle 1984b).

Arroyo fields were typically small in size and few in number. Apparently not all areas in every arroyo were cultivated. The selection of a field site involved an intimate knowledge of local conditions. Fields had to have been flood-prone, but the sheet of water must not have attained a velocity that would have washed out the crop or would have buried it with sediment (Bryan 1929: 445). Channel-bottom weirs were laid out so as to slow the velocity of runoff so that the nutrient-rich silt was deposited (Fogel 1975: 135–136). By retaining moisture, this new sediment resulted in a well-watered fertile planting surface. The simple technology required to build these features has led some researchers to hypothesize that channel-bottom weirs were the earliest form of terracing (Donkin 1979: 32–34; Spencer and Hale 1961: 8). Such terraces are produced by constructing crude rock walls perpendicular to the stream flow, usually in groups or series that range from a few to as many as sixty (see Rohn 1963: 442). The largest series found in the Valley of Sonora includes only three terraces (Fig. 4.5).

Ethnographic comparisons suggest that labor inputs for arroyo agriculture were relatively low (Doolittle 1984b). Weirs probably required no more than a few days for initial construction. Like similar features used in the valley today, construction may have been incremental, taking place automatically, without any direct labor input, as rocks were cleared during the cultivation of the field. Maintenance of weirs was probably minimal. The forming of terraces required no labor because it resulted from the natural process of silt deposition behind the weirs (see Wilken 1976: 416–421). *Onaveño*, the flint variety of maize that is well adapted to dry farming, is known to have been grown in the Southwest at the time of the Spaniards' arrival and it is still grown successfully in parts of Sonora (Miksicek 1979). This variety of maize was probably the principal crop cultivated in arroyo fields. Ethnographic analogs also suggest that in addition to incremental, partial clearance, ground preparation was limited to shallow tillage. Planting was done with a digging stick (Johnson 1950: 10) and the holes were then surrounded by small mounds of soil. Although crops required continual attention to protect them against marauders and pests, planting, periodic weeding, and harvesting constituted the major labor expenditures. As was the case on the floodplain, manuring and other fertilization techniques were not used because the silt and detritus deposition replenished soil fertility annually.

Floodwater farming involving weir terraces and irrigated floodplain farming are at opposite ends of the agricultural intensity continuum. Today arroyo-located runoff farming and water harvesting have evolved incrementally out of floodwater farming. Agricultural ecosystems associated with these kinds of *temporales* represent intermediate forms of agriculture. They have characteristics of floodwater fields in that

Figure 4.5. A series of channel-bottom weir terraces; site Son K:4:114 OU, Appendix B. (Reprinted from the *Geographical Review*, Vol. 70, p. 334, 1980, with the permission of the American Geographical Society.)

they are rainfall-runoff dependent and of floodplain fields in their use of canals. The technology employed in runoff farming and water-harvesting involves shallow tillage (small mounding), small canals, small-channel weirs, some minor terracing, and weeding or hoeing (Doolittle 1984b). It is highly probable that the pre-Hispanic occupants utilized these intermediate forms of *temporales* agriculture because they had knowledge of and used the more intensive forms of agriculture.

AGRICULTURAL INTENSITY

Measuring agricultural intensity has been a task of considerable controversy among scholars concerned with agriculture and agricultural change. Some, such as Boserup (1965; Grigg 1979), consider the frequency of cultivation against land and time, while others, including Brookfield (1972), use the concept of intensity in the traditional economic view, as inputs of capital, labor, and skills against a constant, land. Each scheme has its advantages and disadvantages.

Boserup (1975) and others (Brown and Podolefsky 1976; Turner, Hanham, and Portararo 1977) have demonstrated that an association does exist between the frequency of cultivation per unit area and the level of agricultural production. The unit of land that is cultivated more frequently over a twenty-year period will tend to produce the most food for the same period. Boserup's measure of this frequency, the crop-fallow cycle, can be converted to a form that is suitable for statistical analysis. This conversion requires establishing values for frequency of cultivation. Most cultivation data are reported in annual increments, either as the number of years of fallow or as the number of crops cultivated during a one-year period. Values for cultivation frequencies can be developed by comparing these data to a cultivation unit consisting of one crop for one year. In this scheme a 1/2:10 crop fallow cycle (one crop in each of two years followed by ten years of fallow) is expressed as a 1/1:5 cycle because the standard cultivation unit occurs once for every five years of fallow. This cycle is given a value of 0.16 because one crop is cultivated during a six year period. An annual crop cycle, 1/1:0 (one crop per year with no years of fallow) has a value of 1.00 because the standard cultivation unit is repeated each year. A multiple cropping cycle of 2/1:0 (two crops per year with no fallow years) has a value of 2.00 because the standard cultivation unit is doubled each year. In a slightly more complex example, a 2/1:3 cycle would have a value of 0.50 because two crops are cultivated during a four-year cycle.

Scaling problems result from this procedure because of the exponential increase in values created by the conversion of crop-fallow cycles that usually are reported in annual increments (Turner and Doolittle 1978). Because the scaling problem increases with shorter fallow periods, the frequency-of-cultivation approach provides a more consistent measure for those types of cultivation with longer fallowing than for those with shorter or limited fallowing.

Brookfield and Hart (1971: 106) have noted another problem with the cultivation-frequency procedure. The frequency measure does not account for increases in frequency of cropping. The introduction of new skills and technologies and additional labor inputs might allow cultivation to take place more frequently and might also increase production per unit of cultivation, in effect increasing marginal productivity. The significance of the relationship between cultivation skills and marginal productivity for a variety of types of subsistence agriculture has been established (Brookfield 1972: 31, 34; Geertz 1963: 35), indicating that agricultural technology should be included in the measure of agricultural intensity. Technology tends to increase sharply as the frequency of cultivation rises (Brookfield 1962; Joosten 1962; Ludwig 1968) such that the scaling of techniques, skills, or cropping yields a superior measure of short-fallow cultivation than of long-fallow cultivation.

A combination of the two measures, frequency of cultivation and technology, has been devised by Turner and Doolittle (1978) as a measure that works equally well for all subsistence cultivation and maintains a uniform scale. In this

Table 4.1. Index of Agricultural Technology

Technology (technique, skill, preparation)	Weight
Ground Preparation	
Partial clearance	0.10
Total clearance	0.20
Shallow tillage (mounding, hoeing)	0.30
Deep tillage (ridging, plowing)	0.40
Crop Protection	
Fencing, guarding, or shading	0.10
Erosion Control	
Temporary slope control (contour plowing, mounding)	0.20
Permanent slope control (terracing, tie ridging)	0.30
Leveling (flat surface terracing)	0.40
Hydraulic Controls	
Drainage	
Temporary (small canals)	0.30
Permanent (large canals, field raising)	0.40
Irrigation, minimal control	
Water traps (small-channel wiers)	0.30
Water dispersion (large-channel bottom wiers)	0.40
Irrigation, major controls	
Intermittent water (pot irrigation)	0.30
Constant water (canals, field raising)	0.40
Field flooding (padi)	0.50
Soil Fertility Maintenance	
Burning	0.10
Intermittent weeding	0.20
Constant weeding	0.30
Ash and lime application	0.30
Intercropping or multiple cropping (with nitrogen fixation plants)	0.30
Mulch and manure application (organic fertilization)	0.40
Water-flow fertilization	0.40
Plant Preparations (transplanting)	0.40

Source: Turner and Doolittle (1978).

scheme both frequency of cultivation and technologies are used to measure agricultural intensity. Cultivation frequencies generally range in values from about 0.05 (low temporal intensity) to 2.00 to 2.90 (high temporal intensity). Technological intensity is measured by a hierarchical index of techniques, skills, or procedures used by subsistence cultivators (Table 4.1). For example, a typical long-fallow swidden may be characterized by partial land clearance, a ground preparation value of 0.10, and burning, a fertilization technique with a value of 0.10. The total technique value for this system is 0.20. With a 1/1:20 crop cycle, noted by a temporal value of 0.05, the combined technology-frequency of cultivation measure produces an agricultural intensity figure of 0.25. In contrast, intensive agricultural production from wet (padi) rice cultivation may be characterized by the following techniques and procedures that improve yields: shallow tillage, with a value of 0.30; level terracing, 0.40; controlled field-flooding, 0.50; intercropping, 0.30; organic fertilization, 0.40; waterflow fertilization, 0.40; and transplanting, 0.40. This particular system thus registers a techniques rating of 2.70. With a 2/1:0 crop-fallow cycle, noted by a temporal value of 2.00, padi rice would produce a combined technology-frequency value of 4.70.

This method of measuring agricultural intensity is ideal for comparing different food production methods. Accordingly, it is well-suited for understanding pre-Hispanic agriculture and agricultural change in the Valley of Sonora. Arroyo agriculture characterized by weir terraces involved partial clearance resulting from incremental change, shallow tillage, permanent slope control (terracing), intermittent weeding, and annual cropping for an agricultural intensity value of 1.90. Runoff farming and water harvesting have a value of 2.50 because, in addition to having all the characteristics of the previous agro-ecosystem, these systems also have small canals and diversion weirs. Floodplain irrigation involving total clearance, deep tillage, probably some slope control, large diversion weirs, permanent canals, constant weeding, and intercropping has an agricultural intensity of either 3.2 or 4.2, depending on whether one or two crops were planted annually.

The implications of these relative indices are quite simple. Accepting the concept of labor efficiency and agricultural production, it is reasonable to assume that weir terrace farming and later forms of *temporales* farming were the earliest kinds of agriculture practiced in the Valley of Sonora. As Castetter and Bell (1942: 46–57) have shown, people relying on weir terrace farming also rely heavily on gathered food resources. In the case of the Pima, gathering (primarily of mesquite beans) was 40 to 50 percent of subsistence. Settlements in the valley, therefore, theoretically should be located proximal to both easily worked agricultural lands (Chisholm 1962) and mesquite groves. Indeed, this is exactly where house-in-pit sites are found. The largest early-phase sites are also proximal to the largest relic floodwater farming sites, the large arroyos, and the densest stands of mesquite.

The majority of late-phase sites are floodplain oriented. Increased use of floodplain land for agriculture resulted in a decline in the supply for wild plant resources such as mesquite beans. Deterioration of gathered food resources was neatly compensated for by the increased dependability of and dependence on cultivated foods. Although floodplain agriculture provided increased crop regularity, less chance of crop failure, and more total production, especially if double cropping was employed, it involved greater work than any form of arroyo agriculture. Following the efficiency hypothesis, utilization of the floodplain could come about as the result of any form of stress. It is highly unlikely that any form of environmental degradation, for example drought, would have been responsible. Evidence discussed in Chapter 2 suggests that such events of a magnitude and duration sufficiently severe for change to have occurred did not happen in the Valley of Sonora during pre-Hispanic times. It is more likely that stress was created by population growth (Grigg 1976; Cohen 1977).

CHAPTER FIVE

Demography

Any study of ancient occupance would be incomplete, and therefore deficient, if it did not include an assessment of population. As Denevan (1976) has said, "every major investigation of pre-Columbian cultural evolution and ecology . . . must ultimately raise the question of Indian numbers." Dealing with ancient demography is not an easy task. Data are frequently incomplete (Hassan 1978) and often marked by large variances (LeBlanc 1971). Sometimes the evidence may be misinterpreted (Thompson 1971) because unverifiable, intuitive assumptions frequently have to be made (Swedlund and Armelagos 1976: 34, 53–54), especially when ethnographic and ethnohistoric analogs are used. Although determination of the demographic characteristics of prehistoric people is a perplexing and controversial issue, numerous attempts to reconstruct past populations have been successful. The key to acceptable estimates appears to lie in specificity. Studies that have focused on a limited area, using data only from that area (for example, Clarke 1974), are usually accepted as being more accurate than those studies that purport to be applicable to a wide range of areas. Because the latter use data from several, often distant places (for example, Naroll 1962), their estimates are surrounded by more controversy. Accordingly, the methods employed here use data solely from the serrana and the Valley of Sonora.

POPULATION SIZE

Two widely accepted approaches are commonly used to estimate the size and the density of populations in various situations: estimates based on settlement data (Fletcher 1979: 55–60), specifically the prevalence of house remains, and estimates of potential populations based on agricultural assessments (Turner 1976: 79–82). Discrepancies do result from problems inherent in each of the approaches. The main concerns with the settlement approach are, first, how to account for all sites and, second, the degree to which surface evidence is indicative of past conditions. As discussed in Chapter 3, neither of these problems exist to any great extent with the data for pre-Hispanic occupance in the Valley of Sonora. The principal drawback with the agricultural approach is its inability to handle a range of agricultural practices. At best, only a hypothetical maximum population can be calculated with this technique if the types of agriculture practiced and the amount of lands utilized are known (Hassan 1978: 66–67, 73–77). Considering the evidence presented in Chapters 2 and 4, the problems of estimating a maximum population from agricultural data are minimized in the case of ancient occupance in the Valley of Sonora.

Settlement Approach

Two variables must be considered in order to determine the characteristics of group population by the settlement approach: the number of houses inhabited at any given time and the average number of occupants per house. The former variable has been discussed in Chapter 3. Determination of the latter variable typically requires ethnographic comparisons based on similar, usually contemporary, house and household sizes (Haviland 1972). Accordingly, a small survey of present-day traditional adobe dwellings similar to ancient surface structures was conducted in the Valley of Sonora. The survey revealed that the average house in the valley has 28.3 square meters of floor space and is occupied by 6.3 persons, or has 4.5 square meters of floor space per person. A simple regression analysis revealed that the habitant-house size relationship has an r^2 of 0.96. The present-day houses, though morphologically similar, are somewhat larger than their prehistoric counterparts, probably because the current inhabitants of the valley have furniture and other material possessions that were not used prehistorically. Clarke (1974) made similar findings elsewhere. Contemporary houses average 28.3 square meters and ancient surface structures average 23.2 square meters. If the space occupied by modern goods is taken into account, the average floor space per person is approximately 3.8 square meters in both modern and late pre-Hispanic times. By extrapolation, the average prehistoric household size would have been approximately 6.1 persons. The accuracy and hence importance of this figure should not be taken lightly, as it has ethnohistoric documentation. Using baptismal records provided by the Jesuit missionaries, Sauer (1935: 2) found that between six and seven persons constituted the late prehistoric and early protohistoric serrana household. He further assumed the average to be closer to six persons. Cook (1972: 15) also noted that single-family dwellings in the Southwest as a whole averaged 27.9 square meters of floor space and were inhabited by six people.

A total of 224 houses from 65 settlements were identified for the early phase of occupance in the Valley of Sonora. Using 6.1 persons per house, and assuming that all houses were occupied, a population of approximately 1,400 people is estimated for the valley during this phase. Relic house foundations from the late phase totaled 1,289 from 162 settlements. Application of the 6.1 persons per house figure renders a population of nearly 7,900 people for the late phase of occupance. This figure is only slightly less than the 9,000 persons suggested by Sauer (1935: 28), the only scholar to hazard an estimate of the population of the valley to date.

A maximum population of 7,900 people is probably too low. Indeed, although the figure Sauer derived for the number of persons per house is probably correct, his total population estimate of 9,000 is probably too low also. The data Sauer used were far from complete. Some segments of the population were not included, especially those people living outside the missions. In addition, although his attempt to use baptismal records is meritorious, Sauer's procedure involved little more than speculation on the differences between historic and prehistoric population sizes. Accounting for these discrepancies, Dobyns (1966: 404) concluded that Sauer's endeavor, like those of all other Southwestern scholars who calculated ancient populations (for example, Kroeber 1934: 22; Spicer 1967: 99), "yielded conservative figures."

Two other pieces of evidence suggest that the late pre-Hispanic population of the Valley of Sonora was greater than 9,000: the number of houses that have been destroyed by more recent construction (historical and modern), and new information pertaining to multiple-storied structures. Several present-day towns overlie sites that were occupied during pre-Hispanic times. Residents of Baviacora, Aconchi, Huepac, Banamichi, and several small congregaciones frequently unearth ancient artifacts in their yards. Although the actual number of sites and structures will never be known, it is apparent that the quantity found to date is somewhat smaller than the number actually inhabited prehistorically. Also, Sauer's estimate did not take into account habitation in multiple-storied houses. Every house in the valley was not multiple-storied, of course, and those that were might have had any number of floors. There is, therefore, no way of accurately estimating from relic foundations exactly how large the population might have been. The possibility of error exists because any estimate may be reduced to a mere exercise by manipulation of the variables. Nevertheless, the data clearly indicate that the maximum population was unquestionably greater than 9,000 people.

Agricultural Approach

Agriculturally based estimations of potential population size or density must be viewed with caution because they are contingent on numerous assumptions and interpretations. These estimates, commonly referred to as carrying capacity estimates, rely on formulae that purport to measure, in the context of a particular method of cultivation, the maximum population size or density beyond which the process of land degradation will begin (Brush 1975; Igbozurike 1981). Perhaps the best way to measure carrying capacity is to calculate land support units (LSUs), the amount of land required to sustain a given number of people under specified conditions (Mather and Karan 1978). Data required to compute specific population sizes to densities generally include the intensity and productivity of the agricultural system in question and the amount of cultivable land available (Grigg 1970: 51). This type of information pertaining to the early phase of occupance in the valley is sparse because the amount of land cultivated is unknown. Estimates pertaining to the late phase are easier to assess, not only because the type of agriculture (intensive floodplain irrigation) is known, but also because the total area cultivated can be closely approximated. It is impossible, however, to calculate exactly the total amount of agricultural land in the valley because the area under cultivation changes annually. The figures used here are composites based on information from the 1960 and 1970 agricultural censuses of Sonora (Direccion General de Estadistica 1965, 1975), on unpublished data for the year 1979 to 1980 (S.A.R.H. 1979–1980), and on determinations made from aerial photographs. The largest figure reported from each municipality was used to form a first approximation of agricultural land. Estimates made from the aerial photographs were then used to refine the approximation and thus establish the composite total for the valley. On the basis of these data it was determined that approximately 5,175 hectares of agricultural land have been cultivated in recent years. Of these, 3,975 hectares were gravity-flow irrigated floodplain fields and 1,200 were *temporales* located in arroyos.

The amount of irrigated floodplain land is fairly accurate. The reported data and information derived from the aerial photographs vary only slightly, probably because the floodplain is clearly defined. The amount of arroyo land suitable for agriculture is another matter. The reported figures vary greatly and measurement from aerial photographs is a difficult and subjective task due to the nature of arroyo environs. Because of these discrepancies and problems, the figure used here for arroyo land should not be viewed as an absolute. Nevertheless, the ancient inhabitants of the valley probably had access to at least these same lands. Sauer (1935: 29) argued that there was probably more land available prehistorically because floods in the early part of the 20th century destroyed many irrigated floodplain fields and presumably much arroyo land. The question now, of course, is how many people with aboriginal cultivars and techniques would this land support?

Castetter and Bell (1942: 54–56) found that, on the average, 0.45 hectare of irrigated land provided enough food to feed one Pima annually by double cropping. Similarly, Clotts (1915: 80) found that a per capita average of 0.75 hectare of arroyo bottom land was sufficient to provide enough food for one Papago annually by practicing floodwater farming in the summer. Calculations of the land support units for the floodplain indicate that a minimum of 2.75 hectares was needed to sustain a household of 6.1 persons. The LSU for arroyo land was not calculated because of problems encountered in estimating the amount of these lands suitable for agriculture. If the floodplain figure is appropriate for the Valley of Sonora, nearly 10,500 people or approximately 1,710 families lived in the valley. A larger population would have been possible if additional techniques such as more intensive cropping were practiced. Indeed, it is highly probable that an estimate based in part on Pima figures is too conservative.

Although data are lacking on the Pima, per capita land use estimates from other places and other times suggest that they were not using their land to its maximum capacity considering the technology they possessed. For example, one person requires an average of approximately 2,400 calories per day or 876,000 calories per year (Kirschmann 1975: 233–234). At a rate of 3,400 calories per kilogram (Van Royen 1954: 84; Pimentel and Pimental 1979: 56), this requirement can be fulfilled by producing 258 kilograms or 0.258 metric tons of maize per year. In 1978 Mexico produced 9,616,000 metric tons of maize on 7,184,000 hectares for an average of 1.34 metric tons per hectare (Food and Agriculture Organization of the United Nations 1979: 102). At such a rate, 0.19 hectare was capable of supporting one person for a year. In the Valley of Sonora, 410 metric tons of maize were produced on 180 hectares of irrigated land during 1980 (unpublished data provided by Secretaria de Agricultura y Recursos Hidraulicos) for an average of 2.28 metric tons per hectare; or, in other words, 0.11 hectare of maize was capable of supporting one person annually. Modern maize production techniques, including the use of hybrid varieties, pesticides, herbicides, and fertilizers, were not available to aboriginal cultivators. Nevertheless, the present-day figure is lower than that which was actually possible. A figure such as the 0.32 hectare per person required in the non-rice producing region of China since the 17th century may be more appropriate (Grigg 1974: 88). If such a figure is appropriate then a land support unit of 1.95 hectares of irrigated land was needed to sustain a typical family.

Considering such a low rate of production, it seems strange that the Pima double cropped. Presumably they double cropped extensively rather than single cropped intensively in order to either distribute labor inputs more uniformly throughout the year (for example, Ruthenberg 1976: 192–193) or to decrease the chances of rapidly depleting soil nutrients, especially nitrogen that is removed quickly by maize (Janick and others 1974: 314–316). Assuming the ancient inhabitants of the Valley of Sonora cultivated more intensively than the historic Pima, a population of more than 10,000 and perhaps as much as 15,000 is not beyond question. A sufficient amount of food could have been produced to feed a population larger than the 11,065 enumerated during the 1980 census of the valley (Instituto Nacional de Estadistica Geografia e Informatica 1983). More importantly, they could have produced nearly enough food to feed a population as large as that reported in one of the Spanish explorer's accounts. Obregon reported seeing a population of 20,000 in one serrana valley in 1565 (Cuevas 1924: 148). Although this report might be exaggerated somewhat, it is certainly within the realm of possibility. Furthermore, because his accounts of other geographical phenomena are reasonably correct, there is little reason to doubt Obregon's estimate. It probably suffers only from the usual problems inherent in making quick, on-the-spot estimates.

Despite their methodological shortcomings, the settlement and the agricultural approaches produce similar, albeit conservative, results for the late phase of occupance. Because a great deal of agreement between the two approaches exists for the late phase, the settlement approach used for the early phase probably produced somewhat conservative results as well.

POPULATION GROWTH

The differences between 65 early-phase settlements and 162 late-phase settlements and between 224 early-phase houses and 1,289 late-phase houses suggest a significant population growth in the Valley of Sonora during pre-Hispanic times. An accurate estimate of the annual rate of population growth, however, is a difficult task. The process is confounded by assigning absolute dates to the phases of occupance and by determining exact population sizes for the various phases. Accordingly, a number of determinations, each accounting for specific conditions, must be assessed and compared.

Research on population growth has indicated that the trend for sedentary communities should approximate an S-shaped curve because limited resources eventually produce stressful conditions that tend to slow, and in extreme cases even halt, growth (Cowgill 1975: 509). Such an approach has been shown to be most accurate in other parts of the Southwest where populations reached their peaks between A.D. 1050 and 1400 and then leveled off (Eighmy 1979). In Sonora, however, it appears that the population was still increasing and the environmental base was not yet strained at the time of Spanish contact. Accordingly, an exponential trend seems to be more applicable in this case. Using the standard exponential equation:

$$P_t = a(1 + r)^t$$

where P_t is the population (or a surrogate for population) at a time t and r is the rate of change, population growth curves can be constructed (Shryock and Siegel 1973: 381, 386). It is recognized that the population probably did not grow at a constant rate. Such an assumption, however, is frequently utilized to smooth out short-term fluctuations in order to more clearly illustrate longer term trends (Meadows and others 1972). Although the settlement data indicate a marked population increase, the annual growth rate was not especially large, even if the most liberal of conditions prevailed (Fig. 5.1). Using the latest possible date for the early phase

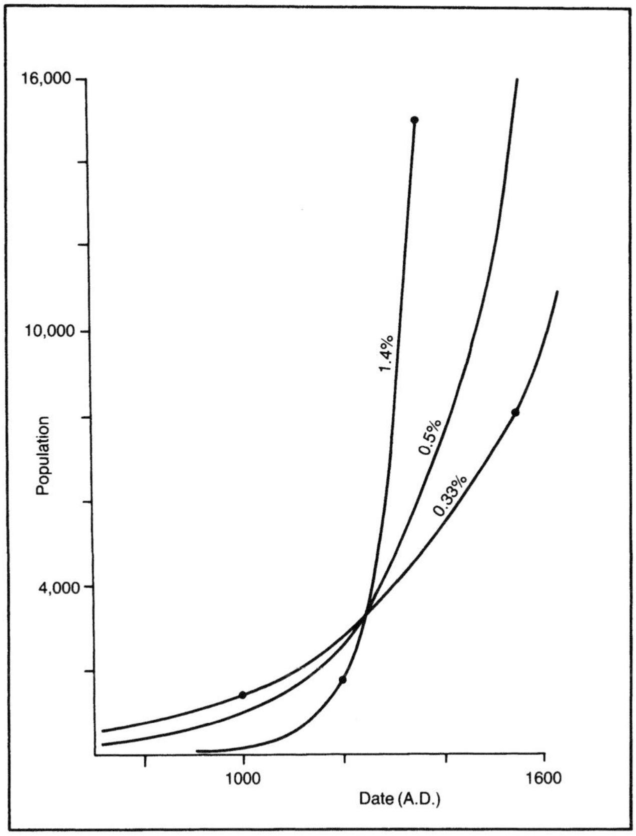

Figure 5.1. Population growth.

(A.D. 1200), the earliest possible date for the late phase (A.D. 1350), and a generous early-phase population estimate of 1,750, the population could have reached 15,000 at the annual growth rate of 1.4 percent. At the other extreme, a maximum population of 7,900 could have been attained at the annual population growth rate of 0.33 percent using the earliest date assigned to the early phase (A.D. 1000), the latest date assigned to the late phase (A.D. 1550), and the conservative early-phase population derived through the settlement approach. Realistically, the rate of change was probably somewhere between these two extremes, perhaps near 0.5 percent (Fig. 5.1). Such a rate is comparable to prehistoric population growth rates in parts of the Valley of Mexico during a period of comparable cultural conditions (Sanders 1972; Parsons and others 1982). The prehistoric population increase in the Valley of Sonora, therefore, could have occurred completely as a result of natural processes (more births than deaths) and, even at a moderate 0.5 percent annual rate of growth, a population of 15,000 could have existed at the end of pre-Hispanic times.

Pailes (1984) has recently argued that a growth rate such as this could not have been possible without immigration. His interpretation, however, appears to be based on misunderstandings of the principal source he cites and the environment in question. Referring to the work of Cowgill (1975), Pailes (1984: 317–318) states that "estimates of 3 or more per 1,000 per year are found to be associated with urban centers during their initial growth surges," and "that when growth rates of 3 or more per 1,000 per year have occurred in preindustrial societies, they have been the exception, not the rule, and they have not been sustained for any appreciable length of time."

Cowgill recognizes that growth rates do not normally exceed 1 or 2 per 1,000 per year over thousands of years. However, he explicitly states: "Surges implying rates of natural increase of from 3 to about 7 per 1,000 per year over regions up to some tens of thousands of square kilometers, sustained over two or three centuries, *have not been uncommon* during the past few thousand years" [emphasis mine]. In regard to urban centers, he (Cowgill 1975: 511) says: "Rates of increase as high as 10 per 1,000 per year or even higher are suggested for the early growth surges of ancient cities such as Teotihuacan . . . but these are concomitant with declining nearby rural populations. . . ." Although occurring only briefly and locally, rates of natural increase greater than 6 per 1,000 have been noted "during the rapid colonization of uninhabited or very weakly defended new territory" (Cowgill 1975: 511).

According to Cowgill's observations, and in opposition to Pailes' interpretation, population growth rates such as those deduced from house counts and agricultural assessments not only could have been possible in Sonora, but indeed were probable. The requisite conditions for such growth certainly characterized the Valley of Sonora between A.D. 1000 and 1400. The locale was sparsely inhabited prior to that time and who is to say that one of the larger sites, for example Son K:4:24 OU (Fig. 3.10), would not eventually have grown to become the size of Teotihuacan had the Spaniards not disrupted the patterns of occupance? Furthermore, in those cases where rapid growth has been recorded, the societies in question were well-nourished (Newman 1962: 25; Santley and Rose 1979). The occupants of the Valley of Sonora, as discussed in Chapter 4, were well-fed and, therefore, were physiologically capable of increasing their numbers by natural means. Immigration, although possible, need not be interjected to explain population growth in the valley. A natural growth rate of greater than 0.3 percent is no more exceptional than the agricultural environs and hence the sustainability of the Valley of Sonora.

POPULATION DISTRIBUTION

The pre-Hispanic population in the Valley of Sonora not only increased dramatically in size but it also underwent some marked changes in spatial distribution. On the basis of settlement data, specifically house numbers, three areas were involved: the arroyos, the floodplain in the southern segment of the valley, and the floodplain in the northern segment.

During the early phase, 13.8 percent of the population resided along the large arroyos (Table 5.1). The remainder was disproportionately distributed between the northern and the southern segments of the floodplain. The areally smaller southern segment contained 56.7 percent of the population, while the larger northern portion contained 29.5 percent. Overall, the southern portion of the valley during the early phase was the population core with more than three-fifths of the total inhabitants.

Table 5.1. Population Distribution in the Valley of Sonora

Valley Area And Phase	Floodplain-oriented Houses N	Floodplain-oriented Houses %	Arroyo-oriented Houses N	Arroyo-oriented Houses %	Total Houses N	Total Houses %
Northern						
Early phase	66	29.5	19	8.4	85	37.9
Late phase	763	59.2	68	5.3	831	64.5
Southern						
Early phase	127	56.7	12	5.4	139	62.1
Late phase	437	33.9	21	1.6	458	35.5
Valley Total						
Early phase	193	86.2	31	13.8	224	100.0
Late phase	1,200	93.1	89	6.9	1,289	100.0

Each relic house is used as a surrogate for a household averaging 6.1 persons.

By the late phase the total population of the northern segment of the valley increased nearly tenfold and the portion that was floodplain-oriented increased almost twelvefold. This growth was markedly different from the modest trebling of population in the southern segment.

Two aspects of the distributional differences between the early and late phases are sufficiently significant to warrant attention. First, although some growth occurred along the arroyos, the relative proportion of the arroyo-oriented population decreased from 13.8 percent to 6.9 percent. This decline suggests that arroyos became increasingly less important for agricultural purposes during the late phase. Second, the high rate of growth in the northern segment created a more uniform population density throughout the valley (Table 5.2). In the early phase each floodplain-oriented household in the northern segment had a land support unit of 40.15 hectares, while a comparable household in the south had a land support unit of only 10.43 hectares. Agricultural land in the southern segment of the floodplain, therefore, was experiencing a relatively greater amount of population stress than was agricultural land in the northern segment. In no place on the floodplain, however, was the hypothetical carrying capacity (minimum land support unit) of 2.75 hectares per household reached.

Table 5.2. Land Support Units per Household in the Valley of Sonora

Valley Area and Phase	Number of floodplain-oriented Houses	LSU per Household (Hectares)
Northern (2,650 hectares)		
Early phase	66	40.15
Late phase	763	3.47
Southern (1,325 hectares)		
Early phase	127	10.43
Late phase	437	3.03

The disparity of population densities during the early phase changed drastically by the late phase. The proportions became exactly reversed. Whereas 37.9 percent of the people lived in the northern segment during the early phase, 64.5 percent inhabited the area in the late phase. The resultant land support units per household then were 3.47 hectares in the northern segment and 3.03 hectares in the southern segment of the valley (Table 5.2). These figures are substantially lower than the respective ratios in the early phase and show less disparity. More importantly, they indicate that throughout the entire valley irrigated floodplain land during the late phase was very close to the hypothetical carrying capacity of 2.75 hectares per household. Of course, both the house count and the land support units derived from Pima correlates are conservative estimates. The maximum late phase population was undoubtedly greater than the number of remnant houses suggests, and the actual land support unit per household for irrigated land might have been as low as 1.95 hectares. Even though the actual values were different from those used here, results of the above analysis are probably accurate because proportionality and consistency are maintained.

Changes in population size and distribution of the magnitude illustrated here obviously had a major impact on the patterns of occupance. With a limited number of mesa-top locales suitable for settlement and a circumscribed agricultural environment, a population increase on the order of five- to nine-fold in a period of only a few hundred years resulted in significant changes in the nature of habitation and subsistence.

CHAPTER SIX

Occupance Interpretations

The evidence presented in the preceding chapters suggests that the ethnohistoric interpretations of aboriginal occupance in the Valley of Sonora at the time of Spanish contact were more accurate than previous archaeological interpretations. On the surface it appears that either the Spanish explorers miscalculated and lied or that the archaeologists misinterpreted their findings. The latter explanation probably has more credence. Although the Spaniards on occasion did stretch the truth for various reasons, they appear to have been quite accurate in their reports on conditions in eastern Sonora. The archaeologists, on the other hand, simply used a survey technique that resulted in their overlooking much important evidence. It must be recognized, however, that this shortcoming is not the fault of the individual researchers, but is largely a function of the state of the science at the time.

Based on an intensive local survey rather than on an extensive regional one, this study provides direct evidence that in late pre-Hispanic and early protohistoric times the occupants of the Valley of Sonora were more numerous, were agriculturally more developed, had a more elaborate settlement system, and had inhabited the valley for a much longer period of time than was revealed through previous archaeological endeavors. Furthermore, occupance was much more complex and developed in the valley during late pre-Hispanic times than it was throughout most of northern Mexico and the American Southwest (Riley 1982, 1987).

Although the data portray conditions in only one small area, they have implications concerning broader issues that involve both the serrana and the larger region. The data provide insight into agricultural land use theory in general and the development of agriculture in the Southwest specifically and into the role of migration and trade in the evolution of complex forms of social and political organization.

AGRICULTURAL CHANGE

A growing population such as that discussed in Chapter 5 requires a commensurate increase in the output of food. Historically there have been only two ways by which an increase in agricultural production has been achieved: either the area under cultivation was enlarged or the output per unit area was increased (Grigg 1970: 42). The particular response chosen by a group in a given environment was presumably the more efficient to yield the higher possible output per unit of labor input. In most cases, expansion of the cultivated area is quick, not too costly in terms of labor inputs, efficient, and, therefore, has been the preferred response for traditional societies (Grigg 1976: 149). This response assumes that additional land similar to that already under cultivation is available. If more land is unavailable, cultivators would be forced to intensify agriculture, that is, to increase the output per unit area and the time expended on the cultivated land (Turner and Doolittle 1978: 298). Recent discussion of this argument was stimulated by Boserup (1965; Grigg 1979), who contended that population increases are responsible for shifts in agriculture from extensive to intensive systems (see also Brown and Podolefsky 1976).

The processes of expansion and intensification are not mutually exclusive, however, but often operate in concert. Elaborating a theme presented by Brookfield (1972), Turner, Hanham, and Portararo (1977) maintained that cultivators are confronted with a variety of agricultural land qualities that are predicated on physical conditions of the habitat and on technology. Land types, designated on their "continuum of agricultural feasibility," range from optimal to marginal in terms of the ease with which they are prepared and maintained for cultivation. Optimal land requires few labor inputs whereas marginal land requires much work. Available technology, of course, is the critical factor in determining the relative ease by which land may be farmed. According to this scheme, agriculturalists should first practice extensive, labor-efficient techniques on optimal lands in order to satisfy production demands. Later, as population stress increases, agriculture should be expanded throughout optimal lands without technological change. When demands can no longer be satisfied within this option, agriculture should be intensified on land already under cultivation, expanded onto previously unused, less optimal land, or intensified and expanded coevally in some combination of these methods. Theoretically, the specified response should be the most efficient in the context of local conditions. In any case, intensification results in decreased efficiency and a stepwise development of agriculture through a continuum of land types (Fig. 6.1), in a classical Ricardian scheme (Ricardo 1817; Hansen 1979; Doolittle 1980).

Systematic analysis of the stepwise development of agriculture requires a temporal component. Studies of agricultural intensification typically have been cross-sectional, based on available data from a variety of areas and time periods (Turner, Hanham, and Portararo 1977). The structure of studies of agricultural expansion, on the other hand, has been temporal, using historical documentation for large

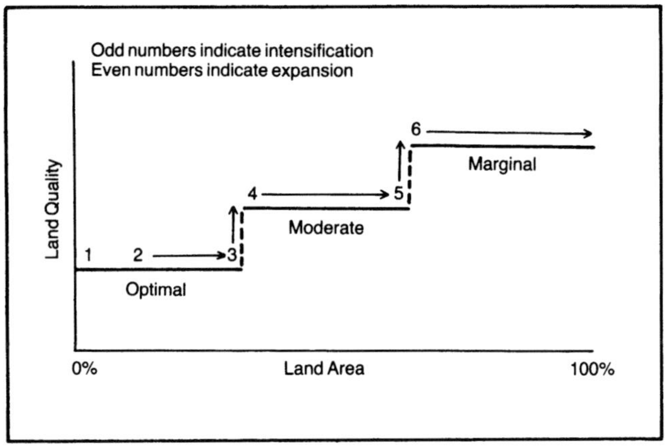

Figure 6.1. Stepwise development of agriculture.

areas (Williams 1970). The areal scale has been an important difference between the two types of studies because those on intensification have focused generally on small groups in highly localized areas and studies of expansion have involved larger regions. The evidence of pre-Hispanic agriculture in the Valley of Sonora ameliorates many of these problems and facilitates the confirmation of a stepwise developmental process. The temporal component is supplied by archaeological data and the focus on one group in one locale avoids a confusion of geographical scales.

On the basis of the Cochise-type metate (see Fig. 3.28), which was used principally for the grinding of wild seeds (Haury 1950), it is reasonable to assume that the earliest occupants of the Valley of Sonora were largely foragers. Later occupants probably practiced both foraging and seasonal cultivation, increasingly relying on an extensive form of agriculture. The earliest evidence of such subsistence activities comes not from the Valley of Sonora but rather from the Bavispe Valley, where people lived in highland caves prior to A.D. 900 and cultivated maize, beans, and squash on nearby lands in the upstream portions of arroyos (Lister 1958: 41–57). Agriculture, however, was not yet a full-time activity. The presence of acorns, pinyon nuts, juniper seeds, walnuts, assorted berries, and deer, turkey, and rodent bones in the caves suggests that hunting and gathering were still important (Lister 1958: 41–57). The most direct evidence of early extensive agriculture in the Valley of Sonora is in the form of channel-bottom weir terraces near the downstream ends of the large arroyos. Today, and presumably in prehistoric times as well, only one crop per year can be produced from such fields and, in all likelihood, the crop would not be large enough to free the population from a partial reliance on wild food resources. The earliest agriculturalists directed their activities toward arroyos because the arroyos cut through virtually all the environmental zones where a diversity of resources could be collected. Although the evidence is tentative, there was a denser arroyo-oriented population during the early phase than during the late phase (Table 5.1). If the predictive value of the theoretical exponential curve (Fig. 5.1) is at all accurate, then it may be reasonable to assume that such an incipient agricultural population occupied the valley prior to A.D. 700 and certainly before A.D. 1000. The later date is in agreement with that from earlier studies (Lister 1958: 41–57).

The early phase, noted by house-in-pit architecture, probably marked a period of major subsistence change with the population located predominantly along the river, but with a surplus of irrigable land. The abundance of land suggests that simple irrigation agriculture was beginning to be practiced only close to the river channel or where permanent water (springs) was available. The part of the valley where such conditions were optimal is in the southern section (Fig. 2.5). Arroyo farming was also probably continuing to be practiced at this time.

The population shift to the northern half of the valley was probably the result of increased stress placed on agricultural lands in the south. In effect, the land support unit of 10.43 hectares per household in the southern segment was reduced to 3.03 hectares because the population grew. Simultaneously the LSU of 40.5 hectares per household in the northern segment was reduced to 3.47 hectares because new lands were brought into production. During the late phase the entire arable portion of the floodplain was probably being used for agriculture and double cropping was becoming increasingly more important. By the time the Spaniards arrived, double cropping was at its zenith (see also Doolittle 1984c).

Two types of agricultural ecosystems were employed in the Valley of Sonora during pre-Hispanic times: direct precipitation and runoff farming of arroyo bottoms, and irrigation agriculture on the floodplain. Although similar in many respects, these agro-ecosystems required disparate labor investments because of dependencies on different water sources. Because of the differing labor requirements, the two systems must be understood in the context of population as a local source of labor supply and consumer demands. The documented population increase and the shifts in population concentration throughout the Valley of Sonora suggest that aboriginal agriculture developed in a stepwise sequence of expansion and intensification. Agriculture originated in the arroyos, the optimal land in terms of labor requirements, and later was expanded and intensified not only to include but also eventually to dominate the floodplain, the marginal land.

DEVELOPMENT OF "STATELETS"

Concomitant with the population increase and agricultural change came several conspicuous changes in settlements—changes in their size, number, hierarchical classification, and distribution. Less obvious, but no less important, was the change in the locations of the nodes, or points of minimum aggregate distance to all other settlements in the respective valley segments. This change is especially significant because it sheds light on the development of a modified form of sociopolitical organization that Riley (1979) has termed "statelets."

As stated in Chapter 1, ethnohistorical reports, specifically those made by the first Spaniards who entered the serrana and the Valley of Sonora during the mid-16th century (the last quarter of the late phase), contain accounts of a complex society that was divided by the discrete valley segments into a number of autonomous social and political units (Riley 1982: 48–50). Each of these statelets was characterized by several distinguishing traits. Many of these traits, such as fortified sites, a pyrosignal communication system, intensive irrigation agriculture, and a (late-phase) settlement pattern in which one very large site was surrounded by numerous small sites (Riley 1980: 42–43), have been substantiated in the preceding chapters. Several traits, such as a celestial religion with a priesthood, a ranked society with a ruling class, and slavery (Riley 1980: 42–43) have not been verified because of problems inherent in the interpretation of social organization from limited archaeological data. However, on the basis of occupance, settlement, and agricultural evidence, the existence of statelets has been confirmed (Doolittle 1984a).

The Valley of Sonora was divided into two statelets, each involving one of the settlements classified as a regional center. As the ethnohistorical data indicate, one statelet included all settlements within the northern segment of the valley. "Previous to Spanish Conquest, the pueblos of Banamichi, Huepaca, Aconchi, Sinoquipe, formed one," according to Pedro Calistro, one of Bandelier's 1884 informers, "which was [centered?] at Ba-de-uachi, near Las Delicias, where the ruins [site Son K:4:16 OU, Figs. 3.15, 3.16] are still visible. After the Conquest, they divided into the four pueblos mentioned" (Lange and Riley 1970: 242). The other statelet involved the smaller southern segment of the valley and was centered at the San Jose site, Son K:4:24 OU (Figs. 3.12, 3.13).

Confirmation of the statelets' existence begs the question of their origin and evolution. The limited amount of archaeological research conducted in the area to date has revealed little about the development of statelets. Indeed, the bulk of that research, that which saw habitation as both late and brief, has been debunked by the settlement data presented here. Two possible scenarios, however, do emerge from the remaining body of research.

One scenario is derived from excavations carried out in the far eastern portion of the serrana during the early 1950s. Lister (1958) found evidence that people moved into the region and began inhabiting caves in the Sierra Madres as northern cultures were expanding southward in Mogollon III times, before A.D. 900. By A.D. 1100, however, these caves were abandoned. Modifying an idea originally proposed by Gladwin (1936) and Sayles (1936), it was suggested that these cave dwellers might have moved eastward, contributing to the rise of Casas Grandes (Mangelsdorf and Lister 1956: 158; Lister 1958: 112–115). This idea is certainly provocative, but it has yet to be fully substantiated. It is equally plausible that the population growth that led to these people's migration into Mexico continued, forcing them to expand westward as well as eastward and to begin living along large arroyos and floodplains in major river valleys, including the Valley of Sonora. Such a scenario is consistent with both the settlement and agricultural evidence presented here.

The second scenario was proffered on the basis of recently collected ceramic data. Pailes (1980: 33–35) envisions the statelet development as the result of Casas Grandes expansion about A.D. 1000, the beginning of the early phase. According to him, this intrusion was intended to control trade routes between the Southwest and Mesoamerica. As was Lister's scenario, Pailes' assumption is little more than speculation. The ceramic evidence he presents is tenuous at best. He frequently cites percentage figures without giving whole numbers, and he uses percentage figures in some articles and whole numbers in others. When the figures that appear in various forms and places are scrutinized together, the only logical conclusion that can be drawn is different from the one Pailes outlines.

Pailes states in a recent publication that the people of Sonora were subjected to a high degree of Chihuahuan influence on the basis that ". . . 96% of the trade pottery in the Rio Sonora valley were Chihuahuan polychromes" (Pailes and Reff 1985: 361), but the data that Pailes cites elsewhere do not offer any support. Although the surveyors on the Rio Sonora project were instructed to look especially carefully for Casas Grandes ceramics and to collect *all* such wares encountered, Chihuahuan ceramics were found very infrequently. In one of his earlier publications, Pailes notes that throughout the duration of the project over 750,000 sherds were collected during both surveys and excavations in the Valley of Sonora (Pailes 1980: 32). Elsewhere he indicates that the total number of sherds from Casas Grandes is only 777 (Pailes 1984: 321). Two conclusions can be drawn from this ceramic data. First, only 0.1 percent of the ceramics found in the Valley of Sonora was from Chihuahua. This is hardly evidence of much cultural contact with Casas Grandes, not to mention domination and the control of trade routes. Second, considering that most intrusive wares did come from Chihuahua, the people in the Valley of Sonora appear to have been reasonably isolated from other Southwestern cultures.

The ceramics from eastern Sonora still remain to be analyzed in detail. Dirst (1979), who assisted in Pailes' preliminary surveys in 1975 and 1976, has attempted to use pottery studies in conjunction with linguistic and ethnographic data in order to investigate the expansion of Casas Grandes influence and its Sonoran frontier. Her findings are tentative, but it is clear that she could not confirm the presence of any Casas Grandes influence in Sonora nor the migration of people westward from Chihuahua. A separate and independent study conducted along the Sonora-Chihuahua border drew similar conclusions. Studying the architecture of Elvino Whetten pueblo and other structures in the Sierra Madre Occidental, Luebben, Andelson, and Herold (1986: 180–181) found that the sierran pueblo had strong architectural affinities to Casas Grandes but was quite different from structural remains found elsewhere in eastern Sonora. Their conclusion, again admittedly tentative, is that Casas Grandes did have some influence in the sierras during its Buena Fe phase (about A.D. 1060–1300) but that influence did not extend westward to the Valley of Sonora.

Overall, the situation in eastern Sonora and particularly the Valley of Sonora appears to be one in which agriculture and population flourished locally without outside stimulation. As previously noted, the population growth indicated by the increase in the number of houses could have occurred without migration.

The apparently sudden development of an inordinately large settlement has been noted as being one characteristic of settlement patterns that owe their existence to long-distance, interregional trade (Vapnarsky 1968). Although there are a few settlements in the Valley of Sonora that have such attributes, it is unlikely these sites were established as trading centers. By his own admission, Pailes (1980: 36) sees the early-phase village as functioning as a local redistribution center. Such a conclusion is, according to the discussion in Chapter 3, borne out by the site's nodal location.

Additional evidence for the emergence of the large settlements as centers of intravalley interaction rather than as trading centers is found in their absolute and relative locations, and changes therein. Settlements established as trading centers, presumably in response to an impetus provided by a dominant trading partner (such as in a colonial situation not unlike that proposed by Pailes) are not usually found near the physical center of their regions. Normally they are located near the periphery of the region on the side closest to the trading partner, and they are rarely nodes of internal interaction (Burghardt 1971; Hirth 1978).

None of the largest sites of the early phase conform to these conditions in the Valley of Sonora. The large sites are not only near the physical centers of their respective valley segments, but they are located at the nodes as well. Furthermore, as the population grew and sites increased both in size and number, the node in the northern half of the valley shifted upstream 6 km (Figs. 3.34, 3.35). By the late phase, a site previously classified as a rancheria had grown into a regional center. This change could only have resulted as a function of intravalley activities, probably increased local exchange. As many studies have shown (for example, Vance 1970), settlements established as long-distance trading centers usually remain dominant even after internal interaction becomes more important than external trade. In those situations in which internal exchange has always been more important than foreign trade, nodes move and settlements may have their relative status altered significantly. Large settlements frequently languish while formerly insignificant settlements may become large centers of interaction (Ettlinger 1981). Such change seems to have taken place in prehistoric times in the Valley of Sonora. The statelets appear to have evolved out of a local redistribution network as the population increased and a variety of lands of different quality were used for agriculture. Considering the changes in the location of the northern segment node, some degree of free economic exchange was probably occurring within the valley at a place convenient to the aggregate population. The node moved as the size, density, and spatial distribution of the population changed. Regional centers emerged only when the society was stratified to the point that permanent capital improvements, such as public architecture, were made at the nodal settlement where intravalley exchange was taking place at the time.

Goods from other areas, of course, are known to have been traded in and passed through the Valley of Sonora (Riley 1976). The large settlements and the statelets, however, did not emerge because of this long-distance trade. The growth of what were to become regional centers preceded any significant large-scale trade. Large settlements were not developed after, or as a function of, existing trading activities. Instead, growing settlements must have become increasingly more attractive to long-distance traders. This finding is in general agreement with both Riley's (1980: 42–43) and Kelley's (1980) ideas concerning the establishment of Mesoamerican-Southwestern trade. A route between these areas probably did not open in Sonora until late in pre-Spanish times. As Kelley (1980: 65) states, "in all probability, this new trail was made possible and profitable by the development of the Sonoran Statelets." The statelets appear, on the basis of settlement evidence, to have developed as a result of internal or indigenous events, independent of other cultures. A population that was increasing without significant immigration appears to have become increasingly dependent on local redistribution, probably to insure against spatial variations in crop yields.

CONCLUSION

When the Spaniards arrived during the first half of the 16th century they found substantial aboriginal occupance throughout the serrana, and especially in the Valley of Sonora. This situation did not change until well after Contact (Riley 1985). A number of factors facilitated the development of the complex human-environmental relationship evident in the statelets. Foremost among these, considering the general aridity of the region as a whole, was the availability and abundance of water year round. The size of the Rio Sonora drainage basin, the river's origin in an area of relatively greater rainfall, and the numerous springs along the course of the channel provide a more than adequate supply of water for both consumption and crop irrigation.

Also of importance were the availability and abundance of a wide variety of wild food resources. Varied terrain with substantial differences in elevation over reasonably short distances, exposure of numerous geological formations, and several soil types have all contributed to the development of distinctive ecological zones and hence a diversity of collectible wild foods. Of these zones, two have special significance for supporting a large population—the large arroyos and the floodplain of the river. Agriculture first became important in the arroyos and later reached a high degree of sophistication and development on the floodplain where the previously mentioned permanent water was available.

Lastly, but certainly not of any lesser importance, was the presence of numerous locales suitable for permanent habitation. The mesa-tops overlooking both the large arroyos and the floodplain were ideal places for permanent settlements. Not only were they located close to agricultural lands and adequate water, but they were centrally located in relation to the other ecological zones where resources could be collected, and they were defensible. Furthermore, some of these mesa-tops were big enough for the development of some very large settlements.

In summary, the evidence presented here indicates that throughout the last 500 to 600 years of pre-Hispanic times, the relationship between the people and the environment in the Valley of Sonora was not static but rather changed almost continually, culminating in a complex pattern of occupance. That occupance began with a small population that was oriented largely toward collecting, presumably in the higher elevations, and as the population grew agriculture became increasingly more important and arroyos were cultivated with greater regularity. Agriculture expanded throughout the downstream reaches of the arroyos out onto the floodplains, eventually becoming highly developed and encompassing most of the formerly riparian forest bottomland. Concomitant with changes in population and agriculture were changes in settlements, which increased in number and size and in the diversity of their locations. The changes in the positions of the settlement nodes suggest that intravalley interaction was increasing throughout the valley during pre-Hispanic times, and that this interaction was centered in the large settlements. When the Spaniards arrived on the scene in the first half of the 16th century, they found elaborate patterns of occupance. Their descriptions of a few large towns surrounded by numerous smaller settlements and of a large population supported by an intensive agricultural system, the hallmark of which was a canal irrigation network, have been verified by the geographically oriented archaeological research reported herein. Thus it is now possible to admire, appreciate, and scientifically depend on the accuracy of the early Spanish accounts that clearly indicate the Valley of Sonora was indeed an oasis in the Gran Chichimeca.

APPENDIX A

Prehistoric Habitation Sites

Data from the 1977 and 1978 surveys in the Valley of Sonora, Mexico
(Rio Sonora Project, William E. Doolittle, principal surveyor)

Site Number	Latitude	Longitude	Area (ha)	Site Orientation	Valley Segment	Bank Side	Houses -in- pits	Surface Structures Single Room	Multi Room	Undiff.	Other Features	Chronology
Son G:16:1 OU	N30°01′30″	W110°12′45″	1.2	River	North	East		6	1	3		Late
Son G:16:6 OU	N30°02′15″	W110°12′50″	0.8	River	North	East		8	1		Historic houses	Late
Son G:16:7 OU	N30°02′45″	W110°12′55″	0.3	River	North	East		7	3		Wall	Late
Son G:16:8 OU	N30°02′50″	W110°12′55″	0.1	River	North	East	1	1				Early, Late
Son G:16:9 OU	N30°02′55″	W110°12′55″	0.1	River	North	East			2			Late
Son G:16:10 OU	N30°03′05″	W110°13′00″	0.1	River	North	East		5	2			Late
Son G:16:13 OU	N30°00′15″	W110°12′25″	0.1	Arroyo	North	East	1					Early, Late
Son G:16:14 OU	N30°01′10″	W110°13′10″	0.1	River	North	West	1					Early, Late
Son G:16:15 OU	N30°01′20″	W110°13′10″	0.2	River	North	West			2			Late
Son G:16:22 OU	N30°02′05″	W110°13′15″	3.0	River	North	West		5	1	6	9 Mounds	Late
Son G:16:23 OU	N30°02′15″	W110°13′15″	0.2	River	North	West		2				Late
Son G:16:25 OU	N30°01′45″	W110°13′15″	0.8	River	North	West	2	3	1	4	8 Mounds, Wall, Roasting pits	Early, Late
Son G:16:26 OU	N30°02′30″	W110°13′30″	0.5	River	North	West	1	1	1	5	2 Mounds	Early, Late
Son G:16:27 OU	N30°03′00″	W110°13′45″	1.0	River	North	West	2	6	4	11	7 Mounds	Early, Late
Son G:16:28 OU	N30°00′55″	W110°14′00″	0.2	River	North	West		3	1	7	2 Mounds	Late
Son K:4:1 OU	N29°46′50″	W110°12′15″	0.4	River	South	East		1	2			Late
Son K:4:2 OU	N29°45′45″	W110°11′30″	0.5	River	South	East				+	Walls	Late
Son K:4:4 OU	N29°46′10″	W110°11′45″	0.4	River	South	East	1	1			Roasting pit	Early, Late
Son K:4:16 OU	N29°57′20″	W110°13′35″	16.0	River	North	West	+	+	+	200+	Public architecture	Early, Late
Son K:4:17 OU	N29°59′15″	W110°11′50″	0.5	River	North	East	1	7		2	Historic house	Early, Late
Son K:4:18 OU	N29°53′15″	W110°12′40″	0.5	River	North	East		3		1		Late
Son K:4:19 OU	N29°47′20″	W110°12′35″	0.6	River	South	East				+	Disturbed	Late
Son K:4:20 OU	N29°56′10″	W110°12′45″	8.0	River	North	East		75	10	+		Late
Son K:4:21 OU	N29°47′30″	W110°13′30″	0.4	River	South	West	6				1 Mound	Early, Late
Son K:4:22 OU	N29°59′40″	W110°12′00″	4.5	River	North	East				+	Cerro de trincheras	Late
Son K:4:24 OU	N29°45′10″	W110°11′15″	10.0	River	South	East	60	65+	20+	+	Public architecture	Early, Late
Son K:4:26 OU	N29°45′07″	W110°12′30″	0.2	River	South	West		1				Late
Son K:4:30 OU	N29°45′30″	W110°12′40″	0.1	River	South	West		1				Late
Son K:4:31 OU	N29°45′15″	W110°12′45″	1.4	River	South	West		3		4		Late
Son K:4:32 OU	N29°45′00″	W110°08′25″	8.0	Arroyo	South	East	12	6				Early, Late
Son K:4:36 OU	N29°57′15″	W110°14′15″	0.1	River	North	West				5		Late
Son K:4:39 OU	N29°57′30″	W110°14′05″	0.2	River	North	West				2		Late
Son K:4:40 OU	N29°52′50″	W110°12′55″	2.0	River	North	East	2	6		7		Early, Late
Son K:4:41 OU	N29°45′20″	W110°11′30″	0.4	River	South	East	7					Early, Late
Son K:4:43 OU	N29°46′00″	W110°12′50″	0.4	River	South	West	1	2				Early, Late
Son K:4:44 OU	N29°46′10″	W110°12′50″	0.5	River	South	West	1	2				Early, Late
Son K:4:46 OU	N29°46′20″	W110°12′50″	0.5	River	South	West	5	2				Early, Late
Son K:4:47 OU	N29°47′20″	W110°13′30″	0.5	River	South	West	5					Early, Late
Son K:4:48 OU	N29°56′45″	W110°17′30″	0.2	Arroyo	North	West				3	4 Mounds	Late
Son K:4:49 OU	N29°48′15″	W110°14′10″	0.4	River	South	West	3	1	1			Early, Late
Son K:4:50 OU	N29°48′00″	W110°13′55″	0.4	River	South	West		1	2			Late
Son K:4:51 OU	N29°47′45″	W110°13′35″	0.5	River	South	West		2	2			Late
Son K:4:52 OU	N29°47′55″	W110°13′35″	0.2	River	South	West	1	1				Early, Late
Son K:4:53 OU	N29°45′45″	W110°12′50″	0.1	River	South	West	3					Early, Late
Son K:4:55 OU	N29°49′05″	W110°14′40″	0.2	River	South	West		1				Late
Son K:4:56 OU	N29°48′40″	W110°14′35″	0.1	River	South	West		1				Late

Data from the 1977 and 1978 surveys in the Valley of Sonora, Mexico *(continued)*

Site Number	Latitude	Longitude	Area (ha)	Site Orientation	Valley Segment	Bank Side	Houses -in-pits	Surface Structures Single Room	Multi Room	Undiff.	Other Features	Chronology
Son K:4:58 OU	N29°49′30″	W110°14′50″	0.6	River	South	West	2	2				Early, Late
Son K:4:59 OU	N29°49′45″	W110°14′55″	0.8	River	South	West		8	4			Late
Son K:4:60 OU	N29°57′50″	W110°14′00″	0.4	River	North	West				+		Late
Son K:4:61 OU	N29°49′45″	W110°15′15″	0.2	Arroyo	South	West		1				Late
Son K:4:62 OU	N29°56′00″	W110°14′20″	0.2	Arroyo	North	West				4		Late
Son K:4:64 OU	N29°52′10″	W110°14′30″	0.2	River	North	West	3					Early, Late
Son K:4:67 OU	N29°52′20″	W110°14′25″	0.2	River	North	West	4					Early, Late
Son K:4:68 OU	N29°52′50″	W110°14′20″	0.8	River	North	West	2	5				Early, Late
Son K:4:69 OU	N29°53′20″	W110°13′55″	0.3	River	North	West	4	4		5		Early, Late
Son K:4:70 OU	N29°58′00″	W110°14′00″	0.1	River	North	West					Cerro de trincheras	Late
Son K:4:71 OU	N29°52′40″	W110°14′20″	0.2	River	North	West		3		1		Late
Son K:4:72 OU	N29°58′20″	W110°12′00″	2.0	River	North	East	5	4		+	20+ Mounds	Early, Late
Son K:4:73 OU	N29°56′55″	W110°17′15″	0.1	Arroyo	North	West	4			3	1 Mound	Early, Late
Son K:4:75 OU	N29°46′30″	W110°11′55″	3.0	River	South	East		+		Several	Disturbed	Late
Son K:4:76 OU	N29°46′45″	W110°12′05″	0.6	River	South	East	3	9				Early, Late
Son K:4:77 OU	N29°47′10″	W110°12′20″	1.0	River	South	East	3	2				Early, Late
Son K:4:78 OU	N29°48′20″	W110°13′10″	0.5	River	South	East	5			+	Disturbed	Early, Late
Son K:4:79 OU	N29°48′20″	W110°13′00″	0.2	River	South	East				5		Late
Son K:4:80 OU	N29°48′05″	W110°12′55″	0.2	River	South	East		2		+	Roasting pit, disturbed	Late
Son K:4:81 OU	N29°48′45″	W110°13′15″	0.2	River	South	East	2	1			Roasting pit	Early, Late
Son K:4:82 OU	N29°49′50″	W110°13′55″	1.2	River	South	East	1	2			5 Mounds	Early, Late
Son K:4:83 OU	N29°54′30″	W110°13′00″	1.5	River	North	East				+	Disturbed	Late
Son K:4:84 OU	N29°56′30″	W110°18′50″	0.1	Arroyo	North	West				+	Historic house	Late
Son K:4:85 OU	N29°51′15″	W110°13′35″	3.0	River	North	East	1	12	1	4	Rock rings, disturbed	Early, Late
Son K:4:89 OU	N29°50′55″	W110°13′45″	0.5	River	North	East		3				Late
Son K:4:90 OU	N29°51′00″	W110°13′45″	0.4	River	North	East		2				Late
Son K:4:91 OU	N29°50′25″	W110°13′50″	1.5	River	South	East		4	2			Late
Son K:4:92 OU	N29°50′10″	W110°13′55″	0.5	River	South	East		3	1			Late
Son K:4:93 OU	N29°50′50″	W110°15′00″	1.0	River	North	West	3	2		2	Mill, disturbed	Early, Late
Son K:4:94 OU	N29°56′20″	W110°14′00″	0.4	River	North	West		3	1	5		Late
Son K:4:95 OU	N29°59′55″	W110°12′40″	0.4	River	North	East				+	Disturbed, historic house	Late
Son K:4:96 OU	N29°52′15″	W110°13′00″	0.1	River	North	East		1		1		Late
Son K:4:97 OU	N29°52′40″	W110°13′00″	0.3	River	North	East	1	1		1		Early, Late
Son K:4:98 OU	N29°57′45″	W110°14′00″	0.3	River	North	West				5		Late
Son K:4:99 OU	N29°45′35″	W110°11′30″	0.2	River	South	East		6				Late
Son K:4:101 OU	N29°53′50″	W110°12′30″	2.0	River	North	East		5	2			Late
Son K:4:102 OU	N29°54′00″	W110°12′50″	0.3	River	North	East		1				Late
Son K:4:105 OU	N29°54′00″	W110°12′15″	0.2	River	North	East					Possible Cerro de trincheras	Late
Son K:4:106 OU	N29°54′00″	W110°12′55″	3.0	River	North	East	1	14		1		Early, Late
Son K:4:107 OU	N29°54′15″	W110°12′30″	1.5	River, Arroyo	North	East		1		3	Roasting pit	Late
Son K:4:108 OU	N29°55′10″	W110°12′55″	1.0	River	North	East				+	Disturbed	Late
Son K:4:109 OU	N29°55′30″	W110°12′40″	0.4	River	North	East	1	3				Early, Late
Son K:4:110 OU	N29°55′45″	W110°12′40″	2.3	River	North	East	10	6				Early, Late
Son K:4:111 OU	N29°56′15″	W110°12′25″	0.3	Arroyo	North	East		2				Late
Son K:4:112 OU	N29°56′25″	W110°12′25″	0.3	River	North	East		2				Late
Son K:4:113 OU	N29°56′30″	W110°12′00″	1.2	Arroyo	North	East	5	1				Early, Late
Son K:4:115 OU	N29°56′10″	W110°12′05″	0.8	Arroyo	North	East				3		Late
Son K:4:116 OU	N29°56′50″	W110°11′30″	5.0	Arroyo	North	East	5	1			8 Possible mound foundations	Early, Late
Son K:4:117 OU	N29°58′05″	W110°12′00″	0.6	River	North	East	3	2		4		Early, Late
Son K:4:118 OU	N29°59′05″	W110°11′25″	0.6	Arroyo	North	East	3			1	Wall	Early, Late
Son K:4:119 OU	N29°54′55″	W110°12′55″	0.9	River	North	East				+	Disturbed, historic house	Late
Son K:4:120 OU	N29°59′30″	W110°13′40″	5.0	River	North	West	2	22	3	18	Roasting pits, rock rings	Early, Late
Son K:4:121 OU	N29°59′20″	W110°13′40″	0.2	River	North	West	1			7		Early, Late
Son K:4:122 OU	N29°54′30″	W110°13′55″	0.4	River	North	West		8	3	7	Rock rings	Late
Son K:4:123 OU	N29°54′15″	W110°13′50″	0.3	River	North	West	1	4	1	2	Historic foundation	Early, Late
Son K:4:124 OU	N29°53′40″	W110°13′55″	0.3	River	North	West	2	1				Early, Late
Son K:4:125 OU	N29°53′50″	W110°13′50″	0.3	River	North	West	1	5	1	1	Trincheras wall	Early, Late

Data from the 1977 and 1978 surveys in the Valley of Sonora, Mexico *(continued)*

Site Number	Latitude	Longitude	Area (ha)	Site Orientation	Valley Segment	Bank Side	Houses -in- pits	Surface Structures Single Room	Multi Room	Undiff.	Other Features	Chronology
Son K:4:126 OU	N29°53′55″	W110°13′45″	0.4	River	North	West	1	2		3	Historic houses, roasting pit	Early, Late
Son K:4:127 OU	N29°54′00″	W110°14′00″	1.5	River	North	West	4	6	2		Trincheras enclosure, public architecture, 1 mound, historic foundation	Early, Late
Son K:4:128 OU	N29°55′00″	W110°14′00″	0.4	River	North	West	2	3			Roasting pit	Early, Late
Son K:4:129 OU	N29°55′10″	W110°14′10″	0.5	River	North	West				4		Late
Son K:4:130 OU	N29°56′00″	W110°14′15″	0.2	River	North	West	3	2		3		Early, Late
Son K:4:131 OU	N29°56′05″	W110°14′15″	0.4	River	North	West				3		Late
Son K:4:132 OU	N29°56′20″	W110°14′25″	1.5	River	North	West	1	1		7	Cerro de trincheras	Early, Late
Son K:4:133 OU	N29°56′45″	W110°14′25″	0.2	River	North	West		2			Roasting pit	Late
Son K:4:135 OU	N29°58′05″	W110°08′30″	0.1	Arroyo	North	East				2		Late
Son K:4:137 OU	N29°55′15″	W110°07′00″	0.1	Arroyo	North	East				2		Late
Son K:4:138 OU	N29°55′00″	W110°05′45″	0.1	Arroyo	North	East					Walls	Late
Son K:4:139 OU	N29°56′00″	W110°20′20″	0.2	Arroyo	North	West				+	Historic house	Late
Son K:4:144 OU	N29°56′20″	W110°20′05″	0.7	Arroyo	North	West	1	3	1		1 Mound	Early, Late
Son K:4:145 OU	N29°56′20″	W110°18′30″	0.4	Arroyo	North	West		3		5	1 Mound, trincheras enclosure	Late
Son K:4:146 OU	N29°54′35″	W110°13′50″	3.0	River	North	East		+		+	Disturbed	Late
Son K:8:1 OU	N29°40′40″	W110°09′05″	1.2	River	South	East		4			Roasting pit	Late
Son K:8:2 OU	N29°43′40″	W110°09′55″	0.4	River	South	East				6		Late
Son K:8:3 OU	N29°43′50″	W110°10′00″	0.4	River	South	East	2			1	Disturbed	Early, Late
Son K:8:4 OU	N29°44′05″	W110°10′10″	0.2	River	South	East		1		2		Late
Son K:8:5 OU	N29°43′35″	W110°10′55″	1.0	River	South	West				1		Late
Son K:8:6 OU	N29°43′45″	W110°10′35″	0.6	River	South	West	2	1		1		Early, Late
Son K:8:7 OU	N29°44′50″	W110°11′45″	0.2	River	South	West				+	Historic foundations	Late
Son K:8:8 OU	N29°44′25″	W110°12′10″	0.1	River	South	West	1				Rock ring	Early, Late
Son K:8:9 OU	N29°44′35″	W110°10′40″	0.3	River	South	East	1	2				Early, Late
Son K:8:10 OU	N29°38′00″	W110°08′15″	0.1	River	South	East				1	Historic house	Late
Son K:8:12 OU	N29°44′20″	W110°12′00″	0.3	River	South	West		1		1	Rock rings	Late
Son K:8:14 OU	N29°44′10″	W110°11′55″	0.1	River	South	West		2				Late
Son K:8:17 OU	N29°44′20″	W110°10′35″	0.7	River	South	East		6	1	1		Late
Son K:8:18 OU	N29°44′30″	W110°10′50″	0.6	River	South	East		3		8	Historic houses	Late
Son K:8:20 OU	N29°44′30″	W110°12′15″	0.1	River	South	West				2		Late
Son K:8:22 OU	N29°40′45″	W110°08′45″	1.0	River	South	East	+	+	+	+	Disturbed	Early, Late
Son K:8:25 OU	N29°45′00″	W110°12′30″	0.2	River	South	West		5	1	1		Late
Son K:8:26 OU	N29°38′30″	W110°07′55″	0.5	River	South	East	6		1	2		Early, Late
Son K:8:28 OU	N29°41′05″	W110°09′40″	0.1	River	South	West		3				Late
Son K:8:29 OU	N29°41′20″	W110°09′50″	0.3	River	South	West				2		Late
Son K:8:30 OU	N29°42′05″	W110°09′25″	0.2	River	South	East	1	3			Borrow pit	Early, Late
Son K:8:31 OU	N29°41′55″	W110°09′10″	0.1	River	South	East				1	Historic foundations	Late
Son K:8:32 OU	N29°44′55″	W110°11′05″	0.2	River	South	East		3			Historic houses	Late
Son K:8:34 OU	N29°41′25″	W110°09′00″	0.8	River	South	East		10	4		Rock ring	Late
Son K:8:36 OU	N29°41′05″	W110°08′45″	0.5	River	South	East				3	Historic house	Late
Son K:8:39 OU	N29°40′55″	W110°08′45″	0.1	River	South	East		2				Late
Son K:8:40 OU	N29°40′15″	W110°08′20″	0.1	River	South	East		2		2	Roasting pit	Late
Son K:8:41 OU	N29°40′15″	W110°08′30″	0.2	River	South	East	1			1	Disturbed	Early, Late
Son K:8:42 OU	N29°40′00″	W110°08′10″	0.1	River	South	East				3	Roasting pit	Late
Son K:8:43 OU	N29°39′50″	W110°08′05″	0.1	River	South	East		2		1		Late
Son K:8:44 OU	N29°39′35″	W110°07′50″	0.1	River	South	East	1	1				Early, Late
Son K:8:45 OU	N29°43′30″	W110°09′50″	0.2	River	South	East		1		4	Historic houses	Late
Son K:8:47 OU	N29°37′45″	W110°07′50″	0.2	River	South	East				+	Disturbed	Late
Son K:8:48 OU	N29°38′30″	W110°08′05″	0.1	River	South	East		2			Roasting pit	Late
Son K:8:49 OU	N29°40′05″	W110°08′20″	0.1	River	South	East		3		2	Historic houses	Late
Son K:8:50 OU	N29°38′20″	W110°08′05″	0.1	River	South	East				2	Historic houses	Late
Son K:8:51 OU	N29°38′40″	W110°07′45″	0.1	Arroyo	South	East		1		1		Late
Son K:8:56 OU	N29°37′15″	W110°08′10″	0.2	River	South	West	2			2	Historic house	Early, Late
Son K:8:57 OU	N29°37′07″	W110°08′10″	0.3	River	South	West		7		4	Historic house	Late
Son K:8:58 OU	N29°36′40″	W110°07′30″	0.1	River	South	East		1				Late
Son K:8:59 OU	N29°36′50″	W110°07′35″	0.2	River	South	East		4		4	Roasting pit	Late
Son K:8:60 OU	N29°37′40″	W110°08′20″	0.1	River	South	West	1				Glyph rock	Early, Late
Son K:8:61 OU	N29°37′30″	W110°08′20″	0.1	River	South	West	2				1 Mound	Early, Late
Son K:8:62 OU	N29°44′30″	W110°08′30″	0.2	Arroyo	South	East				+	Walls	Late

Prehistoric Agricultural Sites and Special Sites

Data from the 1977 and 1978 surveys in the Valley of Sonora, Mexico (Rio Sonora Project, William E. Doolittle, principal surveyor)

Site No.	Type, Features	Latitude	Longitude	Ground Lithics	Flaked Lithics	Ceramics
Son G:16:11 OU	Scatter	N30°00′15″	W110°12′35″		X	
Son G:16:12 OU	Scatter	N30°00′20″	W110°12′35″		X	
Son G:16:17 OU	Signal	N30°00′45″	W110°12′00″			
Son G:16:24 OU	Glyph	N30°02′00″	W110°13′20″			
Son K:4:3 OU	Scatter, roasting pit	N29°45′55″	W110°11′20″		X	X
Son K:4:5 OU	Scatter	N29°45′10″	W110°10′55″		X	
Son K:4:6 OU	Scatter	N29°45′00″	W110°10′55″		X	
Son K:4:7 OU	Scatter	N29°45′00″	W110°10′50″		X	
Son K:4:8 OU	Scatter	N29°46′20″	W110°10′30″		X	
Son K:4:9 OU	Scatter	N29°46′00″	W110°11′25″		X	
Son K:4:10 OU	Scatter	N29°46′15″	W110°12′00″			X
Son K:4:12 OU	Scatter	N29°46′05″	W110°11′25″		X	X
Son K:4:13 OU	Scatter	N29°45′45″	W110°11′50″			X
Son K:4:14 OU	Scatter	N29°45′20″	W110°12′00″		X	X
Son K:4:15 OU	Scatter	N29°46′50″	W110°07′38″	X	X	X
Son K:4:23 OU	Scatter	N29°45′40″	W110°09′20″		X	
Son K:4:25 OU	Scatter	N29°45′02″	W110°12′25″	X	X	X
Son K:4:27 OU	Scatter	N29°45′30″	W110°12′50″		X	X
Son K:4:28 OU	Scatter	N29°45′20″	W110°12′20″		X	X
Son K:4:29 OU	Scatter	N29°45′02″	W110°12′35″	X	X	
Son K:4:33 OU	Scatter	N29°44′50″	W110°08′05″		X	X
Son K:4:34 OU	Weir terrace, roasting pit	N29°44′45″	W110°08′30″	X	X	X
Son K:4:35 OU	Scatter, roasting pit	N29°44′45″	W110°09′00″		X	X
Son K:4:37 OU	Scatter	N29°44′35″	W110°07′50″		X	X
Son K:4:38 OU	Weir terrace	N29°45′25″	W110°08′45″	X	X	X
Son K:4:42 OU	Roasting pits	N29°45′15″	W110°11′30″			
Son K:4:45 OU	Scatter	N29°46′30″	W110°12′55″		X	
Son K:4:54 OU	Scatter	N29°45′50″	W110°12′50″		X	X
Son K:4:57 OU	Scatter	N29°48′05″	W110°14′00″			X
Son K:4:63 OU	Signal	N29°51′40″	W110°14′55″			
Son K:4:65 OU	Scatter	N29°52′15″	W110°14′30″		X	
Son K:4:66 OU	Scatter	N29°52′25″	W110°14′35″		X	
Son K:4:74 OU	Scatter	N29°56′30″	W110°19′15″		X	
Son K:4:86 OU	Scatter	N29°49′40″	W110°12′15″		X	
Son K:4:87 OU	Scatter	N29°49′45″	W110°12′40″		X	
Son K:4:88 OU	Scatter	N29°50′45″	W110°13′45″		X	X
Son K:4:100 OU	Scatter	N29°53′40″	W110°12′30″		X	X
Son K:4:103 OU	Scatter	N29°47′07″	W110°07′15″		X	
Son K:4:104 OU	Roasting pit	N29°50′05″	W110°12′55″			
Son K:4:114 OU	Weir terraces	N29°56′05″	W110°12′25″			
Son K:4:134 OU	Signal	N29°55′20″	W110°17′45″			
Son K:4:136 OU	Scatter	N29°57′50″	W110°11′50″		X	
Son K:4:140 OU	Weir terraces	N29°55′15″	W110°21′30″			
Son K:4:141 OU	Signal	N29°55′30″	W110°22′15″			
Son K:4:142 OU	Weir terraces	N29°54′50″	W110°22′15″			
Son K:4:143 OU	Signal	N29°45′10″	W110°10′35″			

Data from the 1977 and 1978 surveys in the Valley of Sonora, Mexico *(continued)*

Site No.	Type, Features	Latitude	Longitude	Ground Lithics	Flaked Lithics	Ceramics
Son K:8:11 OU	Scatter	N29°43′40″	W110°11′10″		X	
Son K:8:13 OU	Scatter	N29°44′20″	W110°12′05″	X	X	X
Son K:8:15 OU	Signal	N29°43′45″	W110°11′40″			
Son K:8:16 OU	Scatter	N29°43′45″	W110°11′20″		X	X
Son K:8:19 OU	Scatter	N29°44′00″	W110°12′15″		X	
Son K:8:21 OU	Scatter	N29°44′40″	W110°12′15″	X	X	X
Son K:8:23 OU	Scatter	N29°44′50″	W110°12′20″			X
Son K:8:24 OU	Scatter	N29°44′45″	W110°12′20″		X	X
Son K:8:27 OU	Scatter	N29°41′45″	W110°10′30″			X
Son K:8:33 OU	Scatter	N29°44′50″	W110°10′00″	X		
Son K:8:35 OU	Scatter	N29°44′20″	W110°11′15″		X	X
Son K:8:37 OU	Scatter	N29°44′15″	W110°09′20″		X	
Son K:8:38 OU	Scatter	N29°44′15″	W110°09′10″		X	
Son K:8:46 OU	Signal	N29°39′10″	W110°07′40″			
Son K:8:52 OU	Scatter	N29°42′55″	W110°09′00″		X	
Son K:8:53 OU	Scatter	N29°43′00″	W110°08′20″		X	
Son K:8:54 OU	Scatter, roasting pit	N29°42′50″	W110°07′45″		X	
Son K:8:55 OU	Scatter	N29°42′45″	W110°07′30″		X	
Son K:8:63 OU	Weir terraces	N29°44′40″	W110°08′30″			

Distribution of Habitation Sites, Agricultural Sites, and Special Sites in the Valley of Sonora, Mexico

(Rio Sonora Project, 1977 and 1978, William E. Doolittle, principal surveyor)

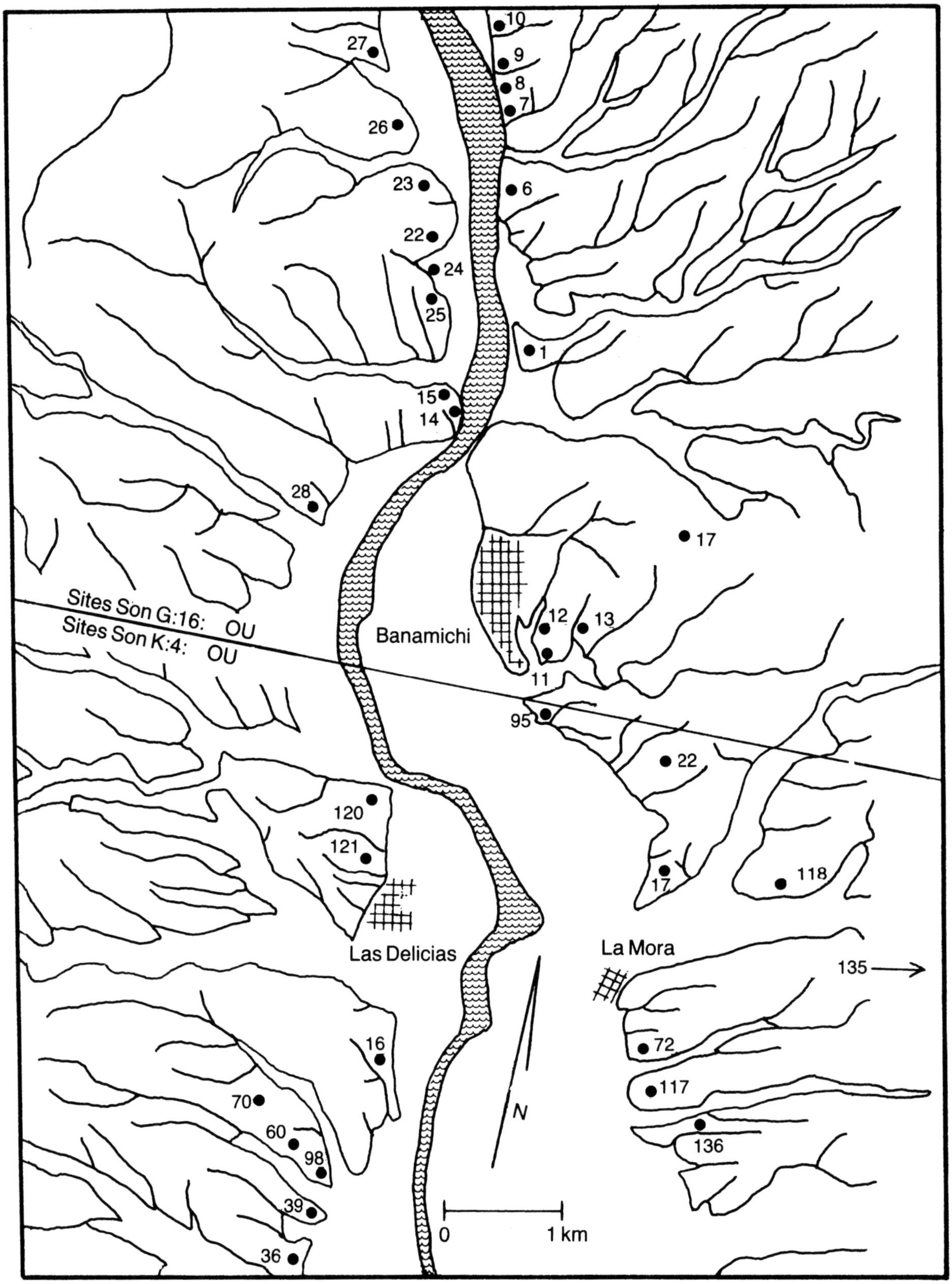

Figure C.1. Sites near the present-day pueblo of Banamichi in the Rio Sonora Valley.

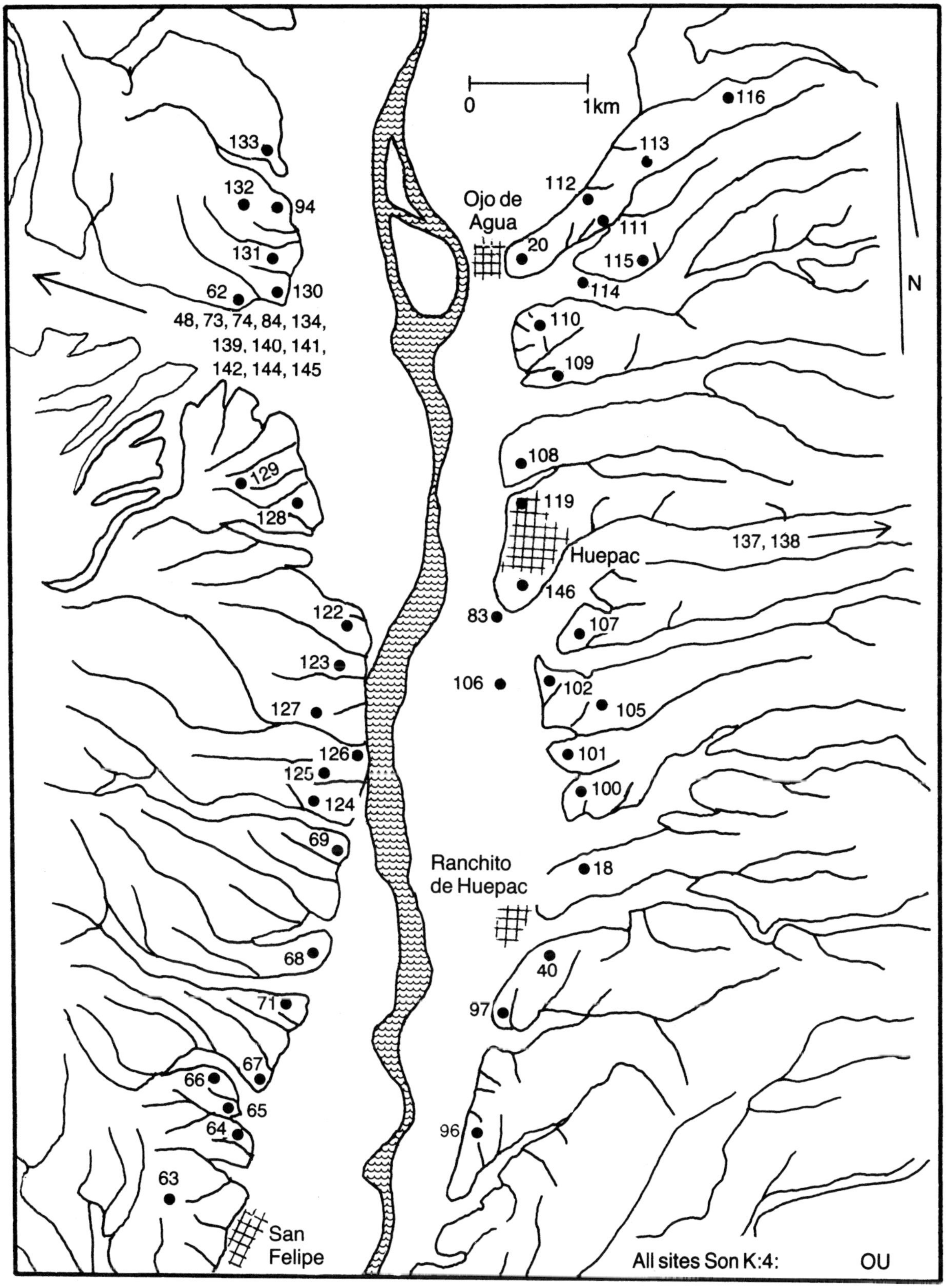

Figure C.2. Sites near the present-day pueblo of Huepac in the Rio Sonora Valley.

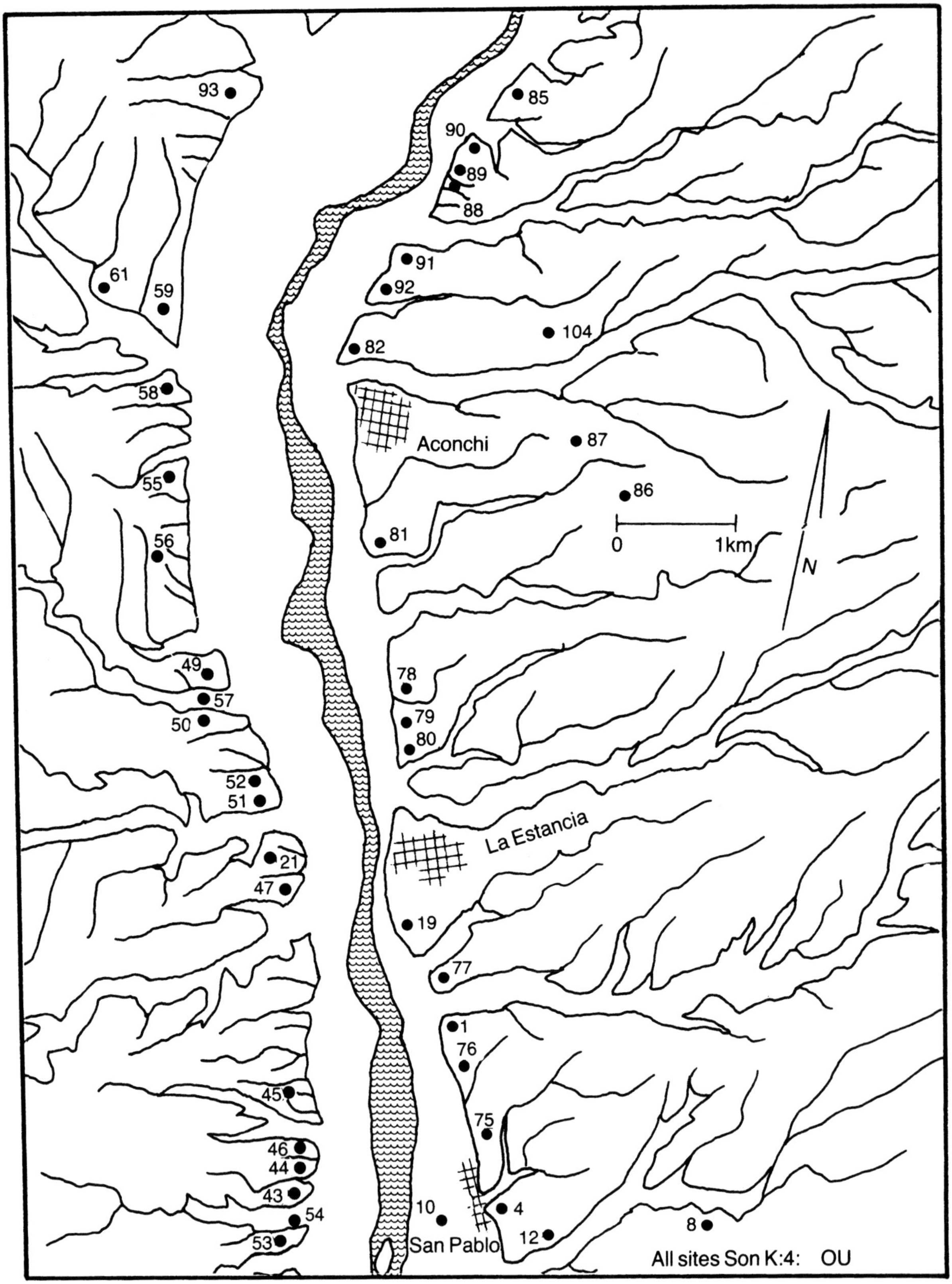

Figure C.3. Sites near the present-day pueblo of Aconchi in the Rio Sonora Valley.

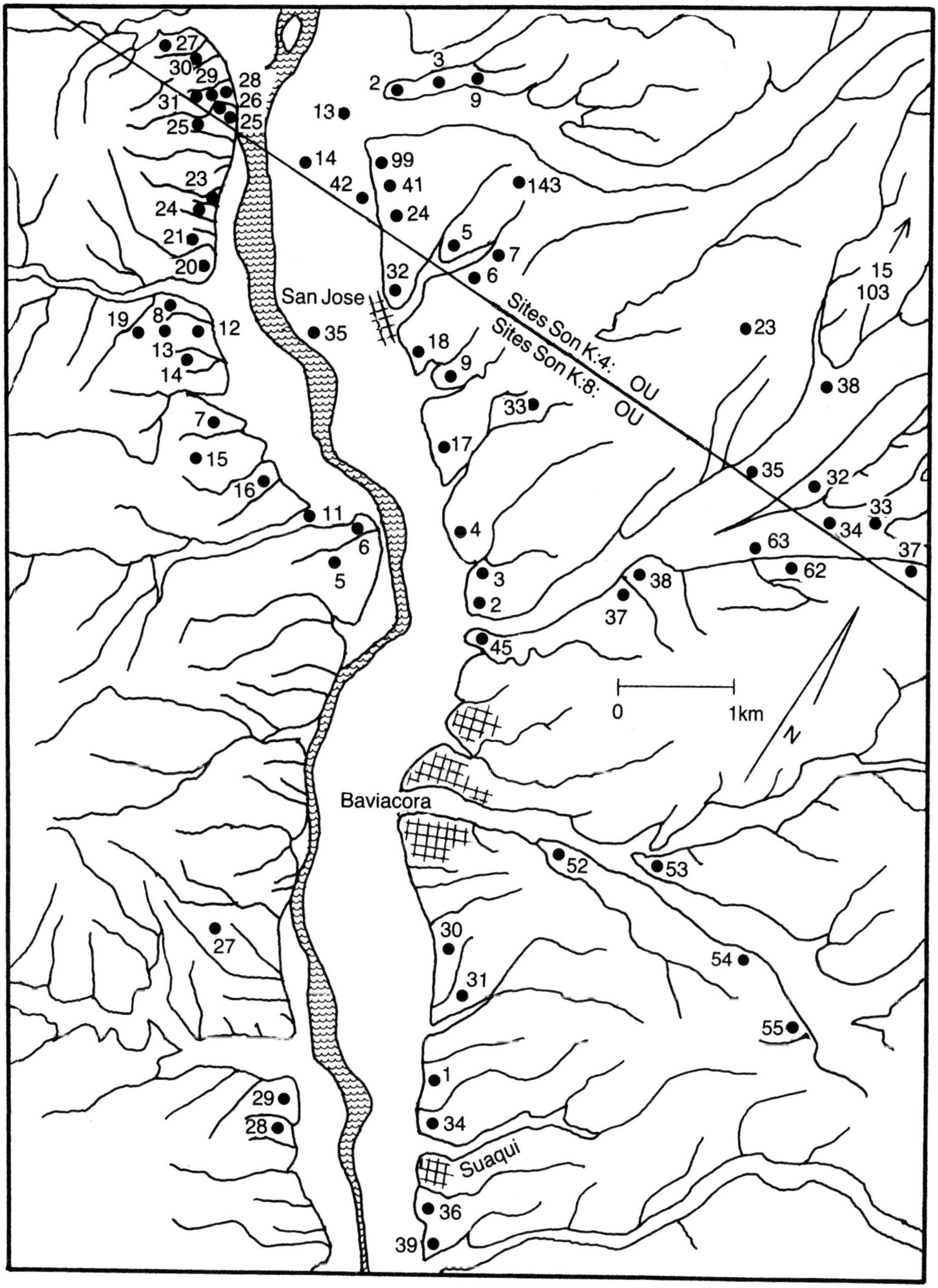

Figure C.4. Sites near the present-day pueblo of Baviacora in the Rio Sonora Valley.

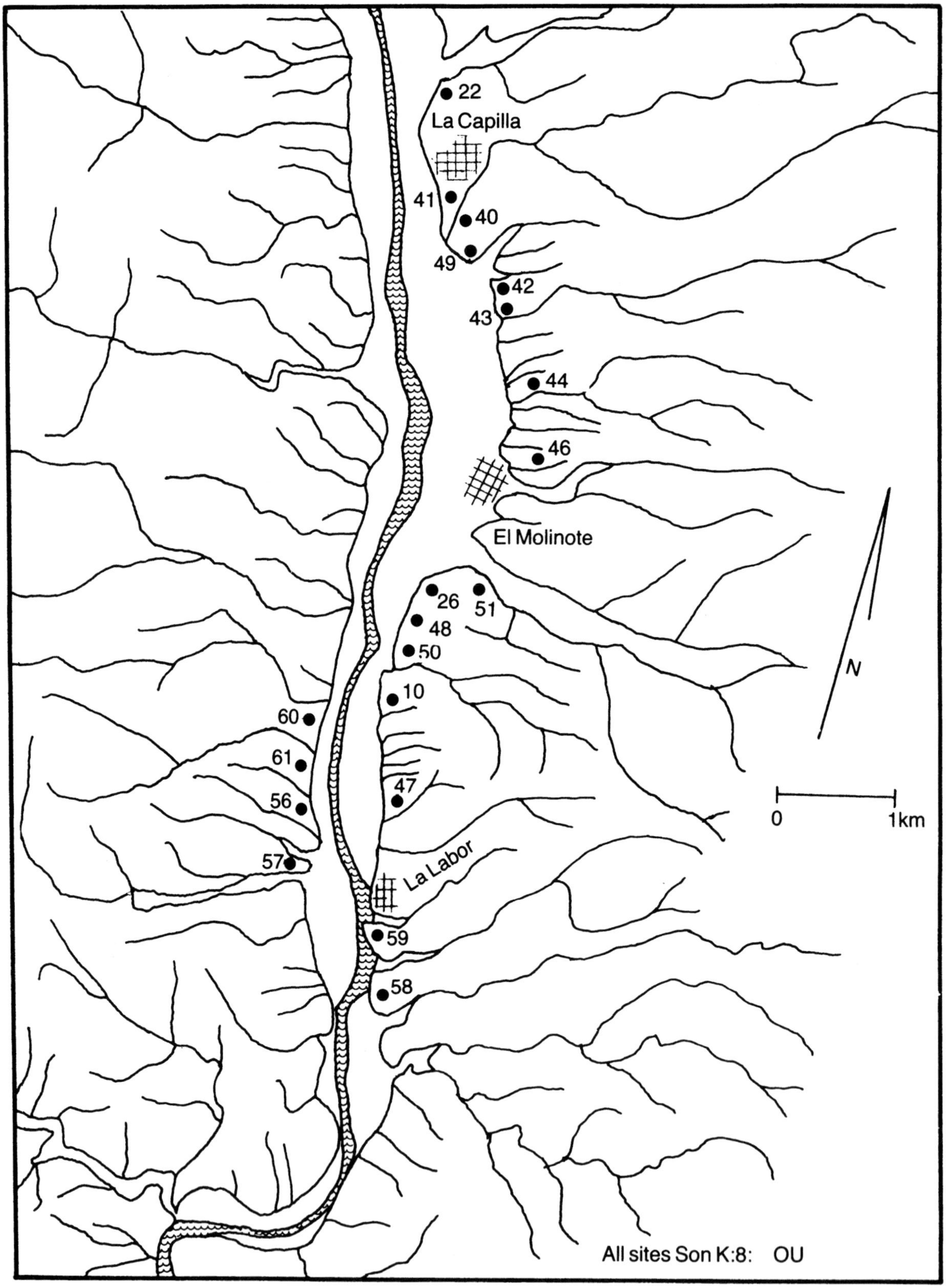

Figure C.5. Sites near the present-day congregacion of La Capilla in the Rio Sonora Valley.

References

Aguirre M., Rafael, and Donald Johnson G.
1983 Current status of the natural resources in the northwest of Mexico. In "Wildlife and Range Research Needs In Northern Mexico and Southwestern United States: Workshop Proceedings," edited by David R. Patton, Jose M. de la Puente-E., Peter F. Ffolliott, Sonoia Gallina, and E. T. Bartlett, pp. 24–27. *USDA Forest Service General Technical Report* WO–36. Washington.

Amsden, Monroe
1928 Archaeological Reconnaissance in Sonora. *Southwest Museum Papers* 1. Los Angeles.

Avila-Gonzales, Jaime
1983 Evaluation of wildlife resources in the higher elevations of the Sonora River basin. In "Wildlife and Range Research Needs in Northern Mexico and Southwestern United States: Workshop Proceedings," edited by David R. Patton, Jose M. de la Puente-E., Peter F. Ffolliott, Sonia Gallina, and E. T. Bartlett, pp. 52–55. *USDA Forest Service General Technical Report* WO–36. Washington.

Bahre, Conrad J.
1984 Cucurpe: A Traditional Agricultural Village in Eastern Sonora, Mexico. In *Latin America: Case Studies*, edited by Richard G. Boehm and Sent Visser, pp. 57–65. Dubuque: Kendall-Hunt.

Bahre, Conrad J., and David E. Bradbury
1978 Vegetation Change Along the Arizona-Sonora Boundary. *Annals of the Association of American Geographers* 68: 145–165.

Bandelier, A. F.
1890 Final Report of Investigations Among the Indians of the Southwestern United States Carried on Mainly in the Years from 1880 to 1885, Part I. *Papers of the Archaeological Institute of America, Americana Series* 3. Cambridge.
1892 Final Report of Investigations Among the Indians of the Southwestern United States Carried on Mainly in the Years from 1880 to 1885, Part II. *Papers of the Archaeological Institute of America, Americana Series* 4. Cambridge.

Bandelier, Fanny (trans.)
1905 *The Journey of Alvar Nuñez Cabeza de Vaca and His Companions from Florida to the Pacific, 1528–1536.* New York: A. S. Barnes.

Bannon, John F.
1955 The Mission Frontier in Sonora, 1620–1687. *United States Catholic Historical Society Monograph Series* 26. New York.

Beals, Ralph L.
1932 The Comparative Ethnology of Northern Mexico Before 1750. *Ibero-Americana* 2: 93–225.

Beardsley, Richard K., Preston Holder, Alex D. Krieger, Betty J. Meggers, John B. Rinaldo, and Paul Kutsche
1956 Functional and Evolutionary Implications of Community Patterning. *Memoirs of the Society for American Archaeology* 2.

Bell, P. L., and H. Bentley Mackenzie
1923 Mexican West Coast and Lower California: A Commercial and Industrial Survey. *Bureau of Foreign and Domestic Commerce Special Agents Series* 220. Washington: Department of Commerce.

Bennett, E. Fay
1977 An Afternoon of Terror: The Sonoran Earthquake of May 3, 1887. *Arizona and the West* 19: 107–120.

Blakemore, Michael
1981 From Way-finding to Map-making: The Spatial Information Fields of Aboriginal Peoples. *Progress in Human Geography* 5: 1–24.

Blanton, Richard E.
1972 Prehispanic Settlement Patterns of the Ixtapalapa Peninsula Region, Mexico. *Occasional Papers in Anthropology* 6. University Park: Pennsylvania State University.
1977 *Monte Alban: Settlement Patterns at the Ancient Zapotec Capitol.* New York: Academic Press.

Bolton, Herbert E.
1949 *Coronado: Knight of Pueblos and Plains.* Albuquerque: University of New Mexico Press.

Boserup, Ester
1965 *The Conditions of Agricultural Growth: The Economics of Agrarian Change Under Population Pressure.* Chicago: Aldine.
1975 The Impact of Population Growth on Agricultural Output. *Quarterly Journal of Economics* 89: 257–270.

Bouscaren, S. J., J. G. Waines, and L. A. Boykin-Bouscaren
1983 Cultivation and Use of Teparies in Sonora, Mexico. *Desert Plants* 5: 38–42.

Brady, Nyle C.
1974 *The Nature and Properties of Soils.* N.Y.: MacMillan.

Brand, Donald D.
1935 The Distribution of Pottery Types in Northwest Mexico. *American Anthropologist* 37(2): 287–305.
1938 Aboriginal Trade Routes for Sea Shells in the Southwest. *Yearbook of the Association of Pacific Coast Geographers* 4: 3–9.

Braniff C., Beatriz
1978 Preliminary Interpretations Regarding the Role of the San Miguel River, Sonora, Mexico. In *Across the Chichimec Sea: Papers in Honor of J. Charles Kelley,* edited by Carroll L. Riley and Basil C. Hedrick, pp. 67–82. Carbondale: Southern Illinois University Press.
1984 Proyecto Rio San Miguel, Sonora. In *Boletin del Consejo de Arqueologia, 1984*, edited by Joaquin Garcia-Barcena, pp. 9–21. Mexico: Instituto Nacional de Antropologia e Historia.

Braniff C., Beatriz *(continued)*

1985 La Frontera Protohistorica Pima-Opata en Sonora, Mexico: Proposiciones Arqueologicas Preliminares. Tesis que presenta para obtener el grado de Doctora en Antropologia, Universidad Nacional Autonoma de Mexico.

Brookfield, Harold C.

1962 Local Study and Comparative Method: An Example from Central New Guinea. *Annals of the Association of American Geographers* 52: 242–254.

1972 Intensification and Disintensification in Pacific Agriculture: A Theoretical Approach. *Pacific Viewpoint* 13: 30–48.

Brookfield, Harold C., and Dorene Hart

1971 *Melanesia: A Geographical Interpretation of an Island World.* London: Methuen.

Brown, David E.

1982a Madrean evergreen woodlands. In "Biotic Communities of the American Southwest—United States and Mexico," edited by David E. Brown, pp. 54–65. *Desert Plants* 4.

1982b Sinaloan thornscrub. In "Biotic Communities of the American Southwest—United States and Mexico," edited by David E. Brown, pp. 101–105. *Desert Plants* 4.

Brown, Paula, and Aaron Podolefsky

1976 Population Density, Agricultural Intensity, Land Tenure, and Group Size in the New Guinea Highlands. *Ethnology* 15: 211–238.

Brush, Stephen B.

1975 The Concept of Carrying Capacity for Systems of Shifting Cultivation. *American Anthropologist* 77(4): 799–812.

Bryan, Kirk

1928 Historic Evidence on Changes in the Channel of the Rio Puerco, a Tributary of the Rio Grande in New Mexico. *Journal of Geology* 36: 265–282.

1929 Flood-Water Farming. *Geographical Review* 19: 444–456.

1940 Erosion in the Valleys of the Southwest. *New Mexico Quarterly* 10: 227–232.

Bullard, William R., Jr.

1962 The Cerro Colorado Site and Pithouse Architecture in the Southwestern United States Prior to A.D. 900. *Papers of the Peabody Museum of Archaeology and Ethnology, Harvard University* 44(2). Cambridge: Harvard University Press.

Buol, S. W., F. D. Hole, and R. J. McCracken

1980 *Soil Genesis and Classification.* Ames: Iowa State University Press.

Burghardt, Andrew F.

1959 The Location of River Towns in the Central Lowlands of the United States. *Annals of the Association of American Geographers* 49: 305–323.

1971 A Hypothesis About Gateway Cities. *Annals of the Association of American Geographers* 61: 269–285.

Butzer, Karl W.

1976 *Geomorphology from the Earth.* New York: Harper and Row.

1982 *Archaeology as Human Ecology: Method and Theory for a Contextual Approach.* Cambridge: Cambridge University Press.

Bye, Robert A., Jr.

1981 Quelites—Ethnoecology of Edible Greens—Past, Present, and Future. *Journal of Ethnobiology* 1: 109–123.

Carniero, Robert L.

1970 A Theory of the Origin of the State. *Science* 169: 733–738.

Castetter, Edward F., and Willis H. Bell

1942 *Pima and Papago Indian Agriculture.* Albuquerque: University of New Mexico Press.

Chang, Kwang-Chih

1958 Study of the Neolithic Social Grouping: Examples from the New World. *American Anthropologist* 60(2): 298–308.

Chisholm, Michael

1962 *Rural Settlement and Land Use: An Essay in Location.* London: Hutchinson University Library.

Christaller, Walter

1966 *Central Places in Southern Germany* (trans. by Carlisle W. Baskin). Englewood Cliffs: Prentice-Hall.

Clarke, Steven K.

1974 A Method for the Estimation of Prehistoric Pueblo Populations. *The Kiva* 39(3–4): 283–287.

Clotts, Herbert V.

1915 Report on Nomadic Papago Surveys to C. R. Olberg, Superintendent of Irrigation. Unpublished manuscript, U.S. Indian Service.

Coe, Michael D.

1964 The Chinampas of Mexico. *Scientific American* 211: 90–98.

Coe, Michael D., and Kent V. Flannery

1964 Microenvironments and Mesoamerican Prehistory. *Science* 46: 650–654.

Cohen, Mark N.

1977 *The Food Crisis in Prehistory: Overpopulation and the Origins of Agriculture.* New Haven: Yale University Press.

Cook, Sherburne F.

1972 *Prehistoric Demography. McCaleb Module in Anthropology.* Reading: Addison-Wesley.

Cooke, Ronald U., and Richard W. Reeves

1976 *Arroyos and Environmental Change in the American South-West.* Oxford: Clarendon Press.

Cordell, Linda S.

1984 *Prehistory of the Southwest.* Orlando: Academic Press.

Cordell, Linda S., and Fred Plog

1979 Escaping the Confines of Normative Thought: A Reevaluation of Puebloan Prehistory. *American Antiquity* 44(3): 405–429.

Covey, Cyclone (trans. and ed.)

1983 *Cabeza de Vaca's Adventures in the Unknown Interior of America.* Albuquerque: University of New Mexico Press.

Cowgill, George L.

1975 On Causes and Consequences of Ancient and Modern Population Changes. *American Anthropologist* 77(3): 505–525.

Crumley, Carole L.

1979 Three Locational Models: An Epistemological Assessment for Anthropology and Archaeology. In *Advances in Archaeological Method and Theory,* Vol. 2, edited by Michael B. Schiffer, pp. 141–173. New York: Academic Press.

Cuevas, Mariano

1924 *Historia de los Descubrimientos Antiguos y Modernos de la Nueva Espana Escrita por el Conquistador Baltasar de Obregon, Ano de 1584.* Mexico: Departamento Editorial de la Secretaria de Educacion Publica.

Daco, A.

1976 Geochemical Explorations: The Washington Mine Area and Vicinity. Unpublished manuscript on file at the office of Cia. Minerales Sotula, S. A. de C.V., Huepac, Sonora, Mexico.

Davenport, Harbert (ed.)
1924–1925 The Expedition of Panfilo de Narvaez by Gonzalo Fernandez Oviedo y Valdez. *Southwestern Historical Quarterly* 27: 120–139, 217–241, 276–304; and 28: 56–74.

Dean, Jeffrey S., and William J. Robinson
1977 *Dendroclimatic Variability in the American Southwest, A.D. 680 to 1970*. Tucson: University of Arizona Laboratory of Tree-Ring Research.

de Azpilcueta, Martin
1630 Carta al Padre Ignacio Zabala. Unpublished letter in the Archivo General y Publico de la Nacion, Mexico. Misiones 25: 1622–1647, folios 234–235.

de Benavides, Manuel
1653 Carta Anua de la Mision de San Francisco Xavier. Unpublished manuscript in the Archivo General y Publico de la Nacion, Mexico. Misiones 26: 1647–1698, folios 391–393.

de Las Casas, Bartoleme
1967 *Apologetica Historia Sumaria*. 2 vols., edited by Edmundo O'Gorman. Mexico: Universidad Nacional Autonoma de Mexico, Instituto de Investigaciones.

Denevan, William M. (ed.)
1976 *The Native Population of the Americas in 1492*. Madison: University of Wisconsin Press.

Di Peso, Charles C.
1956 The Upper Pima of San Cayetano del Tumacacori: An Archaeological Reconstruction of the Ootam of Pimeria Alta. *The Amerind Foundation* 7. Dragoon: The Amerind Foundation.
1974 Casas Grandes: A Fallen Trading Center of the Gran Chichimeca. *The Amerind Foundation* 9. Flagstaff and Dragoon: Northland Press and The Amerind Foundation.
1979 Prehistory: Southern Periphery. In *Handbook of North American Indians*, Vol. 9, *Southwest*, edited by Alfonso Ortiz, pp. 152–161. Washington: Smithsonian Institution.

Direccion General de Estadistica
1965 *IV Censos Agricola, Ganadero y Ejidal 1960, Sonora*. Mexico: Secretaria de Industria y Comercio.
1975 *V Censos Agricola, Ganadero y Ejidal 1970, Sonora*. Mexico: Secretaria de Industria y Comercio.

Dirst, Victoria
1979 *A Prehistoric Frontier in Sonora*. Ann Arbor: University Microfilms International.

Dobyns, Henry F.
1966 Estimating Aboriginal American Population: An Appraisal of Techniques with a New Hemispheric Estimate. *Current Anthropology* 7: 395–416, 446–447.

Donkin, R. A.
1979 Agricultural Terracing in the Aboriginal New World. *Viking Fund Publications in Anthropology* 56. Tucson: University of Arizona Press.

Doolittle, William E.
1979 *Pre-Hispanic Occupance in the Middle Rio Sonora Valley: From an Ecological to a Socioeconomic Focus*. Ann Arbor: University Microfilms International.
1980 Aboriginal Agricultural Development in the Valley of Sonora, Mexico. *Geographical Review* 70: 328–342.
1981 Obsidian hydration dating in eastern Sonora, Mexico. In "Obsidian Dates III: A Compendium of the Obsidian Hydration Determinations Made at the U.C.L.A. Obsidian Hydration Laboratory," edited by Clement W. Meighan and Glenn S. Russell, pp. 155–159. *University of California, Los Angeles, Institute of Archaeology, Monograph* 16. Los Angeles: University of California Press.
1983 Agricultural Expansion in a Marginal Area of Mexico. *Geographical Review* 73: 301–313.
1984a Settlements and the Development of 'Statelets' in Sonora, Mexico. *Journal of Field Archaeology* 11: 13–24.
1984b Agricultural Change as an Incremental Process. *Annals of the Association of American Geographers* 74: 124–137.
1984c Cabeza de Vaca's Land of Maize: An Assessment of Its Agriculture. *Journal of Historical Geography* 10: 246–262.

Doyel, David E.
1979 The Prehistoric Hohokam of the Arizona Desert. *American Scientist* 67: 544–554.

Doyel, David E., and Emil W. Haury (eds.)
1976 The 1976 Salado Conference. *The Kiva* 42(1).

Drake, Robert J.
1954 Sonora Building Foundations. *El Palacio* 61(10): 344–346.

Dunbier, Roger
1968 *The Sonoran Desert: Its Geography, Economy, and People*. Tucson: University of Arizona Press.

Eighmy, Jeffrey L.
1979 Logistic Trends in Southwest Population Growth. In *Transformations: Mathematical Approaches to Cultural Change*, edited by Colin Renfrew and Kenneth L. Cooke, pp. 205–220. New York: Academic Press.

Ekholm, Gordon
1939 Results of an Archaeological Survey of Sonora and Northern Sinaloa. *Revista Mexicana de Estudios Antropologicos* 3: 7–10.

Ettlinger, Nancy
1981 Dependency and Urban Growth: A Critical Review and Reformulation of the Concepts of Primacy and Rank-Size. *Environment and Planning* 13A: 1389–1400.

Euler, Robert C., George J. Gumerman, Thor N. V. Karlstrom, Jeffrey S. Dean, Richard H. Hevley
1979 The Colorado Plateaus: Cultural Dynamics and Paleoenvironment. *Science* 205: 1089–1101.

Ewel, John, Fay Benedict, Cory Berish, Becky Brown, Stephen Gliessman, Moises Amador, Radamez Bermudez, Angel Martinez, Roberto Miranda, and Norman Price
1982 Leaf Area, Light Transmission, Roots and Leaf Damage in Nine Tropical Plant Communities. *Agro-Ecosystems* 7: 305–326.

Felger, Richard S., Gary P. Nabhan, and Thomas Sheridan
1976 Ethnobotany of the Rio San Miguel, Sonora, Mexico. Unpublished manuscript on file at the Centro Regional del Noroeste, Instituto Nacional de Antropologia e Historia, Hermosillo, Sonora, Mexico.

Fish, Merle G., Jr.
1980 *El Cultivo de Roza: Shifting Cultivation in a Dry Forest of Northwest Mexico*. MS, Doctoral dissertation in Geography, University of California, Berkeley.

Flannery, Kent V.
1971 Archaeological Systems Theory and Early Mesoamerica. In *Prehistoric Agriculture*, edited by Stuart Struever, pp. 80–100. New York: Natural History Press.
1972 The Cultural Evolution of Civilization. *Annual Review of Ecology and Systematics* 3: 399–420.
1976a Sampling by Intensive Surface Collection. In *The Early Mesoamerican Village*, edited by Kent V. Flannery, pp. 51–62. New York: Academic Press.
1976b Linear Settlement Patterns and Riverside Settlement Rules. In *The Early Mesoamerican Village*, edited by

Flannery, Kent V. *(continued)*
Kent V. Flannery, pp. 173–180. New York: Academic Press.

Fletcher, Roland
1979 People and Space: A Case Study on Material Behaviour. In *Pattern of the Past: Studies in Honour of David Clarke*, edited by Ian Hodder, Glynn Isaac, and Norman Hammond, pp. 97–128. Cambridge: Cambridge University Press.

Fogel, Martin M.
1975 Runoff Agriculture: Efficient Use of Rainfall. In *Watershed Management in Arid Zones: A Prototype Short Course*, edited by J. L. Thomas and J. N. Fischer, pp. 130–146. Tucson: University of Arizona School of Renewable Natural Resources.

Fontana, Bernard L., J. Cameron Greenleaf, and Donnelly D. Cassidy
1959 A Fortified Arizona Mountain. *The Kiva* 25(2): 41–53.

Food and Agriculture Organization of the United Nations
1979 *1978 FAO Production Yearbook* 32. Rome.

Frazier, Gary W. (ed.)
1975 *Proceedings of the Water Harvesting Symposium*. Phoenix: U.S. Department of Agriculture Agricultural Research Service.

Garcia, Enriqueta
1981 *Modificaciones al Sistema de Clasificacion Climatica de Koeppen*. Mexico: Enriqueta Garcia de Miranda.

Gasser, Robert E.
1977 The Rio Sonora Flotation Analysis. Unpublished manuscript on file at the Department of Anthropology, University of Oklahoma, Norman.

Geertz, Clifford
1963 *Agricultural Involution: The Processes of Ecological Change in Indonesia*. Berkeley: University of California Press.

Gentry, Howard S.
1942 Rio Mayo Plants: A Study of the Flora and Vegetation of the Valley of the Rio Mayo, Sonora. *Carnegie Institution of Washington Publication* 527. Washington.
1982 Sinaloan deciduous forest. In "Biotic Communities of the American Southwest—United States and Mexico," edited by David E. Brown, pp. 73–77. *Desert Plants* 4.

Gifford, D. P.
1978 Ethnoarchaeological Observations of Natural Processes Affecting Cultural Materials. In *Explorations in Ethnoarchaeology*, edited by R. A. Gould, pp. 77–101. Albuquerque: University of New Mexico Press.

Gladwin, Harold S.
1936 Discussion. In "An Archaeological Survey of Chihuahua, Mexico," by E. B. Sayles, pp. 89–105. *Medallion Papers* 22. Globe: Gila Pueblo.

Glass, John B.
1975 A Survey of Native Middle American Pictorial Manuscripts. In *Handbook of Middle American Indians*, Vol. 14, *Guide to Ethnohistorical Sources*, edited by Howard F. Cline, pp. 3–37. Austin: University of Texas Press.

Glassow, Michael A.
1980 Prehistoric Agricultural Development in the Northern Southwest: A Study in Changing Patterns of Land Use. *Ballena Press Anthropological Papers* 16. Socorro.

Gliessman, Stephen R.
1983 Allelopathic Interactions in Crop/Weed Mixtures: Applications for Weed Management. *Journal of Chemical Ecology* 9: 990–991.
1984 An Agroecological Approach to Sustainable Agriculture. In *Meeting the Expectations of the Land: Essays in Sustainable Agriculture and Stewardship*, edited by Wes Jackson, Wendell Berry, and Bruce Colman, pp. 160–171. San Francisco: North Point Press.

Graham, Ian
1980 Spectral Analysis and Distance Methods in the Study of Archaeological Distributions. *Journal of Archaeological Science* 7: 105–129.

Grant, Campbell
1965 *The Rock Paintings of the Chumash: A Study of a California Indian Culture*. Berkeley: University of California Press.
1967 *Rock Art of the American Indian*. New York: Thomas Y. Crowell.

Greenwood, Roberta A.
1969 The Browne Site: Early Milling Zone Horizon in Southern California. *Memoirs of the Society for American Archaeology* 23.

Grigg, David B.
1970 *The Harsh Lands: A Study of Agricultural Development*. London: MacMillan and Co.
1974 *The Agricultural Systems of the World: An Evolutionary Approach*. Cambridge: Cambridge University Press.
1976 Population Pressure and Agricultural Change. *Progress in Human Geography* 8: 133–176.
1979 Ester Boserup's Theory of Agrarian Change: A Critical Review. *Progress in Human Geography* 3: 64–86.

Grove, David C., Kenneth G. Hirth, David E. Buge, and Ann M. Cyphers
1976 Settlement and Cultural Development at Chalcatzingo. *Science* 192: 1203–1210.

Hack, John T.
1942 The Changing Physical Environment of the Hopi Indians of Arizona. *Papers of the Peabody Museum of American Archaeology and Ethnology, Harvard University*, 35. Cambridge: Harvard University Press.

Haggett, Peter, Andrew D. Cliff, and Allan Frey
1977 *Locational Analysis in Human Geography*. Vol. 1. New York: Halsted Press.

Hallenbeck, Cleve
1949 *The Journey of Fray Marcos de Niza*. Dallas: Dallas University Press.

Hammond, George P., and Agapito Rey (trans., eds., and annots.)
1928 *Obregon's History of 16th Century Explorations in Western America Entitled: Chronicle, Commentary, or Relation of the Ancient and Modern Discoveries in New Spain and New Mexico, Mexico, 1584*. Los Angeles: Wetzel.
1940 *Narratives of the Coronado Expedition 1540–1542*. Albuquerque: University of New Mexico Press.

Hammond, Norman
1974 The Distribution of Late Classic Maya Major Ceremonial Centers in the Central Area. In *Mesoamerican Archaeology: New Approaches*, edited by Norman Hammond, pp. 313–334. London: Duckworth.

Hansen, Bent
1979 Colonial Economic Development with Unlimited Supply of Land: A Ricardian Case. *Economic Development and Culture Change* 27: 611–627.

Harlem, Arthur D.
1964 Cerro de Trincheras: Its History and Purpose. *Tlalocan* 4: 339–350.

Harris, David R.
1966 Recent Plant Invasions in the Arid and Semi-Arid Southwest of the United States. *Annals of the Association of American Geographers* 56: 408–422.

Harvey, H. R., and B. J. Williams
1980 Aztec Arithmetic: Positional Notation and Area Calculation. *Science* 210: 499–505.

Harwood, Richard R.
1979 *Small Farm Development: Understanding and Improving Farming Systems in the Humid Tropics*. Boulder: Westview.

Hassan, Fekri A.
1978 Demographic Archaeology. In *Advances in Archaeological Method and Theory,* Vol. 1, edited by Michael B. Schiffer, pp. 49–103. New York: Academic Press.

Hastings, James R. (ed.)
1964 Climatological Data for Sonora and Northern Sinaloa. *The University of Arizona Institute of Atmospheric Physics Technical Reports on the Meteorology and Climatology of Arid Regions* 15. Tucson.

Hastings, James R., and Raymond M. Turner
1965 *The Changing Mile: An Ecological Study of Vegetation Change With Time in the Lower Mile of an Arid and Semiarid Region*. Tucson: University of Arizona Press.

Hastorf, Christine A.
1980 Changing Resource Use in Subsistence Agricultural Groups of the Prehistoric Mimbres River Valley, New Mexico. In *Modeling Change in Prehistoric Subsistence Economies*, edited by Timothy K. Earle and Andrew L. Christenson, pp. 79–120. New York: Academic Press.

Haury, Emil W.
1945 The Excavation of Los Muertos and Neighboring Ruins in the Salt River Valley, Southern Arizona. *Papers of the Peabody Museum of American Archaeology and Ethnology, Harvard University,* 24. Cambridge: Harvard University Press.
1950 *The Stratigraphy and Archaeology of Ventana Cave, Arizona*. Tucson and Albuquerque: University of Arizona Press and University of New Mexico Press.
1976 *The Hohokam Desert Farmers and Craftsmen: Excavations at Snaketown, 1964–1965*. Tucson: University of Arizona Press.

Haviland, William A.
1972 Family Size, Prehistoric Population Estimates, and the Ancient Maya. *American Antiquity* 37(1): 135–139.

Hayes, Alden C., D. Brugge, and W. J. Judge
1981 Archaeological Surveys of Chaco Canyon, New Mexico. *National Park Service Publications in Archaeology* 18A. Washington.

Hedrick, Basil C., and Carroll L. Riley
1974 The Journey of The Vaca Party: The Account of the Narvaez Expedition, 1528–1536, as Related by Gonzalo Fernandez de Oviedo y Valdes. *Southern Illinois University Museum Studies* 2. Carbondale: Southern Illinois University.

Heizer, Robert F.
1958 Aboriginal California and Great Basin Cartography. *Reports of the University of California Archaeological Survey* 41: 1–9. Berkeley: University of California Press.

Heizer, Robert F., and Martin A. Baumhoff
1962 *Prehistoric Rock Art of Nevada and Eastern California*. Berkeley: University of California Press.

Hewes, Leslie
1935 Huepac: An Agricultural Village of Sonora, Mexico. *Economic Geography* 11: 284–292.

Hinrichs, H. T.
1981 New Mexico State Adobe Code. *Adobe Today* 22: 4–9.

Hinton, Thomas B.
1955 A Survey of Archaeological Sites in the Altar Valley. *The Kiva* 21(1–2): 1–12.
1959 A Survey of Indian Assimilation in Eastern Sonora. *Anthropological Papers of the University of Arizona* 4. Tucson: University of Arizona Press.
1983 Southern Periphery: West. In *Handbook of North American Indians*, Vol. 10, *Southwest*, edited by Alfonso Ortiz, pp. 315–328. Washington: Smithsonian Institution.

Hirth, Kenneth
1978 Interregional Trade and the Formation of Prehistoric Gateway Communities. *American Antiquity* 43(1): 35–45.

Hoover, J. W.
1941 Cerros de Trincheras of the Arizona Papagueria. *Geographical Review* 31: 228–239.

Howard, William A., and Thomas M. Griffiths
1966 Trinchera Distribution in the Sierra Madre Occidental, Mexico. *University of Denver Publications in Geography, Technical Paper* 66–1. Denver: University of Denver.

Hrdlička, Aleš
1904 Notes on the Indians of Sonora, Mexico. *American Anthropologist* 6(1): 51–89.

Hughes, P. J., and R. J. Lampert
1977 Occupational Disturbance and Types of Archaeological Deposit. *Journal of Archaeological Science* 4: 135–140.

Hunt, Charles B.
1974 *Natural Regions of the United States and Canada*. San Francisco: W. H. Freeman.

Igbozurike, Uzo M.
1981 The Concept of Carrying Capacity. *Journal of Geography* 80: 141–149.

Instituto Nacional de Estadistica Geografia e Informatica
1983 *X Censo General de Poblacion y Vivienda, 1980, Estado de Sonora,* Volumen II, Tomo 26. Mexico: SPP Programacion y Presupesto.

Isom, W. H., and G. F. Worker
1979 Crop Management in Semi-Arid Environments. In *Agriculture in Semi-Arid Environments*, edited by A. E. Hall, G. H. Cannell, and H. W. Lawton, pp. 200–223. Berlin: Springer-Verlag.

Ives, Ronald L.
1949 Climate of the Sonoran Desert Region. *Annals of the Association of American Geographers* 39: 143–187.

Janick, Jules, Robert W. Schery, Frank W. Woods, and Vernon W. Ruttan
1974 *Plant Science: An Introduction to World Crops*. San Francisco: W. H. Freeman.

Jenny, Hans
1958 Role of the Plant Factor in the Pedogenic Functions. *Ecology* 39: 5–16.

Johnson, Alfred E.
1963 The Trincheras Culture of Northern Sonora. *American Antiquity* 29(2): 174–186.
1966 Archaeology of Sonora, Mexico. In *Handbook of Middle American Indians*, Vol. 4, *Archaeological Frontiers and External Connections*, edited by Gordon F. Ekholm and Gordon R. Willey, pp. 26–36. Austin: University of Texas Press.

Johnson G., Donald, and Luis Carrillo Michel
1977 *Algunos Zacates de Sonora*. Hermosillo: Comite de Fomento Ganadero.

Johnson, Gregory A.
1972 A Test of the Utility of Central Place Theory in Archaeology. In *Man, Settlement and Urbanism*, edited by Peter J. Ucko, Ruth Tringham, and G. W. Dimbleday, pp. 769–785. Hertfordshire: Duckworth.

Johnson, Jean B.
1950 The Opata: An Inland Tribe of Sonora. *University of New Mexico Publications in Anthropology* 6. Albuquerque: University of New Mexico Press.

Joosten, J. H. L.
1962 Wirtscharttiche und Agrarpolitische *Aspekte Tropischer Landbausysteme*. Gottingen: Vortrag.

Kalnicky, Richard A.
1974 Climatic Change Since 1950. *Annals of the Association of American Geographers* 64: 100–112.

Kaplan, Lawrence
1965 Archaeology and Domestication in American Phaseolus (Beans). *Economic Botany* 19: 358–368.

Katz, Solomon H., Mary L. Hediger, and Linda A. Valleroy
1974 Traditional Maize Processing in the New World. *Science* 184: 765–773.

Kelley, J. Charles
1980 Discussion of papers by Plog, Doyel, and Riley. In "Current Issues in Hohokam Prehistory: Proceedings of a Symposium," edited by David Doyel and Fred Plog, pp. 49–66. *Arizona State University Anthropological Research Papers* 23. Tempe: Arizona State University.

King, R. E.
1930 Geological Reconnaissance in Northern Sierra Madre Occidental of Mexico. *Bulletin, Geological Society of America* 50: 1625–1722.

Kirkby, A., and M. J. Kirkby
1976 Geomorphic Processes and the Surface Survey of Archaeological Sites in Semi-Arid Areas. In *Geoarchaeology*, edited by A. Davidson and M. L. Schackley, pp. 229–253. Boulder: Westview Press.

Kirschmann, John D.
1975 *Nutrition Almanac*. New York: McGraw-Hill.

Kochel, R. Craig, and Victor R. Baker
1982 Paleoflood Hydrology. *Science* 215: 353–361.

Kroeber, A. L.
1934 Native American Population. *American Anthropologist* 36(1): 1–25.

Lange, Charles H., and Carroll L. Riley (eds. and annots.)
1970 *The Southwestern Journals of Adolph F. Bandelier: 1883–1884*. Albuquerque: University of New Mexico Press.

Lawton, H. W., and P. J. Wilke
1979 Ancient Agricultural Systems in Dry Regions. In *Agriculture in Semi-Arid Environments*, edited by A. E. Hall, G. H. Cannell, and H. W. Lawton, pp. 1–44. Berlin: Springer-Verlag.

LeBlanc, Steven
1971 An Addition to Naroll's Suggested Floor Area and Settlement Population Relationship. *American Antiquity* 36(2): 210–211.
1980 The Dating of Casas Grandes. *American Antiquity* 45(4): 799–806.

LeBlanc, Steven, and Ben Nelson
1976 The Salado in Southwestern New Mexico. *The Kiva* 42(1): 71–80.

Lehmer, Donald J.
1949 Archaeological Survey of Sonora, Mexico. *Chicago Natural History Museum Bulletin*, December, pp. 4–5.

Lekson, Stephen
1984 Dating Casas Grandes. *The Kiva* 50(1): 55–60.

Leopold, Luna B.
1951 Rainfall Frequency: An Aspect of Climatic Variation. *Transactions, American Geophysical Union* 32: 347–357.

Lister, Robert H. (ed.)
1958 Archaeological Excavations in the Northern Sierra Madre Occidental, Chihuahua and Sonora, Mexico. *University of Colorado Studies Series in Anthropology* 7. Boulder: University of Colorado.

Little, Elbert L., Jr.
1950 Southwestern Trees: A Guide to the Native Species of New Mexico and Arizona. *U.S. Forest Service Agricultural Handbook* 9. Washington: U.S. Department of Agriculture.

Lowe, Charles H., and David E. Brown
1982 Introduction. In "Biotic Communities of the American Southwest—United States and Mexico," edited by David E. Brown, pp. 8–16. *Desert Plants* 4.

Ludwig, H. D.
1968 Permanent Farming on Ukara: The Impact of Land Shortages on Husbandry Practices. In *Smallholder Farming and Smallholder Development in Tanzania*, edited by H. Ruthenberg, pp. 87–135. Munich: Weltfrum Verlag.

Luebben, Ralph A., Jonathan G. Andelson, and Laurance C. Herold
1986 Elvino Whetten Pueblo and its Relationship to Terraces and Nearby Small Structures, Chihuahua, Mexico. *The Kiva* 51(3): 165–187.

Lugli, Piero Maria
1967 *Storia e Cultura della Citta Italiana*. Bari: Editori Laterza.

Lumholtz, Carl
1902 *Unknown Mexico: A Record of Five Years' Exploration Among the Tribes of the Western Sierra Madre; in the Tierra Caliente of Tepic and Jalisco; and Among the Tarascas of Michoacan*. Vol. 1. New York: Charles Scribner's Sons.

Mangelsdorf, Paul C.
1958 Archaeological evidence on the evolution of maize in northwestern Mexico. In "Archaeological Excavations in the Northern Sierra Madre Occidental, Chihuahua and Sonora, Mexico," edited by Robert H. Lister, pp. 96–109. *University of Colorado Studies Series in Anthropology* 7. Boulder: University of Colorado.

Mangelsdorf, Paul C., and Robert H. Lister
1956 Archaeological Evidence on the Evolution of Maize in Northwestern Mexico. *Botanical Museum Leaflets, Harvard University* 17(6): 151–177.

Marshall, J. T., Jr.
1957 Birds of the Pine-oak Woodland in Southern Arizona and Adjacent Mexico. *Pacific Coast Avifauna* 32: 1–125.

Martin, Paul S.
1963 *The Last 10,000 Years: A Fossil Pollen Record of the American Southwest*. Tucson: University of Arizona Press.

Masse, W. Bruce
1981 Prehistoric Irrigation Systems in the Salt River Valley, Arizona. *Science* 214: 408–415.

Mather, Cotton, and Pradyumna P. Karan
1978 The Concept of Land Support Units: Bhutan. *Geografiska Annalar* 60B: 28–35.

McGregor, John C.
1965 *Southwestern Archaeology*. Urbana: University of Illinois Press.

Meadows, Donella H., Dennis L. Meadows, Jorgen Randers, and William W. Behrens III
1972 *The Limits to Growth*. New York: Signet.

Meals for Millions Foundation
1980 *O'odham I:waki: Wild Greens of the Desert People*. Tucson: Meals for Millions Foundation, Southwest Program.

Mendez, Pedro
1628 Carta Anua de la Provincia de Nueva España. Unpublished manuscript in the Archivo General y Publico de la Nacion, Mexico. Misiones 25: 1622–1647, folios 204–205.

Miksicek, Charles H.
1979 From Parking Lots to Museum Basements: The Archaeobotany of the St. Mary's Site. *The Kiva* 45(1–2): 131–140.

Millon, René
1967 Teotihuacan. *Scientific American* 216(6): 38–48.

Minckley, W. L., and David E. Brown
1982 Wetlands. In "Biotic Communities of the American Southwest—United States and Mexico," edited by David E. Brown, pp. 223–268. *Desert Plants* 4.

Mountjoy, Joseph B.
1982 An Interpretation of the Pictographs at La Pena Pintada, Jalisco, Mexico. *American Antiquity* 47(1): 110–126.

Munn, Nancy D.
1973 The Spatial Presentation of Cosmic Order in Walbiri Iconography. In *Primative Art and Society*, edited by Anthony Forge, pp. 193–220. London: Oxford University Press for the Wenner-Gren Foundation for Anthropological Research.

Nabhan, Gary P.
1979 The Ecology of Floodwater Farming in Arid Southwestern North America. *Agro-Ecosystems* 5: 245–255.
1981 Runoff Farming for Dry Lands. *The New Farm*, May/June: 50–53.

Nabhan, Gary P., and Richard S. Felger
1978 Teparies in Southwestern North America: A Bibliographical and Ethnohistorical Study of *Phaseolus acutifolius*. *Economic Botany* 32: 2–19.

Nabhan, Gary P., and Thomas E. Sheridan
1977 Living Fencerows of the Rio San Miguel, Sonora, Mexico: Traditional Technology for Floodplain Management. *Human Ecology* 5: 97–111.

Nabhan, Gary P., Charles W. Weber, and James W. Berry
1979 Legumes in the Papago-Pima Indian Diet and Ecological Niche. *The Kiva* 44(2–3): 173–190.

Naroll, Raoul
1962 Floor Area and Settlement Population. *American Antiquity* 27(4): 587–589.

Naylor, Thomas H.
1983 Review of *The Frontier People: The Greater Southwest in the Protohistoric Period* by Carroll L. Riley. *The Kiva* 49(1–2): 119–121.

Nentvig, Juan
1980 *Rudo Ensayo: A Description of Sonora and Arizona in 1764* (trans., clarif., and annot. by Alberto Francisco Pradeau and Robert R. Rasmussen). Tucson: University of Arizona Press.

Newman, Marshall T.
1962 Ecology and Nutritional Stress in Man. *American Anthropologist* 64(1): 22–34.

Nir, Dov
1974 *The Semi-arid World: Man on the Fringe of the Desert*. New York: Longman.

Noguera, Eduardo
1958 Reconocimiento Arqueologico en Sonora. *Infomes* 10. Mexico: Instituto Nacional de Antropologia e Historia.

Noy-Meir, Immanuel
1973 Desert Ecosystems: Environment and Producers. *Annual Review of Ecology and Systematics* 4: 25–51.

Nuñez Cabeza de Vaca, Alvar
1942 *Naufragios y Comentarios Con Dos Cartas y Relacion de Hernando de Ribera*. Madrid: Espasa-Calpe.

Nye, P. H.
1961 Organic Matter and Nutrient Cycles Under Moist Tropical Forest. *Plant and Soil* 8: 333–346.

Nye, Thomas S.
1972 Mexico, the Closely Guarded Mineral Storehouse. *Mining Engineering*, December: 40–44.

Pacheco, Joaquin F., and Francisco de Cardenas (eds.)
1870 *Coleccion de Documentos Ineditos Relativos al Descubrimiento, Conquista y Colonizacion de las Posesiones Españoles en America y Oceania*. Vol. 14. Madrid: Jose Maria Perez.

Pailes, Richard A.
1978 The Rio Sonora Culture in Prehistoric Trade Systems. In *Across the Chichimec Sea: Papers in Honor of J. Charles Kelley*, edited by Carroll L. Riley and Basil C. Hedrick, pp. 134–143. Carbondale: Southern Illinois University Press.
1980 The Upper Rio Sonora Valley in Prehistoric Trade. *Transactions, Illinois State Academy of Science* 72(4): 20–39.
1984 Agricultural development and trade in the Rio Sonora. In "Prehistoric Agricultural Strategies in the Southwest," edited by Suzanne K. Fish and Paul Fish, pp. 309–325. *Arizona State University Anthropological Research Papers* 33. Tempe: Arizona State University.

Pailes, Richard A., and Daniel T. Reff
1985 Colonial Exchange Systems and the Decline of Paquime. In *The Archaeology of West and Northwest Mesoamerica*, edited by Michael S. Foster and Phil C. Weigand, pp. 353–363. Boulder and London: Westview Press.

Parsons, James J.
1977 Geography as Exploration and Discovery. *Annals of the Association of American Geographers* 67: 1–16.

Parsons, Jeffrey R.
1971 Prehistoric Settlement Patterns in the Texcoco Region, Mexico. *Memoirs of the Museum of Anthropology, University of Michigan* 3. Ann Arbor: University of Michigan.

Parsons, Jeffrey R., Elizabeth Brumfiel, Mary H. Parsons, and David J. Wilson
1982 Prehispanic Settlement Patterns in the Southern Valley of Mexico: The Chalco-Xochimilco Region. *Memoirs of the Museum of Anthropology, University of Michigan* 14. Ann Arbor: University of Michigan.

Patterson, Thomas C.
1963 Contemporaneity and Cross-Dating in Archaeological Interpretation. *American Antiquity* 28(3): 389–392.

Pennington, Campbell W.
1980 *The Pima Bajo of Central Sonora, Mexico*. Vol. 1, *The Material Culture*. Salt Lake City: University of Utah Press.

Pérez de Ribas, Andrés
1944 *Historia de los Triunfos de Nuestra Santa Fe Entre Gentes las mas Barbaras y Fieras del Nuevo Orbe*. (1645.) 3 Vols. Mexico: Editorial Layac.

Pfefferkorn, Ignaz
1949 *Sonora: A Description of the Province* (trans. and annot. by Theodore E. Treutlein). Albuquerque: University of New Mexico Press.

Pimentel, David, and Marcia Pimentel
1979 *Food, Energy and Society*. London: Edward Arnold.

Pineli, Luis
1709 Carta al Padre Mathias de Gani. Unpublished letter in Archivo Historico de Hacienda, Mexico. Temporalidades, Lagajo 325, No. 32.

Plog, Fred T.
1980 Explaining culture change in the Hohokam Preclassic. In "Current Issues in Hohokam Prehistory: Proceedings of a Symposium," edited by David Doyel and Fred Plog, pp. 4–22. *Arizona State University Anthropological Research Papers* 23. Tempe: Arizona State University.

Rahn, Perry H.
1967 Sheetfloods, Streamfloods, and the Formation of Pediments. *Annals of the Association of American Geographers* 57: 593–604.

Raisz, Erwin
1948 *General Cartography.* New York: McGraw-Hill.

Ralph, E. K., H. N. Michael, and M. C. Han
1974 Radiocarbon Dates and Reality. *Archaeology of Eastern North America* 2: 1–20.

Rankin, Adrianne G.
1977 Interim Report: Palynological Investigations, Rio Sonora Project. Unpublished manuscript on file at the Palynology Laboratory, Department of Anthropology, Arizona State University, Tempe.

Redman, Charles L., and Patty Jo Watson
1970 Systematic Intensive Surface Collection. *American Antiquity* 35(3): 279–291.

Ricardo, David
1817 *The Principles of Political Economy and Taxation.* London. Republished 1948. London: J. M. Dent and Sons.

Richardson, H. L.
1946 Soil Fertility and Maintenance Under Different Systems of Agriculture. *Empire Journal of Experimental Agriculture* 14: 1–17.

Riley, Carroll L.
1969 The Southern Tepehuan and Tepecano. In *Handbook of Middle American Indians*, Vol. 8, *Ethnology*, edited by Evon Z. Vogt, pp. 814–821. Austin: University of Texas Press.
1976a Las Casas and the Golden Cities. *Ethnohistory* 23: 14–30.
1976b Sixteenth Century Trade in the Greater Southwest. *Mesoamerican Studies* 10, *Research Records of the University Museum.* Carbondale: Southern Illinois University.
1979 Casas Grandes and the Sonoran Statelets. Paper presented to the Chicago Anthropological Society, Field Museum.
1980 Mesoamerica and the Hohokam: A view from the 16th century. In "Current Issues in Hohokam Prehistory: Proceedings of a Symposium," edited by David Doyel and Fred Plog, pp. 41–48. *Arizona State University Anthropological Research Papers* 23. Tempe: Arizona State University.
1982 The Frontier People: The Greater Southwest in the Protohistoric Period. *Southern Illinois University at Carbondale Center for Archaeological Investigations Occasional Paper* 1. Carbondale: Southern Illinois University.
1985 Spanish Contact and the Collapse of the Sonoran Statelets. In *The Archaeology of West and Northwest Mesoamerica*, edited by Michael S. Foster and Phil C. Weigand, pp. 419–430. Boulder and London: Westview Press.
1987 *The Frontier People: The Greater Southwest in the Protohistoric Period.* Albuquerque: University of New Mexico Press.

Riley, Carroll L., and Basil C. Hedrick (eds.)
1978 *Across the Chichimec Sea: Papers in Honor of J. Charles Kelley.* Carbondale: Southern Illinois University Press.

Robles Ortiz, Manuel, and Francisco Manzo Taylor
1972 Clovis Fluted Points from Sonora, Mexico. *The Kiva* 37(4): 199–206.

Rohn, Arthur H.
1963 Prehistoric Soil and Water Conservation on Chapin Mesa, Southwestern Colorado. *American Antiquity* 28(4): 441–455.

Roper, Donna C.
1976 Lateral Displacement of Artifacts due to Plowing. *American Antiquity* 41(3): 372–375.

Ross, Stanley H.
1968 Metallurgical Beginnings: The Case for Copper in the Prehistoric American Southwest. *Annals of the Association of American Geographers* 58: 360–370.

Ruppé, Reynold J.
1966 The Archaeological Survey: A Defense. *American Antiquity* 31(3): 313–333.

Ruthenberg, Hans
1976 *Farming Systems in the Tropics.* Oxford: Clarendon Press.

Salas, Guillermo
1976 El Periodo Cuaternario de Sonora. In "Sonora: Antropologia de Desierto–Primera Reunion de Antropologia e Historia de Noroeste," coordinated by Beatriz Braniff C. and Richard S. Felger, pp. 63–66. *Centro Regional del Noroeste, Instituto Nacional de Antropologia e Historia, Coleccion Cientifica* 27. Hermosillo.

Sanders, William T.
1956 The central Mexican symbiotic region: A study in prehistoric settlement patterns. In "Prehistoric Settlement Patterns in the New World," edited by Gordon R. Willey, pp. 115–127. *Viking Fund Publications in Anthropology* 23. New York: Wenner-Gren Foundation for Anthropological Research.
1965 *Cultural Ecology of the Teotihuacan Valley.* University Park: Pennsylvania State University, Department of Sociology and Anthropology.
1972 Population, Agricultural History, and Societal Evolution in Mesoamerica. In *Population Growth: Anthropological Implications*, edited by Brian Spooner, pp. 101–135. Cambridge: M.I.T. Press.
1976 The Natural Environment of the Basin of Mexico. In *The Valley of Mexico: Studies in Pre-Hispanic Ecology and Society*, edited by Eric R. Wolf, pp. 59–76. Albuquerque: University of New Mexico Press.

Sanders, William T., and Barbara J. Price
1968 *Mesoamerica: The Evolution of a Civilization.* New York: Random House.

Sanders, William T., Jeffrey R. Parsons, and Robert S. Santley
1979 *The Basin of Mexico.* New York: Academic Press.

Sandomingo, Manuel
1953 *Historia de Sonora (Pusolana), Tomo Primero, Tiempos Prehistoricos.* Agua Prieta.

Santley, Robert S., and Eric K. Rose
1979 Diet, Nutrition and Population Dynamics in the Basin of Mexico. *World Archaeology* 11: 185–207.

S.A.R.H.
1961–1981 Unpublished precipitation data on file at the Secretaria de Agricultura y Recursos Hidraulicos, Residencia Estacion Hidrometrica, Hermosillo, Sonora, Mexico.
1979–1980 Unpublished agricultural data on file at the Secretaria de Agricultura y Recursos Hidraulicos, Subdireccion de Unidades de Riego Para el Desarrollo Rural, Hermosillo, Sonora, Mexico.

Sauer, Carl O.
1932 The Road to Cibola. *Ibero-Americana* 3: 1–58.
1935 Aboriginal Population of Northwestern Mexico. *Ibero-Americana* 10: 1–33.
1954 Comment on Gatherers and Farmers in the Greater Southwest: A Problem in Classification. *American Anthropologist* 56(4): 553–556.
1963 American Agricultural Origins: A Consideration of Nature and Culture. In *Land and Life: A Selection from the Writings of Carl Ortwin Sauer*, edited by John Leighly, pp. 121–144. Berkeley: University of California Press.

1969 *Agricultural Origins and Dispersals: The Domestication of Animals and Foodstuffs*. Cambridge: M.I.T. Press.

Sauer, Carl O., and Donald Brand
1930 Pueblo Sites in Southeastern Arizona. *University of California Publications in Geography* 3(7): 415–458.
1931 Prehistoric Settlements of Sonora, with Special Reference to Cerros de Trincheras. *University of California Publications in Geography* 5(3): 67–148.

Sauer, Carl O., and Emil Haury
1946 Unpublished field notes from an archaeological survey of eastern Sonora in 1946 on file in the Bancroft Library, University of California, Berkeley.

Sawkins, Frederick J., and Daryl A. Scherkenbach
1981 High Copper Content of Fluid Inclusions in Quartz from Northern Sonora: Implications for Ore-genesis Theory. *Geology* 9: 37–40.

Sayles, E. B.
1936 An Archaeological Survey of Chihuahua, Mexico. *Medallion Papers* 22. Globe: Gila Pueblo.

Schacht, Robert M.
1984 The Contemporaneity Problem. *American Antiquity* 49(4): 678–695.

Schiffer, Michael B.
1982 Hohokam Chronology: An Essay on History and Method. In *Hohokam and Patayan: Prehistory of Southwestern Arizona*, edited by Randall H. McGuire and Michael B. Schiffer, pp. 299–344. New York: Academic Press.

Schiffer, Michael B., Alan P. Sullivan, and Timothy C. Klinger
1978 The Design of Archaeological Surveys. *World Archaeology* 10: 1–28.

Schramm, E. F.
1932 *Report on Artemisa Mines Ltd. With a Description of the Ore Deposits Located in Sonora, Mexico*. MS on file, Cia. Minerales Sotula, S.A. de C.V., Huepac, Sonora, Mexico.

Schroeder, Albert H.
1952 *A Brief Survey of the Lower Colorado River from Davis Dam to the International Border.* Boulder City: Bureau of Reclamation.

Schulman, Edmund
1942 Centuries-Long Tree Indices of Precipitation in the Southwest. *Bulletin of the American Meteorological Society* 23: 148–161, 204–217.
1956 *Dendroclimatic Changes in Semiarid America*. Tucson: University of Arizona Press.

Scott, Stuart D.
1966 Dendrochronology in Mexico. *Papers of The Laboratory of Tree-Ring Research* 2. Tucson: University of Arizona Press.

Shreve, Forest, and Ira L. Wiggins
1964 *Vegetation and Flora of the Sonoran Desert*. Stanford: Stanford University Press.

Shryock, Henry S., and Jacob S. Siegel
1973 *The Methods and Materials of Demography.* Washington: U.S. Department of Commerce, Bureau of the Census.

Sillitoe, R. H.
1976 A Reconnaissance of the Mexican Porphry Copper Belt. *Institute of Mining and Metallurgy Transactions* 85: B170–B189.

Smiley, Terah L., Stanley A. Stubbs, and Bryant Bannister
1953 A Foundation for the Dating of Some Late Archaeological Sites in the Rio Grande Area, New Mexico: Based on Studies in Tree-Ring Methods and Pottery Analysis. *Laboratory of Tree-Ring Research Bulletin* 6, *University of Arizona Bulletin* 24(3). Tucson: University of Arizona.

Smith, A. Ledyard
1961 Types of Ballcourts in the Highlands of Guatemala. In *Essays in Pre-Columbian Art and Archaeology*, edited by Samuel K. Lothrop and others, pp. 100–125. Cambridge: Harvard University Press.

Smith, Buckingham (trans.)
1871 *Relation of Alvar Nuñez Cabeza de Vaca*. New York.

Smith, H. V.
1956 The Climate of Arizona. *University of Arizona Agricultural Experiment Station Bulletin* 279. Tucson: University of Arizona.

Soil Survey Staff
1975 *Soil Taxonomy: A Basic System of Soil Classification for Making and Interpreting Soil Surveys*. Washington: U.S. Department of Agriculture.

Spencer, J. E., and G. A. Hale
1961 The Origin, Nature, and Distribution of Agricultural Terracing. *Pacific Viewpoint* 2: 1–40.

Spicer, Edward H.
1967 *Cycles of Conquest: The Impact of Spain, Mexico, and the United States on the Indians of the Southwest, 1533–1960*. Tucson: University of Arizona Press.

Stuiver, Minze
1982 A High-Precision Calibration of the AD Radiocarbon Time Scale. *Radiocarbon* 24: 1–26.

Sullivan, Alan P.
1982 Mogollon Agrarian Ecology. *The Kiva* 48 (1–2): 1–15.

Swedlund, Alan C., and George J. Armelagos
1976 *Demographic Anthropology.* Dubuque: William C. Brown.

Sykes, Godfrey
1931 Rainfall Investigations in Arizona and Sonora by Means of Long Period Rain Gauges. *Geographical Review* 21: 229–233.

Theisen, Gerald (trans.)
1972 *The Narrative of Alvar Nuñez Cabeza de Vaca with Oviedo's Version of the Lost Joint Report Presented to the Audiencia of Santo Domingo*. Barre: The Imprint Society.

Thompson, J. Eric S.
1971 Estimates of Maya Population: Deranging Factors. *American Antiquity* 36(2): 214–216.

Thompson, L. M., and F. R. Troeh
1978 *Soils and Fertility.* New York: McGraw-Hill.

Thorne, D. Wynne
1979 Soil Organic Matter, Microorganisms and Crop Production. In *Soil, Water and Crop Production*, edited by D. Wynne Thorne and Marlowe D. Thorne, pp. 82–95. Westport: AVI Publishing.

Thrower, Norman J. W.
1972 *Maps and Man: An Examination of Cartography in Relation to Culture and Civilization*. Englewood Cliffs: Prentice-Hall.

Tolstoy, Paul, and Suzanne K. Fish
1975 Surface and Subsurface Evidence For Community Size at Caopexco, Mexico. *Journal of Field Archaeology* 2: 97–104.

Trewartha, Glenn T.
1961 *The Earth's Problem Climates*. Madison: University of Wisconsin Press.

Trigger, Bruce G.
1968 The Determinants of Settlement Patterns. In *Settlement Archaeology*, edited by K. C. Chang, pp. 53–78. Palo Alto: National Press Books.

Tuan, Yi-Fu
1959 Pediments in Southeastern Arizona. *University of California Publications in Geography* 13. Berkely: Uni-

Tuan, Yi-Fu *(continued)*
versity of California.

Turnage, William V., and T. D. Mallery
1941 An Analysis of Rainfall in the Sonoran Desert and Adjacent Territory. *Carnegie Institution Publication* 529. Washington.

Turner, B. L., II
1976 Population Density in the Classic Maya Lowlands: New Evidence for Old Approaches. *Geographical Review* 66: 73–82.

Turner, B. L., II, and William E. Doolittle
1978 The Concept and Measure of Agricultural Intensity. *Professional Geographer* 30: 297–301.

Turner, B. L., II, Robert Q. Hanham, and Anthony V. Portararo
1977 Population Pressure and Agricultural Intensity. *Annals of the Association of American Geographers* 67: 384–396.

Turner, Raymond M., and David E. Brown
1982 Sonoran desertscrub. In "Biotic Communities of the American Southwest—United States and Mexico," edited by David E. Brown, pp. 181–221. *Desert Plants* 4.

Tuthill, Carr
1947 The Tres Alamos Site on the San Pedro River, Southeastern Arizona. *The Amerind Foundation* 4. Dragoon: The Amerind Foundation.

Vance, James E., Jr.
1970 *The Merchant's World: The Geography of Wholesaling*. Englewood Cliffs: Prentice-Hall.

Van Royen, William
1954 The Agricultural Resources of the World. *University of Maryland Department of Geography Atlas of World's Resources* 1. New York: Prentice-Hall.

Vapnarsky, Cesar
1968 On Rank-Size Distributions of Cities: An Ecological Approach. *Economic Development and Culture Change* 17: 584–595.

Velazquez-Perez, Jesus, and Carlos Melo-Gallegos
1983 Geographic and ecologic description of the northwest of Mexico. In "Wildlife and Range Research Needs in Northern Mexico and Southwestern United States: Workshop Proceedings," edited by David R. Patton, Jose M. de la Puente-E., Peter F. Ffolliott, Sonia Gallina, and E. T. Bartlett, pp. 5–10. *USDA Forest Service General Technical Report* WO–36. Washington.

Walter, Heinrich
1973 *Vegetation of the Earth in Relation to Climate and the Eco-Physiological Conditions*. Berlin: Springer-Verlag.

Wasley, William W.
1966 The Archaeology of Sonora and Sinaloa: A Review of the Literature and Suggestions for Future Research. Unpublished manuscript on file at the Arizona State Museum, Tucson, Arizona.
1967 Unpublished field notes from an archaeological survey of eastern Sonora in 1967 on file in the Arizona State Museum, Tucson, Arizona.

Wasley, William W., and Alfred E. Johnson
1965 Salvage Archaeology in Painted Rocks Reservoir, Western Arizona. *Anthropological Papers of the University of Arizona* 9. Tucson: University of Arizona Press.

Wellhausen, E. J., L. M. Roberts, E. Hernandez X., and Paul C. Mangelsdorf
1952 *Races of Maize in Mexico: Their Origin, Characteristics, and Distribution*. Cambridge: The Bussey Institution of Harvard University.

Wertz, Jacques B.
1966 The Flood Cycle of Ephemeral Mountain Streams in the Southwestern United States. *Annals of the Association of American Geographers* 56: 598–633.

West, Robert C.
1979 *Carl Sauer's Fieldwork in Latin America, Dellplain Latin American Studies* 3. Ann Arbor: University Microfilms International.

Whalen, Michael E.
1981a Cultural Ecological Aspects of the Pithouse-to-Pueblo Transition in a Portion of the Southwest. *American Antiquity* 46(1): 75–92.
1981b An Investigation of Pithouse Village Structure in Western Texas. *Journal of Field Archaeology* 8: 303–311.

Wheat, Joe Ben
1955 Mogollon Culture Prior to A.D. 1000. *Memoirs of the Society for American Archaeology* 10.

White, Roger W.
1977 Dynamic Central Place Theory: Results of a Simulation Approach. *Geographical Analysis* 9: 226–243.

Wilcox, David R.
1979 Warfare Implications of Dry-Laid Masonry Walls on Tumamoc Hill. *The Kiva* 45(1–2): 15–38.

Wilcox, David R., and Lynette O. Shenk
1977 The Architecture of the Casa Grande and its Interpretation. *Arizona State Museum Archaeological Series* 115. Tucson: Arizona State Museum, University of Arizona.

Wilford, John N.
1981 *The Mapmakers*. New York: Knopf.

Wilken, G. C.
1976 Traditional Slope Management: An Analytical Approach. In *Hill Lands: Proceedings of an International Symposium*, edited by J. Luchok, J. D. Cawthon, and M. J. Breslin, pp. 416–422. Morgantown: West Virginia University and the West Virginia Forage and Grassland Council.

Willey, Gordon R., (ed.)
1956 Prehistoric Settlement Patterns in the New World. *Viking Fund Publications in Anthropology* 23. New York: Wenner-Gren Foundation for Anthropological Research.

Williams, M.
1970 The Enclosure and Reclamation of Waste Land in England and Wales in the Eighteenth and Nineteenth Centuries. *Transactions of the Institute of British Geographers* 51: 55–69.

Winship, George P. (trans. and ed.)
1904 *The Journey of Coronado 1540–1542 from the City of Mexico to the Grand Canyon of the Colorado and the Buffalo Plains of Texas, Kansas, and Nebraska*. New York: A. S. Barnes.

Wiseman, Fred M.
1976 Aplicaciones de la paleoecologia a la arqueologia de Sonora. In "Sonora: Antropologia del Desierto—Primera Reunion de Antropologia e Historia de Noroeste," coordinated by Beatriz Braniff C. and Richard S. Felger, pp. 73–76. *Centro Regional del Noroeste, Instituto Nacional de Antropologia e Historia, Coleccion Cientifica* 27. Hermosillo.

Woosley, Anne I.
1980 Agricultural Diversity in the Prehistoric Southwest. *The Kiva* 45(4): 317–335.

Yang, Tien Wei, and Charles H. Lowe, Jr.
1956 Correlation of Major Vegetation Climaxes with Soil Characteristics in the Sonoran Desert. *Science* 123: 542.

Index

Abstract

The inhabitants of eastern Sonora, Mexico were reported by the 16th century Spanish explorers to be more populous and culturally more advanced than other groups in northern Mexico and the southern portion of the American Southwest at the time of European contact. They had a complex settlement system involving a few large centers surrounded by numerous smaller sites. Their varied architecture involved a number of different types of both residential structures and public architecture. These people possessed a well-developed agricultural complex with a variety of crops that were grown in two seasons with the aid of canal irrigation. Trade was important, as was defense and long-distance communication through the use of a pyrosignal network. In spite of their reported achievement, the ancient people of this region have been the subject of few archaeological investigations, which has contributed to the common interpretation that the region was sparsely populated by people who were little different from the rest of the nomadic Chichimecs who occupied northern Mexico.

This study concerns an intensive, systematic analysis of relic settlements and agricultural features in the Valley of Sonora. Evidence indicates that the ethnohistorical accounts of the Spanish are accurate and that the generally accepted archaeological interpretation needs major revision. A four-tier settlement hierarchy involving numerous, uniformly spaced sites existed by A.D. 1500. Two sites were especially large and contained public architecture, including ball courts. Most of the settlements, however, were small, agriculturally oriented hamlets and rancherias that tended to be located proximal to the floodplain throughout the valley. The pattern for settlements dating as early as A.D. 1000 was considerably different, involving a three-tier hierarchy with relatively fewer sites and only one moderately sized dominant village. Many of these smaller sites were oriented toward large arroyos where runoff agriculture was practiced.

Changes in settlement patterns, especially movement of the node, or point of minimum aggregate distance between one site and all others, are interpreted as meaning that developments occurred without external influence or migration. Increased economic complexity involving a shift from a predominantly subsistence orientation to a rudimentary market system is interpreted from the settlement and agricultural evidence. The contacts and trade that existed with neighboring groups and with distant peoples probably were consequences rather than causes of changes evident in the occupance data.

Sumario

Los reportes de los exploradores españoles del siglo XVI muestran que los habitantes de la región oriental del estado de Sonora, México fueron más numerosos, y más avanzados culturalmente que otros grupos del area el cual es actualmente el norte de México y el suroeste de los Estados Unidos al tiempo de la llegada de los europeos. Este grupo de sonorenses tenía un sistema complejo de poblados consistiendo de algunos pocos grandes centros de población rodeados de otros más pequeños y más numerosos. Tenían una arquitectura muy variada de estructuras residenciales y públicas. Esa gente poseía un sistema de agricultura muy desarrollado con una gran variedad de cosechas las cuales eran cultivadas durante dos temporadas del año con la ayuda de acequias de irrigación. El comercio era un factor importante y también los sistemas de defensa y una red de comunicaciones por medio de señales de fuego. A pesar de esos logros ya mencionados, los antiguos habitantes han sido objeto de muy pocas investigaciones arqueológicas, lo cual hace creer que la región estaba poblada con muy poca gente y esos no se diferenciaban mucho de los chichimecas nómadas, los cuales ocuparon el norte de México.

Este estudio se compone de un intenso análisis sistemático de los poblados antiguos y su agricultura en el valle de Sonora. La evidencia que tenemos enseña que las relaciones etnológicas-históricas de los españoles fueron acertadas y que las modernas interpretaciones arqueológicas comúnmente aceptadas necesitan una revisión general. En el año de 1500 D.C. había una jerarquía de poblados con cuatro niveles. Los sitios eran numerosos y situados a espacios regulares. Dos de estos lugares eran especialmente grandes y con arquitectura pública, incluyenda campos deportivos. Sin embargo, eran pequeños la mayoría de los poblados y rancherías cuya actividad principal era la agricultura. Tenían también la característica de encontrarse situados en las áreas de riego natural a lo largo del valle. La muestra de poblados que datan desde el año de 1000 D.C. presenta una diferencia considerable. Había una jerarquía con tres niveles que tenía relativamente menos sitios y solo un sitio de tamaño moderado. Muchos de estos pequeños poblados se encontraban situados cerca de los grandes arroyos donde practicaban agricultura de temporal.

Los cambios en el patrón de poblados y especialmente el movimiento del lugar central o punto de distancia mínima entre un sitio y los demás, se ha interpretado así que el desarrollo ocurrió sin cualquier influencia externa o la migración. Los contactos y el comercio que tenían con grupos vecinos y con gentes más distantes probablemente fueron los consequencias y no las causas de los cambios que vemos en las épocas de ocupación.